STRICTLY
SPEAKING

STRICTLY
SPEAKING

Reid Buckley's Indispensable Handbook on Public Speaking

REID BUCKLEY

McGraw-Hill

NEW YORK   SAN FRANCISCO   WASHINGTON, D.C.   AUCKLAND   BOGOTÁ
CARACAS   LISBON   LONDON   MADRID   MEXICO CITY   MILAN
MONTREAL   NEW DELHI   SAN JUAN   SINGAPORE
SYDNEY   TOKYO   TORONTO

Library of Congress Cataloging-in-Publication Data

Buckley, Fergus Reid.
Strictly speaking : Reid Buckley's indispensable handbook on public
speaking / Reid Buckley.
  p.   cm.
Includes index.
ISBN 0-07-134610-4
  1. Public speaking—Handbooks, manuals, etc. I. Title.
PN4121.B7785   1999
808.5'1—dc21   99-21413
                                                    CIP

McGraw-Hill

A Division of The McGraw-Hill Companies

1 2 3 4 5 6 7 8 9 0   DOC/DOC   9 0 4 3 2 1 0 9

ISBN 0-07-134610-4

Printed and bound by R. R. Donnelley & Sons Company.

McGraw-Hill books are available at special quantity discounts to use as premiums and
sales promotions, or for use in corporate training programs. For more information,
please write to the Director of Special Sales, McGraw-Hill, 11 West 19th Street,
New York, NY 10011. Or contact your local bookstore.

This book is printed on recycled, acid-free paper
containing a minimum of 50% recycled, de-inked
fiber.

To my students:

past, present, and future . . .

if any

CONTENTS

PREFACE
Why Anyone Should Want to Learn to Speak

Why should anyone subject himself to the trouble of learning to think and speak on his feet? Well . . .

Some twenty years ago, at a remote corner in the hinterlands of South Carolina called Ellerbee Mill, a ferocious bear of a man thrust the barrel of a 30.06 deer rifle into my stomach and growled at me, "I'm going to blow your effen belly off the road. I'm going to drop you in the ditch."

I had surprised him poaching on private land, shooting a rifle across a public intersection, and killing a doe, for which, of course, he had no "tag," or permit.

In the act of accosting him, I had my shotgun slung carelessly over my right shoulder; he, however, had wheeled into me, rifle grasped at hip level, by the suddenness and unexpectedness of his movement getting the drop on me. He was backed by his brother, in a pickup truck, and by a young man who prowled behind my back holding a .12 gauge semiautomatic shotgun, presumably loaded.

The fellow holding the rifle kept repeating, "I'm going to blow your effen belly off the road; I'm going to drop you there in the ditch soon as it gets dark enough!" That was about half an hour off, I judged. I started talking to the man, who was demented, obsessed with his abstract hatred for the landed, or by his standards, wealthy plutocrat, of which I was the accidental object. I knew I had to keep talking to him in order to distract and defuse his emotional surges—when the muzzle of the rifle trembled in his hands—when his right hand convulsively gripped the trigger guard. "Don't shoot him," pleaded his brother, "No need to shoot him." But my assailant kept repeating, "Ain't no effen sumbitch going to tell me I can't hunt where I want. I'm gonna blow this effen sumbitch off the road. I ain't gonna wait for dark. It's gettin' dark enough now. I'm gonna let him have it now!"

He got himself so exercised, I feared that the finger on the trigger would convulse, yank back, and that he would, in fact, blow me to kingdom come. I had hunting companions—my wife, friends—who, I prayed, would shortly come looking for me. If witnesses showed up in time, I did not think he'd dare carry out his threat.

And so I kept talking. What powers of sweet persuasion did I summon to my aid? Well, one brilliant gambit that occurred to me was this: "You can't shoot me here," I said to him belligerently, sticking my chin out and leaning over the muzzle of the rifle to stare him right in the kisser.

"Yeah," he cried, "and why not, Mistuh; you tell me why I can't shoot you here?"

"Because," quoth I, with dazzling lucidity (I cannot, in retrospect, believe I actually spoke these words), "this is a public road, that's why. It's illegal to shoot a person on a public road."

It didn't matter, as it turned out. My object was to engage his intellect in matters removed from his obsession with killing me, to spin cobwebs over his intentions, to distract his rage, to compel him to engage with me in a dialogue. Any dialogue. I asked him if he thought it was rich Yankee arrogance for me to object to his shooting across an intersection that was walked every evening by children coming home from school? Was that unreasonable? I *demanded* to know. On the contrary, wouldn't it have been truly despicable had I not given a damn about the danger to little boys and girls who were that moment strolling back and forth on the road before us? What did he think of that? Did he have an answer for that?

I kept after him, badgering him on dialectical levels. Every time he heated up—the rifle prodding me in the gut, rage washing across his face, causing his hands and arms to shake from desire—when those explosive moments of almost uncontrollable homicidal fury welled up in him, I kept talking, speaking reasonably, unemotionally, at times, forsooth, wittily—grinning at him, shrugging my shoulders. For thirty minutes I talked that fellow out of pulling the trigger. I don't know whether, like MacBeth or Hamlet or King Lear, I spoke in rolling iambic pentameter, in rich and striking figures of speech, and sometimes also in couplets, but when finally the Blazer 4-wheeler rolled up and my gallant wife (and friends) leaped out to the rescue, shotguns in hand, it was over, and I was still alive.

Your life may not hang in the balance; your livelihood may. What the art of public speaking boils down to is, crudely stated, selling; morally analyzed, imposing one's will. The paramount reason for putting oneself to the trouble of learning the forensic craft is that one wishes to persuade someone else (or a lot of people) to think as one thinks, do as one suggests, buy what one sells, adopt the policy that one promotes. (Or *not* pull the trigger.) Therein the prize: dominion over the minds and spirits of one's audience, power over their capacity for action. According to Plutarch, Plato declared:

> . . . the art of public speaking . . . is . . . the government of the souls of men, [whose] chief business is to address the affections and passions, which are as it were the strings and keys to the soul, and require a skillful and careful touch to be played on as they should be.

We all have something to say, sell, or espouse. There is none of us who isn't engaged daily in the business of playing the strings and keys to someone's soul, of trying to get that person or those persons to do our bidding—one way or another, but chiefly by gentle persuasion. Every ingredient of the craft of public speaking is necessary to that quotidian task of selling oneself and selling one's case (or bill of goods). The better you are at speaking on your feet before a thousand people, the better do you develop a skillful and careful touch to play on, the better will you be one-on-one, or one before a few. Unfortunately, though you may be naturally gifted one-on-one and do pretty well exerting your sway over a small group in informal circumstances, these faculties and powers do not automatically transfer to the stage or to a public performance. You have to train yourself for that test.

HOW TO USE THIS BOOK

Think of it as a checklist. All of a sudden you discover that you must give a talk next Monday at a town meeting or at your business's annual romp in Bermuda or to the PTA of your daughter's high school. You wish to die.

Don't. Go at once to the Table of Contents and select what may be relevant to your immediate need. Where feasible, I've divided the text into two sections. When you get into a chapter, the first items you will read will be the quick fixes for next week's performance.

You may wish to read no more than that. But when you feel the urge to dig a little deeper, peruse the material under each special heading that you'll find following the quick fixes, such as:

Sweat, Blood, Toil, and Tears: Surpassing Yourself

The wording of this heading is adapted to the material, but what you will find beneath it are examples of things you should or should not do or more complete discussions of the elements you'll need to discharge your obligation and become an able public speaker.

Once again: Why *is* it you wish to become good at speaking on your feet? Winston Churchill responded to that query in an unpublished (can you believe that?) essay:

> Of all the talents bestowed upon men, none is so precious as the gift of oratory. He who enjoys it wields a power more durable than that of a great king. He is an independent force in the world.

Reid Buckley
Camden, South Carolina
Comillas, Cantabria, Spain

ACKNOWLEDGMENTS

I want to thank Carolyn Krupp of IMB Literary for her pugnacious marketing of the manuscript, Betsy Brown of McGraw-Hill for her sensitive editing, James Bessent for his meticulous copyediting, and senior editing supervisor Jane Palmieri for her painstaking coordination of all the pieces. My thanks also to retired coach Hilda MacMahon, senior coach Carolyn Hammond, master coach Harriet G. DuBose, my editorial assistant, Caroline L. Buxton, and director of the Buckley School, Karen Miller, for their contributions to the chapter on character defects; and the last for diligently undertaking the chore of formatting and turning out sundry copies of the manuscript.

My thanks go also to Martha D. Moore and her administrative assistant, Roxanne Martin, for coming to my succor at several critical junctions; and, of course, most particularly, as always, to my long-suffering, nevertheless beloved wife, Tasa.

PART 1

DRY BONES

The Short List of Dos and Don'ts

CHAPTER 1

10 CARDINAL SINS THAT AMATEURS COMMIT

or How Not to Gape Your Mouth So Wide That Your Tonsils Fall Out . . .

Herewith the cardinal sins that business people and professional folk typically blunder into when they open their mouths in public.[1]

CARDINAL SIN 1

Never succumb to self-satisfaction . . . and never trust an innocent.

Someone will see through you. The most sympathetic-appearing person in the audience may be your enemy. Gird yourself for battle always by cleansing your spirit of pomposity and a false sense of your importance. (For more on pomposity see Chapter 18.)

A Tale with a Moral

One can't conceal the dread truth from everybody, not all the time. At a flossy country club luncheon a few years ago the silverthatched tycoon

---

[1] Most of the material in this chapter is based on an article, "The 10 Commandments of Public Speaking," by Reid Buckley, published by *FYI* in the Christmas issue of 1996. My thanks for their permission to reproduce it here.

held forth on the benefits to the community of the arts center he was funding.

Guests listened with rapt attention—or so it seemed—tittering at his jests, nodding heads solemnly at his aphorisms. His wife, sitting next to him on the dais, stared up at her spouse with the rictus of a worshiping smile on her face—twenty minutes. I was fascinated, watching her. Her expression never varied. (She brought to mind Pat Nixon: bouffant blond hair, impeccable white linen suit.) Her husband went on and on, winding at last into his peroration, at which time my attention was distracted by a 13- or 14-year-old who was seated at a round table below the dais, in front of me: his daughter.

She was struggling with a yawn. She resisted, but the corners of her mouth were as though tugged away from her pretty little teeth by iron grapples. She could not suppress the eruption, which was prodigious. It tripled the cubic volume of her mouth, and it came forth loudly, like sixty pounds of air pressure escaping the inner tube of a tractor's tire. *Aaaaawwwwwooooooooeeeeeooooo!* At which—this was amazing!—her mother burst into a silver carol of laughter, provoking titters and then howls from everybody in the room except the great man, who glared at wife and daughter in crimson-cheeked fury.

This is my first counsel. Don't let the apple of your eye reveal to all the world the hollow person that you have become. If you cannot suppress your arrogance and conceit, avoid blunders; learn to dissemble the truth. The remedy? Speak so briefly and so self-effacingly that neither innocence nor astuteness will smoke you out.

CARDINAL SIN 2

Never begin a speech with a joke.

. . . Not even if it's funny. Nothing betrays the amateur faster.

Forget Cicero. Don't be so eager to ingratiate yourself. All you may earn is contempt. Get to your point directly. Lace your text with humor, sure, but let it boil up out of the text, uncanned.

Humor must be necessary to be legitimate. It must advance the argument. If your talk can get along without the anecdote (a humorous aside is different), let it. (For more on the uses of humor, see Chapter 17.)

An Example of Having Fun
and Contriving Humor out of Necessity

It happens that I possess a nose that a Roman senator would envy—or maybe a toucan.

I'd had a skin cancer removed from its bridge one winter, which, given the tightness of the skin there, necessitated clamps to hold the suture together, in turn necessitating a very large and protuberant bandage. I had to go on lecture tour, and at the first two stops I became aware of hosts and audiences resolutely attempting to avoid staring at my proboscis. The effort produced great distress in these good folk as they went walleyed facing me. I guessed what they were thinking: either, "Jeez, what a schnozzle that fellow must have had before the doctors worked on it," or, "What a lousy surgeon that poor guy got."

Their preoccupation with my nose was getting in the way. So I confronted their secret thoughts, telling my audiences on the third night,

> Big noses have played a significant rôle in my family since I can remember. My father had a patrician, his enemies said piratical, nose. One afternoon in the late 1920s, John Pierpont Morgan II was expected for tea. He was driving all the way out to Sharon, Connecticut, from New York City (three hours in those days) to talk to my father about oil. Now he, Mr. Morgan, was endowed with the humongous humdinger of schnozzles, fleshier than Jimmy Durante's, as rubious as that of his illustrious progenitor, J. P. Morgan I.
>
> Our mother was petrified [I went on], not by Mr. Morgan's nose, understand, by the reaction she feared it might kindle in her children. "Alöise," she said; "John," she said; "dear sweet Priscilla," she said; "and you, naughty and incorrigible Jimmy!" she said: "do not, for heaven's sake, stare at Mr. Morgan's nose. He is very important to your father, who needs money to drill wells in unlikely places. Just come in when I call for you. Boys, bow. Girls, curtsy. Under no circumstances stare goggle-eyed at—Jimmy!—snicker at—John!—make a crack about—Alöise!

(darling Priscilla, you wouldn't think of it!)—Mr. Morgan's nose. Just bow, curtsy, and run off."

Well, my older siblings did just that, to Mother's intense relief. They bowed, curtseyed, and skedaddled. Emitting a sigh—sugar tongs in one hand, cup and saucer in the other—our mother turned to her guest, asking, "And now, Mr. Morgan, how many lumps of sugar will you have in your nose?"

"Stare away," I concluded to my audiences, "We'll both feel better."[2]

CARDINAL SIN 3

Shun the conditional tense.

Use an opaque black felt pen to wipe outcroppings of the conditional tense from your text. It's weak. It's tentative. And nothing conduces more certainly to giving the impression that one is a windbag. "I would suggest." "I would submit to you." It spills into the subjunctive before one can say would-that-it-were, which sounds stilted. Stick to the present tense. (For more on using good clean English, see Chapter 10.)

CARDINAL SIN 4

Spurn rhetorical flourishes.

Fluff language, filler talk, sheer verbosity, spurn them. "I'd like to begin by." Begin, damnit! Don't hem and haw. "I submit to you." If you mean that, you don't know what you're saying. "My distinguished colleague." Oh, balls. "If you will." Not on your life, baby! "Think about it!" (For more on verbal flatulence vs. good clean declarative English, see Chapter 10.)

More on Such Banes

"Think about it!" has become a plague. When used to sum up a thought, the adjuration is usually accompanied by a portentous frown

---

[2] I learned only in May of 1995 that this story is apocryphal family lore, but I didn't know that at the time.

and a Nixonian shaking of the wattles. It assumes a moral superiority that is quite indefensible.

In this same category belongs the deadly phrase "Let me share with you . . ." I don't want it. Keep it to yourself. Don't impose on me your compulsion to regurgitate your miserable soul. When one hears that awful, touchy-feely, falsely humble ingratiation, one *knows* that one is in for a slathering of sentimentality or a revelation of such gruesomely intimate character that it transgresses decency. *Larry King.*

Share nothing from the stage or banquet table. Let me tell you about sharing. One can share a blanket, split peas, a cookie, a seat, knowledge. One may even share a Kleenex, in a pinch. One cannot share pain ("Have some, it's on me!"), an experience, an emotion, an idea, an intellectual state, an opinion, good taste or bad.

CARDINAL SIN 5

Avoid vulgar, with-it, faddish in-phrases like PC.

Do you remember "the bottom line?" Time was when one could read nothing without bumping up against it. "The bottom line" belongs in an accountant's statement, possibly with reference to a *Sports Illustrated* swimsuit issue.

"The bottom line," "getting down to the nitty gritty," "politically correct," even "immanentizing the eschaton": such reductions, when fresh, can be okay. But they must be fresh. The moment they bubble up in weekly news magazines or on TV talk shows, they are used up. (For more on quips and decent English, see Chapter 10.)

The Awful Peatbog of Fashionable Phrases

Even when newly minted, there's something repulsive about them. They assume superiority also. They are PLU talk.[3] My gastric juices rise to the gorge when a member of the chattering classes or some denizen of the Beltway disparages political correctness. I bet Al Gore lectures Tipper on the perils of PC every night.

---

[3] People like us, dummy!

CARDINAL SIN 6

Do not quote anything from anyone unless you have read the book.

. . . Or are thoroughly familiar with the authority's work and have thought long and hard about it. Oh, sure, there are juicy quotations that can be irresistible and safe to use, but served-up opinions, aphorisms, or *pensées justes* outside the area of one's competence sound somehow as though they have been horsed into the text for show, not truly marinated in the speaker's mind.

As a rule, any quotation longer than fifty words is a mistake. Twenty-five words is better by half. But even brief, pointed, nifty quotations can be an addiction. The repetitive *thud-thud-thud* of clever ironies dulls the audience's minds, which don't need that (see below). It's the old rhetoric of shock at work.

CARDINAL SIN 7

Never indulge in an unlikely allusion, either.

Unlikely for you, that is; the kind of thing commercial speech-writing outfits are apt to plunk into the text to dress it up. Count on this: almost nobody who quotes Plato has read Plato.

Quit being pretentious. One cringes when captains of industry recite Ovid or when fund-raisers knock off Zen Buddhist koans or when retired NFL linebackers solemnly deliver their critiques of pure reason.[4] The speaker should avoid dressing himself in borrowed clothes, for fear some brat in the audience (maybe even a beloved daughter) will shout that he is wearing none. (For more on canned wisdom, see Chapter 10.)

How Even a Chief Executive Can Blunder

Ronald Reagan had a stable of shrewd speech writers, but memory winces at his greeting of the Pope at the Miami airport back in 1987.

---

[4] See *The Critique of Pure Reason*, by Immanuel Kant, 1781.

It was nightfall, recall. The weary pontiff was met by Reagan at the foot of the jet's gangway. Our hero's welcoming remarks were larded with references to scholastic philosophy that fitted him as gracefully as a fighter pilot's cap fits Bill Clinton. Rarely did Ronald Reagan permit himself to look or sound foolish, but the half-smile that played on John Paul's lips as, with bowed head, he endured those uncharacteristically sententious presidential words, gave the game away. *He* knew that Ronald Reagan had not read a word of Thomas Aquinas, and so did everybody else—on the tarmac and watching the news.

On the other hand,

CARDINAL SIN 8

Do not rely on the slightest gleam of intelligence that you believe you detect in your audience. Aim at the gut!

This is like relying on the gleam of compassion one detects in the eye of a Swiss banker, which turns out to be his glass eye. In the aggregate, even Nobel laureates are dumber 'n dirt. Before they quit the auditorium your audience have forgotten what you said. So quit appealing to their intelligence. Everything you say should be exquisitely wrought, wise, witty, and wonderful, but you must aim at the gut, at implanting in the audience a good feeling about you. "Sound fellow! I agree with every last jot and tittle, whatever they were." In this consists the genius of Bill Clinton's stump speeches: their warm and fuzzy sincerity, totally resisting analysis, but making their point with the public just the same. *All* the same,

CARDINAL SIN 9

Never fail to treat every member of your audience as the juror over your conscience, for whom you will exert your best effort proving the validity and justice of your case.

Humility of spirit is the vital attribute of the speaker. Conceit is his enemy. The speaker who disrespects his audience (dumb clucks that they maybe) is a fool.

Condescension on the Part of the Speaker Can Forfeit Everything

This was former Senator Bob Dole's weakness in the 1996 campaign. He allowed the perception that those who don't agree with him can't tell the difference between a mud slide and mudslinging. That may have been the case, but it's rude nevertheless, and it lost him California. (For more on Bob Dole and one-liners, see Chapter 2. For more on humility of spirit and conceit, see Chapter 18.)

CARDINAL SIN 10

Never accept a booking in Pennsylvania.

. . . Or Wisconsin or Minnesota or the Dakotas. Why? As a tribe, they can be audiences that speakers conjure in their nightmares (shades of Adlai Stevenson). It's as though nuances sail by their heads like Frisbees in a high wind, and they are bereft of a sense of humor.

Be careful not to press your luck when addressing an audience comprising mostly the Dutch, Germans, Slavs, or Scandinavians—or folk deep in the boondocks. People way out in the country may think it discourteous to laugh, even when they understand the humor, which, if it is tinged with sophistication, will not be often. Pray for an audience of urban Jews, Irish, Spaniards, Poles, and Trappist monks. (They laugh at everything.)

Why Only Had He Been Shot, Would Mark Twain Have Preferred to Be in Philadelphia . . .

Years ago, after a booking in Harrisburg, my path crossed that of the late Russell Kirk, the phenomenal man of letters, who had lectured at a nearby college.

Over lunch, he said to me, "Were you aware that Mark Twain dreaded giving talks in the Commonwealth as much as you and I do? Why, one night he was addressing a rural York County audience that never cracked a smile. One farmer in particular unsettled him, a tall, gaunt, lean fellow in his mid-fifties, with a lantern jaw and gnarled fists, who stared grimly up at him out of steel gray eyes. Twain swore to himself, 'I'm going to crack that fellow's shell if it's the last thing I do.' With this object fervently in mind, he aimed the final twenty minutes of his wittiest remarks at that farmer and that farmer only . . . only to see them bounce off that impervious brow and fall shattering to the floor. Twain had done his darnedest, but he had failed.

"Afterwards," Kirk went on, "at the apple cider and doughnuts reception, the farmer stomped up to Twain, saying, 'Mr. Clemens, sir, that speech you gave was so funny I could hardly keep from bustin' out laughing.'"

CARDINAL SIN 11

Never speak after George Will.

. . . Nor before him, for that matter. Which is why these 10 Cardinal Sins stretched into 11.

It's like going before or after a stand-up comedian crossed with Samuel Johnson. George Will has been accused of delivering a litany of erudite one-liners, but that charge is in the order of postulating a surfeit of caviar. (There's no such thing.) Never make the mistake of trying to compete with a phenomenon. Ask to be excused. Cough up blood. If that's impractical, courage! Keep your remarks brief, low-keyed, and utterly unrelated to what the star has said or plans to say. If his talk is going to be political, stun the audience with your grandaunt's recipe for pecan pie. Then wait for a better night.

CHAPTER 2

10 COMMANDMENTS THAT ALL SPEAKERS MUST OBSERVE

The moment class began, he would seize us by our throats, launching into complex distinctions with nary a concession to the 8 o'clock hour, the stupor induced by springtime, or our dull student minds.

I'm talking about Yale's great cosmologist, the diminutive Paul Weiss, within the span of whose skull dwelt a universe measured in light years. "The indeterminateness of the indeterminate," he would cry in his high nasal voice, flinging his hands dramatically heavenward (once his wristwatch on its elastic metal band flew out the window to land two stories down on the strip of lawn bordering the school building. Stopping in midsentence, astonished, he scampered out of the classroom, down two flights of stone steps, out into the soft sunshine, retrieved his timepiece, scampered back up the stairs, bursting into the classroom with the triumphant shout), ". . . is determinately what it is!"

He never missed a beat. And no more gripping teacher did Yale College boast. We sophomores struggled—oh, and how we struggled! But we hung breath-bated on every syllable that issued from Paul Weiss's mouth, fascinated by him, our minds wholly engrossed by the difficult concepts he was introducing.

This is what you must do with your audience.

COMMANDMENT 1

The very first paragraph of your talk should shock the audience with its complexity and difficulty, or with its outrageousness.

Uh-huh. From the outset, you must compel your audience to sit up in their seats and pay closest attention.

The latest corporate buzz phrase is "executive presence." That's what you want to establish the moment you take command of the stage, and the best way is to rattle your audience's brains.

Sweat, Blood, Toil, and Tears: Surpassing Yourself

Remember what Plato told us was the purpose of public speaking: "government of the souls of men." Well, dominion over the minds and hearts of men goes to the heart of "executive presence," and this is achieved by challenging the ability of your audience, bang from the nonce, to keep up with your mental broadsides.

Mind, one does have to play with "delicate strings" the intellectual capacity of those to whom one is speaking. One doesn't attempt expounding knotty concepts to Yale sophomores in the springtime, nor any time to brokers, golfers, or joggers, nor to anyone in Hollywood who hasn't yet slept in Abe Lincoln's bed, or who truly believes that wolves don't bite. That's folly. It's like trying to get a medical doctor to say something simply, or a lawyer to say something cheaply.

But that's not your problem, you lament. You are not Paul Weiss. You have nothing so difficult nor so complex and original to say. You're not even Yogi Berra. To which I answer: I plumb do not believe you. Truly, I do not. Every human being in this planet above the IQ level of a toll collector on a highway has rich lodes inside him to mine, if he'll dig for them. Dig! Else, never display the insolence of claiming the attention of your fellow men from a podium. Go mutter someplace in private, or bore your spouse, or telephone Dick Morris. (For how to discover something to say, see Chapter 6.)

COMMANDMENT 2

Having first shocked them, soothe, placate, and coddle your audience.

You have them now on the edges of their seats, roused from post-prandial stupor or fully recovered from last night's too many cocktails (or from watching Al Gore dance the *Macarena*).

Slacken the reins in this second paragraph. Permit your audience to breathe a little.

Surpassing Yourself . . .

You must conduct some audiences across tricky terrain by the hand, sheering clear always of the twin reefs of arrogance and condescension.

"You may not be familiar with Godel's Incompleteness Theorem," you might observe (assuming for some reason you began talking about Godel's Incompleteness Theorem, which would not be my advice), "but the essence is actually simple, originating in a letter from St. Paul to Titus, in which he recounts that a Cretan stated, 'Cretans are always liars.' If this is true, you see, it's false. If a Cretan condemns all Cretans as liars, then he himself is one, and what he tells you is a lie."

Maintain this easy conversational tone, using the simplest language. Push your luck now with a similar thrust. Say: "Suppose you hear someone declare, 'This statement is false.'" Continue: "At once there are problems. If *that* statement is true, then it's false, but in addition, if it's false, then it's true." Gently paraphrase: "You see, if there is truth in his declaration that his statement is false, then it is false because he speaks truly; but if what he says is false, then his declaration is true."

At this point, smile broadly and move on. Since audiences are generically so obtuse that they never truly follow your reasoning, and since this particular audience is by definition coin-collector dumb, (a) they don't know whether you've spoken nonsense, and (b) they're too intimidated to challenge you. *Remember, it's okay to repeat a sentence in some difficult passage or to rephrase what you have just said by way of explication, but never, ever, resort to a chart or any other visual aid.* (For more on the proper way of placating an audience, see Chapter 19.)

COMMANDMENT 3

Above all, convey humility of spirit.

You may be bright, you may be distinguished, you may have achieved a whole lot in your lifetime, but if you do not possess humility of spirit, your words will be the mere tinkling of brass cymbals. The pompous or self-satisfied speaker begs for the ice pick to punch holes in the full sail of his vanity.

Humility of spirit is a grace. One cannot fake it; but through the intensity of your desire to persuade the audience to your point of view, and through the utter sincerity of your belief in what you are saying, you will subjugate the ego to the message and gain the good-will that is the necessary precursor of persuasion. (See Chapter 20, the explication of point 10, for more on carrying the audience.) If you come off as a snotty SOB, you'll gain the day only despite the obstacle of yourself. But if love is the well from which you draw, your audiences will be predisposed to be moved by your reason. (For more on humility of spirit, see Chapter 19.)

COMMANDMENT 4

Do lightly salt your speech with acerbic topical wit if it is apposite.

You've established that you are a serious customer.

You've tempered the opening blast of your remarks with a less rigorous second paragraph, permitting the audience to catch up with you and feel a little more comfortable. You've next conveyed your humanity and the gentleness that wins souls (the chief business of the art of public speaking). Now you need to lighten the atmosphere further with shafts of your native wit. (For more on the uses of wit and humor, see Chapter 17.)

Digging Deeper into the Subject: Surpassing Yourself

Late in the 1996 Presidential campaign, the scandal of Indonesian contributions to the Democratic Party's war chest billowed across the air waves, with even James Broder venting his disgust in a column and ABC's wholly cynical Peter Jennings lifting his elegant eyebrows in distaste. Bob Dole was in his last desperate days.

He was pressed by reporters for his reaction to this latest scandal. Did he launch into a moralistic rant about sleaze in high places? That wouldn't have been like the man. He went with the grain of his character (as all of us should). In that dry, blunt, plainspoken prairie accent, he said:

The President and Mrs. Clinton aren't available for comment, I hear. They're undergoing treatment for Lippo-suction. [*Here he paused a moment while the press caught on—liposuction . . . Lippo Bank—and then erupted in laughter.*] Bill Clinton never heard of Mr. Huang. They say he's visited the White House sixty-five times in the past ten months, but no, Bill Clinton had to check with his store of FBI background files to find out who the man was. [*Laughter.*] Yes. I heard the President and his staff are being funneled through two security checkpoints every time they leave and enter the White House. The first is a lie detector, the second wipes out the memory of the lie. [*Chuckles, laughter, derisive hoots.*] With Bob Dole you won't need that.

This is a masterful performance by Bob Dole, I think you'll agree. (I made it up.) He never steps out of character; he adroitly reminds the press that here is just one more abuse of power by a White House that has become notorious for straining public credibility. Exploit your humor in that manner most natural to you, slipping the knife in with deft thrusts. The balance has to be just right. Never permit humor to overshadow the bite of what you say, but by framing your barbs in witty fashion, you disarm criticism of yourself. "The Senator was on a roll, wasn't he? I mean, you could tell he was enjoying himself . . . but the points he raised about this Administration are right on target."

There are several subpoints to reflect upon:

- Almost before you have thought up your one-liners people may not remember who John Huang was or that the corporate conglomerate he fronted for was Lippo Group, Lippo Bank, Lippo Plaza, Lippo Everything.

- As I write, the scandal continues making news, but by the time you read this reference to it, it will be stale. Quips of a topical nature enjoy the briefest half-life. I invented these, as I've confessed, but someone else is sure to pick them up. Gags travel by osmosis. Tell your quips once, never repeat them. (For more on gags and humor generally, see Chapter 17.)

- Never risk giving the impression that you aspire to double for Bob Hope. (That's why the rule is *lightly* to salt your talks with such jabs or asides. Gravitas—executive presence—and wit are congenial; gravitas and cheap shots of the nightclub comedian genre are incompatible.)

- Don't fret because you imagine you're not verbally clever. You don't have to be Seinfeld. Taking 10 minutes to brood on the unending stream of idiocies that characterize this dismal age will pop material in your mind. The only talent required of you is to retain independent judgment; that is, that you refrain from being one of the idiots at whom the idiocies of the age are aimed.

- As mentioned above, don't ever sacrifice sense to fun. Your witticisms *must* be to the point, dumping you back into your topic. (That is why I concluded the sequence, "With Bob Dole you won't need that.")

COMMANDMENT 5

Argue to the core.

Never divagate.

Never be seduced by an amusing or even fascinating story that not only sins for being irrelevant to your topic but that does not actually advance the analysis you are presenting.

Illustrating your point is not the purpose of an anecdote. *Deepening the understanding* of your case is what your anecdotes must do. Weed and weed and weed. Cut and cut and cut. (For more on building a case, see Chapter 10.)

Avoiding Digging a Pit for Oneself

Many executives and professionals make the fundamental mistake of approaching a speech as their Grand Occasion, which may never be repeated.

And so they attempt to stuff the sausage with all the suet it can bear, until the skin is bursting. What they have accomplished is to guarantee that, indeed, *never* will they be asked to address an audience again, not if anyone can help it.

<u>Do this</u>. Read your talk to yourself so often that you, the author, become unutterably bored with it, causing you to edit and sharpen it to the effect that you won't bore your audience the first time.

The companion injunction is this:

COMMANDMENT 6

Be not only succinct, be brief.

. . . And briefer yet.[1]

This is also the age of the bullet, the six-second sound bite. Any speech exceeding thirty minutes is a mistake.

I'm not suggesting that you may be a bore one minute past half an hour, but that your contemporary audiences possess little stamina of concentration and (on their part) insufficient humility of spirit to listen for more than thirty minutes to the Archangel Gabriel announcing doomsday. (For more on brevity, see Chapter 10.)

When Brevity Isn't Permitted

There are circumstances when you may not be permitted your good sense.

High schools and colleges, for example, demand that you consume a full fifty-five minutes. They don't want the kids roaming corridors for longer than it takes them to get to the next class, inasmuch as, given the leisure, they tend to mug, rape, and zap one another. Which is awkward. (And messy.) If you are *compelled* to hold the floor longer than you wish, arrange for a question and answer period. In fact, whenever you speak thirty minutes or more, always . . .

COMMANDMENT 7

Arrange for a question and answer period.

. . . Of ten to fifteen minutes.

It breaks up the monologue; it involves the audience; it can clarify points.

---

[1] In her latest book (*Simply Speaking*, ReganBooks, 1998), Peggy Noonan insists that twenty minutes is the maximum allowable length nowadays, and she adduces the powerful authority of Ronald Reagan.

Organizing a Q&A Session

- **Insist that a chairman field the questions.**

Acoustics are almost always poor in lecture and banquet halls. People cough, dishes clatter. Even when mikes are placed here and there for the audience to speak into, what people say is often mumbled, disorganized, unintelligible. If the chairman restates the questions, everybody knows what is being asked, and meanwhile you have gained a few seconds to think up answers.

- **Have the chairman insist that questions not exceed fifteen seconds, and try to keep your responses crisp, under a minute.**

Audiences detest it when a few wannabe orators or ideological fanatics grab their chance to rant into a floor mike. And few lapses in judgment or consideration are so infuriating to an audience than that of the speaker who, having just held forth for thirty minutes, launches into a protracted answer to the first question flung at him. Don't attempt to respond to every nuance suggested by a complex question. (Say, frankly, this would take too long; the audience will sympathize.) Select that aspect of the question that can be knocked off or expounded in the most economical manner.

- **Be gracious about difficult questions that may damage your case to which you do not know the answer.**

Thank the person—from the heart. Tell him (or her): (a) "You've brought up something I've never before thought of," or (b) "I'd never heard of that study until you mentioned it," or (c) "Those statistics are news to me and I have no answer to them." Then say, in the first case, (a) "But thanks to you, I'll be giving it a lot of thought"; in the second case, (b) "Now that you've brought the study to my attention, I'm going to be sure to read it"; in the third case, (c) "But thanks to you, I'll look at them, check them out, and decide what bearing they have." *Then ask for that person to pass his name and address up to the chair,* permitting you to drop him a note when you've done what you promise.

Nowhere is it written that you may not flatter opponents who earn your respect. They'll think well of you as a person and give your case a more sympathetic consideration. By being candid when you don't know the answer, you will have enhanced the credibility of everything else you said that evening, and you will have gained respect.

- **Be prepared for sleazeballs.**

The most unexpected questions sometimes pop up from the floor, bearing little relation to the topic of the evening. Be considerate, kind, and unstuffy, but explain that since this particular query is personal, or on another subject, it would be unfair to take the time of the whole audience to address it. Then say you'll be happy to do so after the evening has come to a close, if the person will come up to the stage. Americans seem to be possessed by a consuming curiosity about one's personal life. Many have come to the lecture not to hear what you have to say about your topic but to hear you say it. They are celebrity-struck, and they seem to assume that all people in public view are as willing to display their souls in public as Demi Moore or Sharon Stone their private parts. It's as though they believe they have a *right* to inquire anything they please of anyone who exposes himself on a stage, and that you, the unlucky speaker, are obliged to gratify them. This morbid, salacious, unhealthy curiosity has been uncinched by those awful television talk shows, where audiences crowd studios to listen to indescribable human refuse tell in detail how their daddies beat them or how their priest or minister seduced them. There doesn't seem to be any *pudeur* left in this country. (One wonders, would Bill Clinton have been possible before Oprah Winfrey?)

Be friendly always on stage, but don't acquiesce in permitting yourself to be made an open target for nasty, insolent, or prurient personal questions. Cut the churl off at the knees. Should he ask, say, "Haven't you ever enjoyed a one-night stand, Mr. Jones?" reply, "Since I can only assume from the disgusting insolence of your question that you enjoy boasting in public about being unfaithful to your spouse, I'm tempted to ask you about your infidelities, but I doubt anybody here is interested. Next question." Even if he persists, he'll be shouted down.

COMMANDMENT 8
*Keep in stock an anecdote that sums up
and pleasantly illustrates your thesis.*

Never, ever, not ever do ye forget: the audience (like conservatives) are the stupid party. By the time you have answered the last question, they have forgotten the body of your text.

Summing Up for the Audience

As a conservative, I used to bemoan the corruptions that inevitably attend concentration of power. Lord Acton, absolutely.

Having dealt with the last volley from the floor, I often closed the evening by recounting that when I was 11 years old and living in Mexico, I discovered that since time immemorial, Mexicans have suffered from corrupt government. "This is one social malady that can't be blamed on Hernán Cortés," I'd say, "but Mexicans alleviate the pain by their rollicking sense of humor. One Sunday, the *Excelsior*, Mexico City's *NY Times*, displayed a cartoon on its front page of Diogenes, in Greece, with his lantern, looking for an honest man. Adjacent was a second cartoon of Diogenes, this time in Mexico, looking for his lantern." Adding (*ho-ho-ho*), "In Washington he'd be looking for his toga as well."

COMMANDMENT 9

Contrive always to get five minutes to yourself before the performance.

You need repose to wash the sediment of cocktail or supper party chatter out of your mind.

You *must* concentrate on your material before launching into it. Talk to whoever is running matters. Tell him or her that you need to withdraw from the hurly-burly. They'll understand. Those five or ten minutes to yourself before a performance can be as refreshing and important and *energizing* as a midday nap.

What to Do When Circumstances Conspire against You

Seclusion isn't simple to arrange when you're at a banquet, penned in by supper partners.

Before the event, practice in the mirror expressions of instant gastric extremity. A glance at your distress will prompt fellow guests to excuse you.

Oh: at a luncheon or banquet, the rule is take one alcoholic drink before you get up to speak, a stiff one if need be, but never two.

COMMANDMENT 10

Always complete dressing before you mount the stage.

Women are, on the whole, fastidious about first impressions, but men commonly fall into the vice of buttoning their jackets or hauling up on their back seats by the belt as they walk to the lectern. Or worse. (But you'll have to read on for that.)

Just keep in mind that the time to tighten the knot of your tie, or tuck that handkerchief into a breast pocket, or check your teeth in a compact mirror to make sure no lipstick has stuck to them, or that they are still there, is before you mount the podium. (For more on dress, see Chapter 11.)

A Horrible Example

Back in the 1950s, a youth of many parts—a visionary, a horseman, a saltwater sailor, author of temple-tumbling books—was seeking funds for a literary venture that was destined to become the decisive political journal in the final years of the twentieth century.

Handsome, debonair, charming, and amazingly young, he spoke before a Duchess County audience that reeked of old New York wealth and old New York stuffiness. Applause greeted him when he strode on stage. Alas, he had neglected to zip up; and as he threw himself into his pitch, a white tail of his shirt peeped through the opening of the fly and hung saucily there, swishing back and forth with the vigorous twists and turns of his body. Kinfolk in the front row hissed at him; he smiled down on them benignly, oblivious . . . flinging himself so completely into his appeal that he planted both fists on his hips and thrust back on the small of his spine, which had the effect of thrusting his pelvis forward. Which . . .

Would you believe that he raised $300,000 that night?

Which goes to show that if you know how to govern the souls of men, you can make your point, even if your trousers are down about your ankles.

PART 2

SPEAKING SITUATIONS

How to Survive Next Week's Talk

INTRODUCTION

You must first choose.

Depending on what group you're addressing, what is it that you want to accomplish? Is your principal purpose:

- To ingratiate yourself?
- To educate or enlighten?
- To advance a policy?
- To raise money for some charitable or political purpose?
- To seek support for yourself or your candidate?

Depending on that decision, the prescriptions that follow must be modified by you.

Suit your purpose. I've been arbitrary here, assuming that if you are speaking to business associates (Chapter 3), your primary objective is to present facts, challenge old assumptions, or seek commitment to new policies; if to a fraternal organization (Chapter 4), your primary objective is to ingratiate yourself by giving your audience a good time; and if you are speaking on behalf of a political position or candidate, or for a cause (Chapter 5), what you are there for is to raise money and garner votes.

This is probably too arbitrary and restricted. You'll have to measure which mix you desire, for which individual occasion.

ASSUMING THE TACTICAL ADVANTAGE

This enlarges on the advice given under Commandment 1, Chapter 2, recommending that the speaker take his audience by the throat.

Should you be engaged in debate or find yourself—in your capacity as a professional or executive (not to speak of being in politics)—in a controversial or polemical situation, use these tactics:

1. Choose to counterpunch always; elect to go second or last.

2. Disarm the opposition as cleverly and engagingly (read *insouciantly*) as you are able.

3. Go for the jugular.

Sweat, Blood, Toil, and Tears: Surpassing Yourself

All three can be taken care of in a bundle.

At a scholarly Buckley School of Disciplined Thinking seminar in May of 1996, the question of judicial restraint was debated by the brilliant young scholar Paul Rahe and Judge Robert Bork.

Paul Rahe was slated second. With immense charm, he began by acknowledging the heavy debt that he and all Constitutional scholars owe to the rigorous analyses of Robert Bork; he then proceeded for fifteen shriveling minutes to lambast Judge Bork's case, leaving him not limb nor life nor seemingly shred of dignity to cling to. At the end of it, hushed heads turned to the heavily hunched and bearded figure of the judge, who had sat immutably under the barrage, and who now rose for his five-minute rebuttal, which he began, "So wonderful was your argument, Paul, that I rejoiced that it had nothing to do with mine."

Choosing to be last, or being cunning in exploiting the precise dramatic moment and marshaling the verbal wit to do so, is an art that only experience in the rough and tumble of life can bestow. But be cautious. In his defense before the Athenian Senate, Socrates (on trial for his life) began in words of exquisite grace, not dissimilar to those of Judge Bork, saying:

> How I have felt, O men of Athens, at hearing the speeches of my accusers, I cannot tell; but I know that their persuasive words almost made me forget who I was, such was the effect of them; and yet they have hardly spoken a word of truth.

What a way to grab the attention of one's audience, court their favor, yet lay rascals low! Despite which, Socrates was famously adjudged guilty and sentenced to death.

The moral is this: Verbal eloquence alone will neither disguise truth nor persuade malice. Ask Bill Clinton.

CHAPTER 3

SPEAKING OBLIGATIONS RELATED TO YOUR BUSINESS OR PROFESSION

Even though the notion of earning one's bread by the sweat of one's brow, either in office or consultancy, may be repugnant, *EVERYONE SHOULD READ THIS FIRST SECTION*; thence skipping to the chore most approximating the one one faces. If rules and exhortations are repeated, that's for a reason.

A definition may be necessary. No matter how exalted *his* condition, how lowly *theirs*, the superiors of any speaker are his audience (just as His Holiness the Pope is the servant of the servants of God). The immediate superiors of the president of a corporation are his board and its chairman, over which sit in judgment the stockholders. The superiors of any officer in any organization are his immediate boss and, in the wider perspective, the bosses of his boss, which at the highest level are once again the stockholders.

BESEECHING THE AUGUST INDULGENCE AND FAVOR OF YOUR SUPERIORS

And now an admission: so long has it been since I served as CEO of a Fortune 500 company that I sought counsel from friends and graduates[1]

---

[1] They are James L. Ferguson, retired Chief Executive Officer of General Foods; C. L. "Jerry" Henry, former CFO of DuPont, presently Chairman, President, and CEO of Johns Manville Corporation; Brian J. Lipke, Chairman and CEO of Gibraltar Steel Corporation; and Edwin Russell, CEO of Minnesota Power, Inc. For more on their individual comments, see Appendix A.

of The Buckley School, to whom and for which I am grateful. That so many of their recommendations coincide or overlap strengthens their authority. Here's the short list:

1. Keep it simple; keep it short.
2. Remember, you're selling both yourself and your ideas.
3. Prepare, rehearse, polish.
4. Take the "temperature" of your audience; be sensitive to whatever private agendas may be lurking.
5. Be patient.
6. Abolish slides and other visual aids unless absolutely necessary.
7. Give the bad news first.
8. Learn how to turn on the light switch.
9. Shun jargon, hi-tech twaddle, business babble, the third person, and the passive voice.
10. Confess that you don't know the answer when you don't know the answer.

These adjurations are basic for all occasions in which you, the speaker, are seeking approval, either of past performance or a new course of action. Much the same principles apply when you wish to sell a product to potential clients. Taking them one by one:

Sweat, Blood, Toil, and Tears: Surpassing Yourself

1. Keep it simple; keep it short.

Never run longer than an hour and a quarter, which is fifteen minutes too long. If you possibly can, contain your presentation to less than sixty minutes.

Be focused: deliver your report in crisp, concise language. (For more on these important considerations, see the Part 4 Introduction and Chapter 10.) Don't waste people's time with what they know; give them something new, exercising your imagination. And be sure to alert them beforehand whether the meeting requires action or is for informational purposes only. (I'd be reluctant to occupy the attention of my CEO or board solely for the informational value of what I have to say. Something demanding a decision at their supreme level should be at the core of my text, even though that decision needn't be made at once.)

For Heaven's sake, do not bore your CEO or the board. Neither be so bold, new, and revolutionary that you totally upset them by straining their imaginations beyond their capacity to comprehend this novel thing you are proposing.

Never forget that in a business report, substance is more important than style, though substance clumsily expounded may lose the day to a flashier competitor. One of the beauties of reading John Maynard Keynes or John Kenneth Galbraith is that though intellectually you can be assured that what they write is specious, it's almost always stylish and entertaining. One of the horrors of reading a speech by Al Gore or Bill Clinton is that even should you agree 100 percent with what they say, it's so pedestrianly put that you may wish you loved Newt Gingrich. The (sobering) fact of the matter is that even in the supposedly hardboiled business arena, style defeats substance deplorably often, because style is *seductive*, which explains equally corsets, hoop skirts, human skin deepfried in palm oil, glitz, and the spectacle of that old fool Walter Cronkite blubbering in public over the memory of JFK.

2. Remember, you're selling both yourself and your ideas.

Your ideas may be persuasive on their own, but it's you who must put them across. This is where style enters: an adroit and graceful presentation can make palatable even uncomfortable reforms or departures. You must stand by them. They will stand up depending on your stature: your reputation for sense and clearheadedness; the compelling sense of what you say at this moment. Check, double-check, triple-check for evidence you may have misconstrued and errors of logic that escaped your vigilant first reading. All human beings are subject to blunders in fact and logic. Never will you be impeccable in both, or even either.

The manuscript of a book is read seven, eight, ten times by the author; then it is read and criticized by his editor, presumably a professional (mine for this book is both a pro and a doll); then it is rewritten and read once or twice or three times more by the author; then it is submitted to the editor and a copy editor; then the galleys or page proofs are sent to the author for final correction. Notwithstanding all this, the moment the author opens the published book, he discovers that he dated the Treaty of Utrecht 1317 (instead of 1713); spoke of the vested virgins in the Greek temple; lauded a Bach concerto for its *classical* construction; somehow omitted a whole half line that was the bridge between *A* and *B*, and without which *B* is incomprehensible, though nice; and wrote of high *chiché* when he meant *chic*, or *quicke* when he meant *quiche*, which, to add insult to injury, he detests. To his dismay, he discovers blunders by the dozen, including two or three *he had corrected in the galleys* that, like a virus with a molecular memory for the vicious form, somehow reverted to their wrongheadedness; as when some dodo somewhere substituted meritorious for meretricious, when (damnit!) he meant meretricious, and so corrected it back on the page proof, and it came up meritorious anyhow.

These unforfendable gremlins, which seem to breed within the nature of any transposition from the mind to the printed page, cause woe sufficient without chancing any more howlers through sloppiness or laziness. Don't become *paranoiac* about scanning your text and scanning it and scanning it again; simply keep in mind that your job is at stake, your head is on the block, your spouse a widow, your children orphans . . .

3. Prepare, rehearse, polish.

In a conversation with your superior, you may be compelled to wing what you want to say; you are obliged to answer his questions. But when you are putting together a report for a company gathering at which your boss and the board may be present, do all the sweating beforehand, mentally rehearsing your text. Don't risk that awful popping out in beads of perspiration once you're on your feet, thinking the terrible thought: *I should have reasoned this through and cleaned my argument up before opening my mouth.* Few agonies are so terrible: maybe being summoned by the headmaster for some serious infraction when you are 15 years old, or being summoned by

St. Peter for final judgment. For more on this, see Chapter 9, Organizing the Written Article or Speech.

4. Take the "temperature" of your audience; be sensitive to whatever private agendas may be lurking.

Don't blunder into the cannon's mouth. Privately sound out your audience before making your presentation. If you know for a fact that your boss or the CEO is going to detest what you believe is your duty to tell them, prepare inwardly for the consequences, do your best to make your point as seductively (stylishly) as possible, and unless it is absolutely necessary, hold back your gunfire until a more propitious opportunity presents itself. If you know for a fact that certain members of the board will detest your message, and if confrontation is unavoidable because you cannot, in good conscience, keep silent, seek out allies on the board. Enlist their support before you charge up San Juan Hill. (For more on this subject, see page 39.)

5. Be patient.

. . . Both strategically and tactically.

Think twice about advancing a controversial position, keeping your counsel and husbanding your resources until you have gathered sufficient allies (see item 4 above). Once you have decided that a decision cannot be delayed, be painstaking in expounding, explaining, and defending your view. Expect incomprehension, skepticism, and hostility. These reactions are natural when what one has to say is both interesting and different. Never take any protest personally, and never blame your opponents for their opposition. You invited it.

This is important. Do not ever treat people who disagree with you as your enemies or, worse, as nitwits. (The second is the greater insult.) Never permit the faintest odor of condescension or contempt to escape you. Be good-humored always. Acquire the capacity for infinite tact. Be sensitive to all those extraneous considerations that may be disturbing others. Are your proposals endangering anyone's job? Will someone's authority suffer, the range of his responsibilities be cut back? Is there the implication in your report that some exalted personage has done a bum job? Suffer personal attacks graciously, and learn from them. (For more on patience, see page 43.)

6. Abolish slides and other visual aids unless absolutely necessary.

A very high officer of a very major hi-tech defense contractor came to us several years ago in distress. He was a graduate of the Executive Seminar in Communication Skills, yet he was in crisis. Joshua had fit the battle of Jericho, the Berlin Wall had come tumblin' down, military spending by Congress was being cut back, and contracts on which his company depended heavily were drying up. An extraordinary emergency meeting of the board and all the division chiefs of the corporation had been scheduled. Our client had been told by the CEO, his immediate superior, that he was to make a major presentation at that meeting, at which (a) the future of the company would be decided, and (b) his future with the company would be decided.

He sent in advance a technician who was to confer two days with our writer, Kathleen Parker, before he himself arrived for eighteen hours of drill. The speech he had drafted was written in a foreign language closely resembling English as spoken by Bushmen in the Great Kalahari Desert, as far as any non-techwonk might have observed. Not only was the jargon absolute, the text was fifty pages long, sufficient for an address of two hours, and ninety-eight visual charts and graphs were included in the package. Kathy and then I rewrote the talk from first word to last, between us cutting it to forty minutes. Despite screams of outrage from the technician and the deep tremors of our client, we abolished all but two of the charts, eliminating the overhead projector. I had to jawbone the poor fellow. He could not conceive of making his presentation without the crutch of those excruciatingly boring and redundant (and ultimately meaningless) visual aids. He worried that his boss would be scandalized. (The technician waxed hysterical as, one by one, we tossed his creations out.) But we prevailed, and the consequence was (a) our client's company successfully revolutionized its way of doing business in the direction our client proposed, and (b) he chalked up a major personal success, his CEO complimenting him on the clarity, economy, and lucidity of his talk, which, "Thank *God*," he said, "contained none of those damned charts and other visual distractions."

The techniques of executing some forbiddingly complicated process, as, say, a surgical procedure, may demand visual explications. But this is special and rare. Visual aids are used by people *as an expression of their insecurity*, when there is no necessity for them as a means of diverting attention from themselves, or as a tacit confession of their inability to make anything clear verbally. They are also a pernicious "distraction," as our client's CEO put it, from where the focus ought to be, which is on the speaker. In Spain there's an adage about fighting girth as one grows older: *el culo o la cara*. It's either the ass or the face. The one expands or the other withers. Either the speaker or his visual aids are going to star. One or the other will engross attention. Eschewing charts and slides and transparencies *whenever possible* compels the speaker to chisel his prose so that what he says is lapidary in its clarity. His language should compel the audience to visualize what he is saying. This effort on the part of the audience, demanded by the complexity (no less lucidity) of what the speaker is imparting, commands the absolute attention of the audience, which requires strenuous effort on the speaker's part, in his writing and in his delivery. The speaker will sweat, oh my; he will be bone-tired when he finishes. But his audience will be rapt: challenged, absorbed, educated. When the speaker finishes, the spell he has wrought may continue a few moments, to be broken by a thunderous round of applause. (We can dream.) (For more on this subject, see page 54, later in this chapter. The advice, remember, is culled from experts.)

If you *must* resort to charts and statistical tabulations in support of your position, hand these out prior to your talk. Stuff them in those kits that business people are handed when they arrive at conventions. Pass them out at breakfast, or as people enter the lecture hall. Don't plod through the information contained in these handouts. Select from the mass of data those facts and figures that are significant or essential for a solid understanding of the case you are making. Never say in the course of your talk, "You'll find on page 17 of the looseleaf binder in your laps the growth of respiratorial allergies in the United States over the past twenty-five years relative to the increased incidence of redheads of Irish extraction and the simultaneous spread of unscrubbed industry smokestacks from urban centers to the suburbs." Why not? Because disturbing numbers of people in your audience will start thumbing or flipping through that binder, searching for page 17 (and when finding it, become bemused by other information on the page or become infatuated with and pore over a chart they mistakenly flip to beyond page 17, which happens to relate to a subsequent point you wish to make), meanwhile (in either instance) totally breaking intellectual connection with you, while your voice continues to buzz, as background static in their skulls. You lose your audience not when you make reference to the advance materials but when you call attention to them and invite your audience to transfer their attention from you to what's in their hands.

Say, either at the beginning of your talk or at the end, "The kits we've passed out to you contain the empirical evidence for what [I'm going to say] [I've just said]. Study that information at your leisure. If you have any specific questions about anything, ask me [when I'm through] [now]."

7. Give the bad news first.

Doing anything else invites charges of disingenuousness and suspicion that the speaker is craven.

Also, who wants to leave an audience on a sour note?

8. Learn how to turn on the light switch.

My friend Joe Sullivan is a top-drawer chief executive officer and an Irishman of irascible temperament. Second-level management aspiring to the first level often blunder, he tells me, at the most elementary level. "They spend time trying to get the overhead projector going, looking for the light switches. The impression they give is that they didn't adequately prepare the presentation in advance."

A persistent nightmare revisits my attempt to sell Abercrombie & Fitch an ingenious contraption invented by Alfonso Urquijo, banker and internationally renowned Spanish sportsman, that permitted the shotgunner to test himself in his office against every conceivable flying target, incoming and going away. It worked through the random rotation of metal templates in a projector, which cast the shadows of ducks or pigeons or pheasants against any solidly colored wall. These images sprang into view by surprise and from all angles. The gunner swung at them with his favorite weapon, to whose barrels had been affixed a specially designed flashlight that cast an intense beam at the pull of the trigger. Sighting along the barrels, one saw when the vivid circle of light encompassed the target shadow, or failed to.

Running a single template was the equivalent of a round of skeet or clay pigeons—maybe better. Tens of thousands of busy executives would rush to buy and install this boon in their offices.

"But does it work?" asked the president and CEO, leery of any complex mechanism made in Spain. (This was the 1960s.)

"Absolutely," quoth I. "Infallibly," quoth I. "Gloriously," quoth I.

The entire high command of that then-august sporting goods emporium (with whom I had done business before, exporting leather shellbags) assembled in the board room on the tenth-floor offices of their Madison Avenue store to view the marvelous invention. I am not mechanically inclined. The fact is, everything mechanical since the inception of the industrial age is in conspiracy against me and has been since I came into this world, perhaps because that occurred in France. Yet I had been instructed in the use of this machine: I set up the projector, plugging its cord into the 220/115 transformer and that into a handy socket on the baseboard; selected and inserted a template in just the way I had been taught; and clipped the flashlight under the muzzles of a sleek Purdy .20 gauge, which I handed ceremoniously to the chairman of the board. Then, as I began describing the wonders that we were all about to witness, I sought the projector's switch to turn the machine on.

My inquiring hand and fingers failed to locate it. Rapid further tactile explorations did not discover it. My tongue wagged on, both hands now flitting rapidly across the top, along the sides, in front, back, and under the projector's bottom, to nil avail: no toggle, button, or lever revealed itself. At last, I left off talking, devoting myself candidly to my desperate search. "Maybe it's attached to the cable," suggested the chairman kindly, peering under the table top. "I think I see it!" exclaimed the president and CEO, getting on hands and knees to examine one of those European on/off switches that are situated along the length of the cord. But that wasn't it. "Here, let me take a look," said a burly executive vice president, shouldering me out of the way to examine the projector. But he had no better luck than I ... nor did anyone else. Hilarity began the search, exasperation ended it. A half-hour later, I departed with my marvelous invention.

Take nothing for granted; make certain everything that needs to work does work and that you know where the critical switch is located,[2] the most important of which is that critical switch in the minds of the board.

9. Shun jargon, hi-tech twaddle, business babble, the third person, and the passive voice.

CEOs generally are not horses' asses; they are, in the vast majority, sophisticated, literate, and respecters of simplicity. They abide needlessly convoluted syntax and polysyllabic language as little as the rest of us. They *may* be SOBs; they are not fools. Business writing has evolved with the evident purpose of thwarting the understanding, as an idiom to hide behind. Its object is the reverse of clear meaning; it is obfuscation. Its end is to help the author evade responsibility for what he says and to conceal beneath verbiage the barrenness of his mind. It's wonderful. It's a blessing to cowardice and mediocrity. *But don't try pulling this with top-level management.*

They know the game. Like the hot blade of a knife, their intelligences cleave through pretentiousness and pomposity. They perceive at once when the subordinate does not know what he's talking about and is trying to cover for his inadequacy by needless circumlocutions and by resorting to tongue-thickening mush. A good speech may not be sufficient to exalt you; a turgid speech will squash you.

10. Confess that you don't know the answer when you don't know the answer.

Tell it straight, and when you are stumped, resolve to dig up the answer at first opportunity, e-mailing, faxing, or otherwise communicating it to your boss (the CEO and the board). (See Chapter 2, Commandment 7, for more about this.)

---

[2] In the case of the Spanish shadow box, cunningly, just beneath the knob focusing the lens.

Always assuming that you are not a fool, candor beats know-it-all any time. In admitting ignorance there is commendable humility of spirit. Know-it-all wearies. He's gunning for your job, you can be sure of that. Besides, he is often so complacently certain of his knowledge that he is subject to enormous errors of fact and calculation. The quick-and-ready answer can be refreshing, the glib answer never is.

I have a wonderful story illustrating this point that I choose not to tell you in this book.[3]

PREPPING OR PEPPING OR ADJURING YOUR SUBORDINATES

Generally adhere to the rules for addressing your superiors given above, hewing to these in addition:

1. Do not condescend.

2. Speak in simple language, but avoid slang, obscenities, and profanity.

3. If you wish to congratulate your subordinates for a good job, do so with sincere fervor, but spare exaggeration.

4. If you are compelled to chide your subordinates for sloppy performance, do so with perfect candor.

5. Be lavish with humor, but do not permit it to put your message in second place.

6. Never stoop to being a barracks lawyer—you represent management, not the union.

7. Do not curry favor in any way.

8. Do not disseminate gossip about the people above you or make disparaging remarks about them or tolerate disparaging remarks about them.

9. Do not permit yourself to be the prey of factions.

---

[3] The reason? Refer back to Chapter 1, Cardinal Sin 2, and forward to Chapter 17.

10. Don't, for Heaven's sake, seek to ingratiate yourself by making reference to your past glories on the baseball diamond, the football field, the ice rink, or the basketball court.

That last is in the order of Bill Clinton boasting about his military record. And even if you were an all-American jock, one glance at your belly now dispels the adolescent glory.

None of the other rules require comment, but do keep vividly present that when compelling your subordinates to listen to a talk by you, it is *they* who sit in judgment.

TELLING IT TO YOUR BOARD

Well, of course, you *don't*. You're smarter than that.[4]

As well as corporate boards, this topic comprehends philanthropic and civic committees of all kinds. It divides into four parts: preparation, exposition, resistance, and follow-through.

Preparation

1. Be as cunning and wise as Ulysses: in advance of the meeting, thoroughly prepare:

   • The evidence supporting your recommendations

   • The diplomatic landscape

   • The staging and technical requirements of the meeting

2. Never play politics.

3. Put yourself in the shoes of your target audience.

4. Decide what is salient about your message.

---

[4]For this exalted contingency I enlisted the savvy of Vern A. Ketchem, retired CEO of Kelvinator International and White Consolidated Industries, Intl., who has been a close collaborator of The Buckley School these past ten years ("Carload Ketchem" was his soubriquet in the business, because that's the way he sold household appliances to the Saudi Arabians, by the freight car load); Joseph F. Sullivan, retired Chairman, President, and CEO of Blue Cross/Blue Shield and Companion Insurance of South Carolina, and longtime member of the school board; and fellow youthful miscreant, Joseph H. Williams, retired President and CEO of The Williams Companies, which, under his able direction, metastasized. I have cribbed from their spoken and written advice in full, shamelessly.

Sweat, Blood, Toil, and Tears: Surpassing Yourself

1. Be as cunning and wise as Ulysses . . .

Advises Vern Ketchem: Thrash out your proposals with your personal staff or close friends. Make certain that what you are going to say is backed by the evidence. Ask yourself: What exactly are my objectives? (Determining these helps keep the presentation within bounds.) Are you suggesting a major departure from normal operations, that is, a long-term major shift in products, direction, and emphasis? Then ask yourself: What kind of a board am I dealing with? Is it a policy-making board, or is it one that likes to micromanage? Is it hostile, friendly, or flexible? Depending on the character of the board, determine what your best approach may be.

Commence the process of persuasion early. Test the waters first with your board's chairman, sounding him out in personal conversations. Outline for him the circumstances that motivate (or compel) the proposal you wish to make. Get his approval to go ahead with it and to gather necessary backup evidence. (If your chairman is unalterably opposed, your pitch is dead on arrival, unless you resolve on a palace coup.) Go next to the executive committee, assuming your business has one. Test those waters to find out who favors your position. Thoroughly brief potential allies. Secure enough support to go to the full board, but only when you are sanguine that you will win. If you're not that sure, you need to do more groundwork. If the sell isn't easy, you may need to resort to a consultant for technical advice.

2. Never play politics.

Corporate politics is a bane. Defining your objectives, however, testing the predisposition of individual members of the board and the obstacles that you are likely to encounter in selling your recommendations, and endeavoring gently and subtly to predispose board members to your point of view aren't to be mistaken for divisive and potentially invidious conniving.

3. Put yourself in the shoes of your target audience.

Says Joe Williams: "[The Board's] knowledge of your business, its capacity to learn, and its need to know. Most corporate boards [comprise] very bright, very busy, very distracted people, often with considerable diversity in [their] makeup. The directors look in on your business perhaps ten times a year, and they have very full lives to occupy them between meetings. Your own board, however, may have a more specialized character that needs to be evaluated before you decide how to style your presentation." He echoes here the frustrations that Jim Ferguson, another frequent outside board member, rails against—the CEO or reporting officer who makes no allowances for diversity of background and proceeds as though everyone has been suckled at the pap of his particular corporate "culture" and is thus conversant with all the buzz concepts and acronyms is both thoughtless and parochial.

4. Decide what is salient about your message.

Again from Joe Williams: "Decide what the board must learn from your presentation and then focus the message so that they can . . . retain it." If the issue requires a decision from the board, "think about what they will need [for the purpose] and then sharpen your focus on these points. Leave out the romance, and don't try to answer all questions in the presentation, but be prepared," he warns darkly, "to answer intensive questioning following your presentation."

The Exposition

1. Convey meaning, not information.
2. Never surprise your board.
3. Get to the point: be short, sweet, and crystal clear.
4. Help the board arrive at a decision.
5. Don't be evangelical.
6. Be flexible and willing to modify your plan, should it prove necessary.
7. Having obtained board approval for your main policies, proceed to feasibility plans, backup, and so forth.
8. Rehearse the whole presentation.
9. Avoid the egregious pitfalls.
10. Be patient.

Sweat, Blood, Toil, and Tears: Surpassing Yourself

1. Convey meaning, not information.

Writes Joe Williams: "Good . . . presentations inform the board about the meaning of the facts and use information to support the thesis. It is okay to assume the board isn't current on the issue, so give them sufficient facts [so that] a decision [can] be reached. But also assure that the board has done its homework and has read the informational materials in advance."

Almost all graphs, slides, and overhead visuals are needless. They convey redundant information without plumbing the significance of it, and they should be ruthlessly expunged. Anyone who does not comprehend this injunction is doomed to be second rate. (See also point 6 of the opening section of this chapter.)

2. Never surprise your board.

"Never!" says Joe Sullivan emphatically, "—with either good or bad news. Send out packets of concisely composed advance materials. Reveal what you are going to discuss in the agenda. At $30,000, $40,000, $50,000 a year honorariums, directors do their homework. They want to know in advance what they may want to ask at the meeting. They are highly sensitive to their fiduciary responsibility."

3. Get to the point: be short, sweet, and crystal clear.

Growls Joe Sullivan, the dearest wishes of corporate directors across the land: "Keep the entire meeting brief—not more than an hour and a half, unless for some extraordinary reason." Insists Joe Williams: "*Management* is paid to investigate all aspects of an issue thoroughly and to make recommendations to the board. The *board* is paid to evaluate management's recommendation. The board meeting is not an open forum to debate all aspects of an issue without recommendation."

Why is this central advice so widely ignored? Joe Williams told me over the telephone that when he was yet a young CEO making a presentation to the board of The Williams Companies, the late Les Worthington, former Chairman of U.S. Steel, took him aside in avuncular fashion and said, "You know, Joe, I have very little free time. And all that information you gave us on why we should look into the Middle East as a company and all those interesting anecdotes simply didn't help me as a member of the board come to a decision." The temptation to embellish is natural, understandable, and immature. It's also thoughtless. I have a private prayer: *Lord, protect me from the thoughtlessness of youth and the selfishness of old age.* Petitioners before boards and those who sit on them should recite it.

4. Help the board arrive at a decision.

"Facilitate this," urges Joe Sullivan, speaking as a veteran of bad board trips, "by having answers ready for their questions." Inadequate answers indicate inadequate preparation; which is typical of second-level management aspiring to the top level. Questions that are likely to surface and the corresponding answers should be foreshadowed in the advance materials, to which the presenter may make reference in the event someone on the board has been negligent about studying his homework.

5. Don't be evangelical.

You never went to suggest that objective evaluations have been subordinated to enthusiasm. You do not ever want to fall prey to the overweening surety that can undermine reason, circumspection, and the sense of proportion. On the other hand . . .

The cool, detached, dry, apparently diffident presentation may inadvertently convey lack of personal conviction that the course advocated is correct. It may convey also an absence of personal commitment. Charges up San Juan Hill are not successfully carried that way. *Sans* the *faux bourdon* of passion, no one is moved and nothing is achieved; too much and the cause is scuttled. I am personally impressed by the person who, despite his evident advocacy, anticipates objections and sets forth in painstaking detail all the reasons or evidence detrimental to his recommendations. I trust that person's judgment.

6. Be flexible and willing to modify your plan, should it prove necessary.

This advice from Vern Ketchem follows on the cautionary note above. The signal of the fanatic—of the absolutist and rigid mentality—is unwillingness to compromise. Along with arrogance, incompetence, duplicity, and fanaticism, nothing puts off the wise old heads of board members faster.

7. Having obtained board approval for your main policies, proceed to feasibility plans, backup, and so forth.

Vern Ketchem warns against a common failure. Once approval in principle has been wrested from the board, the supplicant—you, the presenter—must follow through with the blueprint for action. All ideas have consequences, some of which are bound to please not everybody. It is best to state them immediately, on the strength of the granted approval. Then there can be no recriminations. Joe Sullivan adds here that it pays to put "your cantankerous board member on the planning committee, thus compromising his opposition. Keep your cool," he counsels. And get even: "Make sure the enemy on the board isn't reelected."

8. Rehearse the whole presentation.

Need this be emphasized? Yes. In every detail, including the technical ones mentioned above.

9. Avoid the egregious pitfalls.

Of which Joe Williams lists: "The personal pronoun, acronyms, running overtime, repeating information and data presented in the handout, slide machine that doesn't work; breaking wind."

To which I agree . . . saving his distaste for the personal pronoun. He is dead wrong about that. (See points 1 and 2 on page 46.)

10. Be patient.

This last, sage counsel by Vern Ketchem honors his silver hair, what's left of it. Don't overreach. Don't ask for more than you are going to get. Don't frighten your board with your importunate hurry. A suddenly chronic adverse environment may require radical solutions, but make straight the way for them. Cultivate the consent of your board before asking for it. (For more on this subject, refer back to point 5 on page 31.)

What about resistance and follow-through, mentioned at the outset? They've been covered along the way.

Considerations for Listening to a Board Presentation

But Joe Williams adds five important considerations from the point of view of the director, which aid in arriving at a decision and which alert anyone who is making a presentation to what is expected of him:

1. *What is the point?* Do I get a clear understanding of the recommendations and the reasoning behind them?

2. *Do I believe the point?* Does the presenter believe the point? Did he/she present it fairly, evaluating the pertinent issues? Is it management's position or just the individual's?

3. *Have the board's standing questions been answered*—i.e., Profitability? Risk? Stakeholder impact (employees, communities, shareholders, political transactions)?

4. *Would I make this decision if I owned the business?*

5. *What is the CEO/staff dynamic?* Where in the organization is the inspiration for this recommendation? Is the CEO driving the issue, or is it a burning subsidiary issue; that is, are the organizational issues internally driven or clouding the issue apart from its own merits?

Tremendous tips. Any executive preparing a report for his or her directors should keep these five considerations in mind . . . should *frame* his or her proposals keeping them in mind. The best way to obtain agreement is exercising the imagination, putting oneself in the shoes of the other.

Obfuscating the Facts to Your Stockholders

It is said that reports to stockholders are exercises in deceit.

Now that statement is outrageous calumny. You'll note right off that no authority is given for it: "It is said." Yeah. By whom?

1. Shun the third person and the passive voice.

2. Shun acronyms and other jargon.

3. Do not make verbs out of nouns and nouns out of verbs.

4. Use homely words derived mostly from the Anglo-Saxon, short declarative sentences, and where possible, confine yourself to the present or future tenses.

5. Do not wax eloquent.

6. Tell the story you have to tell simply.

7. Do not cram your text with figures that can be found in the financial and P&L (profit and loss) statements.

8. Do not fawn over your employees in false, ritualistic, despicable language.

9. Do not commit a second falsity (as well as do violence to logic) by referring to your hired help as "associates."

10. Should ever you refer to the corporation, when directly addressing stockholders, as "your company," offer your tongue to a white-hot poker.

Sweat, Blood, Toil, and Tears: Surpassing Yourself

There are now imaginative, stylish, clear, informative, and gracefully written corporate annual reports and letters to stockholders, among them (standing out in my memory) the 1996 DuPont production and Coca-Cola's 1997 effort. In general, however, corporate and professional prose is so dreadful that I am put into a bad temper merely contemplating it. It is reprehensible for several major reasons: (1) the writer seeks to deceive, (2) the writer seeks to impress, (3) the writer seeks to evade responsibility for past actions or present recommendations, (4) the writer grovels, or (5) the writer seeks to glorify himself.

I am not able to assert which segment of the business and professional world is truly the worst offender. For the past several years, however, we (at the School) have been getting a lot of students from the major financial institutions, and they—some of them, not all: the cocky young—sin most noxiously because underlying such a lot of what they write is professional arrogance. Nothing can be more irritating, or more dangerous to their judgment as financial analysts, to the degree that the habits of pompous, clumsy, opaque, or incorrectly structured syntax may denote vain, clumsy, opaque, or incorrectly structured thinking. Some faces seem to invite the fist. The Wall Street yuppy, male and female, is a special breed of cockroach that begs for the heel.

I greet these at our one-day workshop, called Writing to Make Your Point: Style, Wit, Persuasion (taught primarily by the talented Kathleen Parker), with an ill-tempered (is there another sort?) tirade, which in this book comprises the Introduction to Part 4, Putting the Damn Thing Down on Paper. Meantime:

1. Shun the third person and the passive voice.

2. Shun acronyms and other jargon.

Joe Williams's distaste for the personal pronoun, recorded earlier, may stem from its abuse by the vainglorious officer. I grant that littering a page with too many references to one's sagacity, vision, enterprise, and executive savoir faire is poor form. Otherwise, my old friend is wrong.

"It is thought . . ." *No*: "*I* think . . . " "It is recommended . . ." *Absolutely not:* "*I* recommend . . ." or "*We* recommend . . ." The SEC's surprising recent diktat[5] declaring that it will no longer tolerate jargon and excessive acronyms in reports to itself or to stockholders, nor use of the third person or objective case, is a major blow against mummified, obscurantist, and pompous corporate prose, which is stylistically a bane, and worse, may indicate intentional deception. Speak and write plainly. Stand by what you say.

3. Do not make verbs out of nouns and nouns out of verbs.

This is a tedious argument and often a matter of personal taste. Begin with a noun that is ugly in English, French, and Spanish, verbalize it, and what do you get? "Enthused." How would you define that state? As "infused with enthusiasm"? What excuse is there for the airline injunction to use one's seat cushion "for flotation purposes," instead of "to float on"? Have we gained by verbalizing the noun "impact"? Personally, I rather like "to access," which we acquired through computerese, though I fear the coming of "to egress." And I fly into a

---

[5] First week of April 1997: a most blessed event, to be remembered.

rage when I hear sports announcers opine that the Miami Dolphins need to "offense" better or the Pittsburgh Steelers should "defense" more crushingly. Such illiterate defacements of the noble language we have inherited are inexcusable.

Watch out for them.[6]

4. Use homely words derived mostly from the Anglo-Saxon, short declarative sentences, and where possible, confine yourself to the present or future tenses.

5. Do not wax eloquent.

6. Tell the story you have to tell simply.

Recount for your audience, the stockholders, a narrative of events of the past year. If possible, insert drama or a modicum of suspense in the tale you tell.

> We began 1998 wondering whether the lean pickings of the past three years had taught us the right lessons, whether we had analyzed the new business environment correctly, and whether the hard work and often painful refocusing of our energies would, in fact, pay off. First quarter results were ambivalent— I suppose some of you were startled when analysts downgraded the company from a "buy" to a "hold." I imagine a lot of you were distressed, and I'm sure more than a little concerned, when second quarter results showed such spare apparent progress and the market reacted by shaving ten points off the stock.
>
> I confess that we in management were also anxious, even discouraged, by how slowly the reforms we instituted and the new directions in which we had taken the business reflected on the profit and loss statement. When third quarter results posted a 2 percent rise in operating profits, one could feel the

---

[6] This is, of course, the age—which will go down in infamy—when the Anglican Church ravaged the Book of Common Prayer and when the Holy Roman Catholic Church in America delivered Douay to the Goths and the Vandals.

relief surging from the assembly line up through the front offices. Relief and jubilation. That modest uptick, following on nine straight flat or regressive quarters, proved to everyone in the company that we'd done it. The payoff was finally at hand. It wasn't until fourth quarter results that the market at last woke up to what was going on; but when we were able to announce a 32 percent surge in sales for the year, operating profits of $2.3 billion, a 62 percent reduction in short-term debt, and a jump in earnings per share from $1.44 to $2.10, Wall Street took notice and the company's stock spurted to its present levels of between $75 and $80 the share . . ."

The point of this imaginary scenario is to indicate how reporting good news to stockholders can be dramatized through narrative techniques using the simplest conversational language. The tone is personal and direct, elated, yet neither vain nor immodest. There's some self-congratulation, and why not? Management showed the courage of its convictions and those convictions prevailed. Succeeding paragraphs might enter into details: how this or that division happily marketed the new product; injected fresh energy into old products; discovered a glitch in the production line that had long escaped analysis, correcting it; or opened a rich new vein where everyone else thought the ore was played out; and so forth. *Simply.*

7. Do not cram your text with figures that can be found in the financial and P&L (profit and loss) statements.

Fourth quarter results showed a 23% increase in sales over the same period last year, from 4th Quarter $1.61 billion in 1998 to 4th Quarter $1.98 billion in 1999, resulting in an 11% increase in net earnings before taxes over the same period last year, from 4th Quarter $342.65 million in 1998 to 4th Quarter $380.34 million in 1999, resulting in a net 7.6% increase in 4th Quarter per share earnings for 1999 over 1998, from 4th Quarter earnings per share of $3.10 in 1998 to 4th Quarter earnings per share of $3.37 in 1999.

This sort of thing is indigestible and needless. For an oral report, the financial comparisons can be supplied in handouts or exhibited on charts. In the written report, sidebars can highlight the relevant statistics. *The oral and written texts should confine themselves to the significant results.* Try it this way:

> Fourth quarter earnings improved over this time last year, as expected, producing a moderate 11 percent increase in net earnings. This is a little better than comparative industrywide results, but not much. Per share earnings, on the other hand, were disappointing: a mere 7.6 percent increase, or $3.37, compared to 1998's $3.10. We expected better results . . .

And so forth. The professional analyst will go zip to the financials, wasting no time on pretty talk or veiled apologies or (in bad cases) attempts by the president or CEO to put a good face on rot. Stockholders come to the meeting wanting to know the momentum. Is the company stuck in the mud, sinking out of sight, or slogging determinedly through a trough of boggy terrain toward firmer, higher, happier ground; or is it—excitingly—poised to leap ahead? That's the story to tell us lowly investors, us laypeople: plainly, honestly, adducing figures and percentages where necessary that support the assumptions, but, prithee, sparely.

8. Do not fawn over your employees in false, ritualistic, despicable language.

In my capacity as an owner of DuPont (see anon), I prevailed on the new president, Charles O. Holliday, Jr., to address himself to this matter in the 1998 report; which he did, splendidly, as follows:

> I had an assignment in DuPont about 15 years ago in Corporate Plans to work on a mission statement for the company. In the process of doing that I read every CEO letter, annual report, and corporate mission statement I could find. Each of them, somewhere toward the last paragraph, said something like "people are our most important asset." So after reading 50 or 100 of these things, I questioned if they really meant what they said.

Unctuously patting employees on the back at the tail end of reports is condescending, patronizing, and insincere. If you truly appreciate the people who work for you, recount anecdotes about them: in the written report, using sidebars; orally, as interjections. For example, continuing the report to stockholders improvised above:

> . . . Wall Street took notice and the company's stock spurted to its present levels of between $75 and $80 the share.
>
> Our stock may not long stay pegged to that range, either. Sherwood Amos and Ella Brownell, analysts in the Poughkeepsie gasket plant, long suspected that greater efficiency could be wrung out of the software governing the new production system. All July, August, and September they puzzled over parameters, sifting data through synthesizers until—Woody Amos told me—their "eyeballs spun." Then one evening in the first week of October, Ella Brownell telephoned him at his home to say, "Woody, I think I've got it. Will you check these deviations for me?" Which he did. Between them that following week, they patched the entire automated plastic extrusion/injection process, to the end that where formerly it took us three hours to produce 1800 high-tensile-strength gaskets, we are today producing 4000 of the gaskets in the same three hours . . . and expect within six months to be extruding them at a rate of 7000 every three hours. Oh, by the way, Ella Brownell was diagnosed twelve years ago as suffering from Parkinson's disease; for the past two years she has carried on with her work from a wheelchair.

The pithier the example, the better, of course, but perfunctory treatment of the extra efforts and accomplishments of employees is insulting. All employees reflect in the glory of the few, and it is, in fact, the corporate ethos in the ranks that encourages independent thinking and foments initiative.

9. Do not commit a second falsity (as well as do violence to logic) by referring to your hired help as "associates."

As much as you may esteem them, little could be more condescending than to style them as such.

This is fashionable usage in a number of large corporations—like wall-less, "open" offices that feign a democracy of collaborative endeavor. Come on!

This illusion not only reflects inflation of language, a cardinal sin to which business is peculiarly tempted, it also represents false, sentimental, and despicable thinking (for its intention to deceive). "Associate" may denote merely "fellow worker," true, but in common understanding the word conveys the second dictionary meaning, which is "partner," or "companion," bearing within it the assumption of equality of status.

An associate in the true sense is a partner owning a respectable percentage of the PA or corporation. He cannot be dismissed in the same arbitrary fashion that an employee may be dismissed. He is not given orders. He is not bound to time clocks. He receives not a salary or wage, but a share of the profits, corresponding either to his equity in the company or to the proportion of his contribution to those profits (the lawyer's hours, the doctor's roll of patients), or both.

Come on! A true associate is a principal: he generates major revenue by personally dispensing the service that earns it, or he has contributed in a major way to the founding capital structure that makes the business or the service possible. The bland sort of *faux* egalitarianism that seeks to inflate the status of employees to that of "associates" blurs distinctions and (I'd bet; I can't assert my assumption as fact) is regarded with contempt by many of the hired help it is supposed to flatter. "Yes, indeed, I'm an associate of Roger Milliken, and just the other day I said to him, Mr. Milliken, sir—I mean, *Roger* (sir)—that fabric you selected for the interiors of the new BMW account isn't the one I'd have chosen; so if you don't mind, Roger (old chap), I'm changing it." Uh-huh. Roger Milliken, who personally owns a third of Milliken Mills, translating into a couple of billion-plus dollars, may be a benign and charming autocrat; he is the boss nonetheless.

Do not play this sleazy game in your stockholders report.

10. Should ever you refer to the corporation, when directly addressing stockholders, as "your company," offer your tongue to a white-hot poker.

The same principle of ridiculous inflation characterizes this routine locution in stockholders reports.

Nobody would have dared dispute that the Ford Motor Company was old Henry Ford's motor company, public or not—one was invited to ask for any color enamel on the Model A, so long as it was black. At age 78, that grand old protectionist and benevolent despot, Roger Milliken, rules Milliken Mills with an iron will (he'll claim that this isn't so) and in a true sense may call it "his" company (he made it what it is). Bill Gates is the founder and resident genius and a major share-holder of Microsoft, and admissibly can be possessive about it. Permissibly, Microsoft can be referred to as *his*. The legion of charming, yachting, horse-raising descendants of Pierre Samuel DuPont de Nemours, however, though in the aggregate possessing millions of shares of that great company, do not individually (nor even collectively) "own" it.

Descend on down the feeding chain. DuPont's outstanding stock numbers 1,120,900,000 shares, of which I happen to boast 3800, or 0.0000339013 percent;—for which I am exceedingly thankful, but which percentage I can't even articulate, it's so infinitesimally small. Yes, I "own" a teeny-weeny, itty-bitty piece of the action, but is DuPont in any significant sense "my" company?

Only by metastasizing from the ridiculous to the sublime; only in the falsely subservient usage of too many company reports. This is dishonest. We stockholders, no matter the insignificance of the number of our shares, do have irreducible proprietary rights recognized by law.[7] But it is as foolish to presume from this statutory guarantee to status of ownership of the corporation as to presume that because my maternal great-grandmother was a Mary Lee, originally of St. Louis, who may or may not have been collaterally related to the Virginia Lees, that I am in any meaningful sense a member of that illustrious family and may go about proclaiming the graybearded paladin of the Confederacy as my cousin . . . marginally removed.

---

[7] Which in my opinion, for what it's worth, *should* be reduced in order to reflect reality; by issuing voting stock in the ratio of 1:1/10th of 1 percent of the total stock outstanding.

DISARMING SECURITIES ANALYSTS

. . . The dread last of critical business-related performances—the oral presentation before savvy, cynical, skeptical merchant bankers, securities analysts, and examiners from the SEC.[8]

1. Do everything possible to abolish slide shows, overhead projections, flip charts, and other visual encumbrances.

2. Be simple, lucid, and unpretentious; practice the appearance of total candor.

3. Cover everything that you wish institutional investors or securities analysts to know, and be sure to prepare answers for what you anticipate may be their main concerns.

4. Clarify from the nonce any potential imputation of conflict of interest.

5. Tell the bad news first and explain what you have done to fix it.

6. Be passionate, but be credible. If there is a downside, state it.

7. Demonstrate your competence as an executive and manager through the presentation itself.

8. Gear the specifics of your presentation to the audience.

9. Be sensitive to nuances of interest or concern in your audience, and be nimble: be prepared to adapt your presentation to those nuances, shortening this to emphasize that.

10. Emphasize your company's competitive strengths in its own industry.

---

[8]I've had recourse to several experts in these matters also—graduates of my school, people who have been in one way or another associated with it. One is the corporate vice president and national sales manager of PaineWebber, Robert E. Bedritis; another is the managing director of Equitable Securities Corporation, of Nashville, W. Howard Cammack, Jr.; and a third is a recently retired officer of what may be the world's foremost financial institution. She has been instrumental in putting together deals computed in the billions of dollars. For personal reasons, she prefers not to be identified.

Messrs. Bedritis and Cammack sent me letters with their prescriptions; she submitted to me what she entitled "Basic Guidelines to Follow When Giving Presentations to Institutional Investors." The three documents comprise the basis of what follows.

11. Develop a plan for discussing your company's competitive weaknesses.

12. Ask questions yourself to clear up any misunderstanding.

13. Allow ample time for Q&A.

14. Practice the Q&A diligently.

15. Always conclude by saying thank-you.

Sweat, Blood, Toil, and Tears: Surpassing Yourself

1. Do everything possible to abolish slide shows, overhead projections, flip charts, and other visual encumbrances.

I don't fear repeating myself on this theme because, oh! how we have had to struggle with people who come to us for help in IPO presentations: to persuade them that *the focus of hard-bitten analysts or investors during the interval of the presentation is on the person,* the presenter, *not on the facts and figures.*

Before or after, they'll subject the details to keenest scrutiny. But at the time the person is telling his story or making her pitch, they are sizing that person up as a human being (trustworthy or not) and as a professional (competent? realistic? both feet on the ground?). Anything that distracts from the impression the speaker makes is a liability.

Remember, there can only be one star, the speaker or the slide show, the speaker or the flip chart. Visual "aids" are visual distractions; they are often obstacles to the purpose of the presenter, which is to persuade the audience that he or she is credible, hence that the product he or she is selling is credible. (I realize that this is a logical fallacy.) Supply them with the facts and figures beforehand, do. Prepare a handsome kit for them to take to their offices when you are gone. Bring up the charts, or slides, or overhead projections, if you must, after you are finished with your delivery, in connection with the answer to a question. But even then, keep ever in mind that a smooth, lucid, coherent reply to a question, unembellished, can have conclusive effect in the mind of the listener. You may make your sale then. Don't permit extraneous visuals to diminish that effect.

2. Be simple, lucid, and unpretentious; practice the appearance of total candor.

Be neither brash, flip, cocksure, too assertive, exaggerated, nor overly enthusiastic. Be quietly confident, forcefully understated. Don't attempt to impress; *be* impressive.

Practice looking as open and honest as St. Peter, even when you may be concealing something, putting a good face on a negative factor, purposely playing loose with and even distorting fact, covering a hidden agenda, or plain lying. I am not recommending that you do any of these bad things, mind, but I have been around too long to be ingenuous. If you are in fact a scoundrel, perpetrating a deception, practice the bland innocence of the swindler and the con man.

That brass you must acquire, though you may be as innocent as a newborn lamb. The threshold of indignation in some people is high. Others blush easily: when disconcerted, or when it may be insinuated by a hostile analyst or investor (this is rare) that they are not telling the whole truth, though they are doing their honest best to the limits of their knowledge. Some people look guilty at the sound of a traffic cop's siren, coming apart, prepared to babble that yes, they did rob the bank, did commit the murder. When preparing for an IPO or SEC presentation, with your confederates practice fielding hard questions, cutting remarks, unjustified insinuations—observing yourself in a mirror as you speak—until the rush of blood to the cheeks is controlled, until the lips quit twitching, the facial tic vanishes, the beads of sweat on the brow (or up by the hairline) dry up. Then you are ready.

4. Clarify from the nonce any potential imputation of conflict of interest.

A New Age soft drink company wanted to go public. The three principals came to us for coaching. They were unprepossessing. Their leader was a flashy, fast-talking entrepreneur from upstate New York, who murdered the English language. Not yet 30 years old, he had already made several millions of dollars, which he let us know. The two colleagues whom he had selected to manage the company and carry the burden of the presentation were little improvement. The first, the proposed CEO, was in his late fifties and wore an expression of morose abstraction throughout; the second, the proposed CFO, was clever and well-informed, but with his black little eyes and glittering teeth, he somehow gave the impression that he was about to raid a hen coop and suck all the eggs. It transpired (a) that a holding company owned by the entrepreneur, which he used to organize such ventures as this, was going to be relieved of a substantial burden of debt owed to it by the soft drink company once it went public, and (b) that he personally was going to be enriched by several millions of dollars' worth of stock (at the public offering price) that he held in security against that debt.

There was nothing illegitimate in the benefits to the entrepreneur, but these two items were not made clear in the initial verbal presentation; they were buried in the financials. Had it gone uncorrected, this disingenuousness, in conjunction with the personalities of the three men, would have soured a lot of analysts and investment bankers. We arranged to have the entrepreneur state right up front, in his two-minute introduction, that he stood to profit handsomely (and deservedly) from the public offering.[9]

5. Tell the bad news first and explain what you have done to fix it.

Never risk ignoring, eliding, or concealing a negative factor (unless, of course, you are the scoundrel alluded to above). Deal with it squarely, get it out of the way. (See tip 11 on page 58.)

6. Be passionate, but be credible. If there is a downside, state it.

Your job is to persuade people to put their money where your mouth is. Greed is the lust you must whet. And greed is so universal and so strong a motivation that it is easily aroused—which works in your favor. But greed does not respond to pallid exposition, nor, when combined with experience—as will be the case in hard-bitten merchant bankers and stock analysts—is it insensible to exaggerations and fatuous expecta-

---

[9]We worked hard drilling the entrepreneur in humility and the felicity of participles and function of single negatives, the CEO in amiability and the function of the human smile, and the CFO in giving less of a resemblance to a ferret or a weasel. They floated their stock successfully. I did not buy any.

tions. Your claims must be credible, which credibility is gained by fairly presenting the ambiguities. (See tip 11 on page 58.)

7. Demonstrate your competence as an executive and manager through the presentation itself.

My wise old godfather, Warren Smith, used to drum into me, "There is no such thing as a bad business; there are underfinanced or poorly managed businesses." Seeking to go public is a way of getting that financing without incurring debt. The presentation that convinces investment bankers of the viability of the venture should also convince them that it will be in competent hands.

It surprises how little attention many entrepreneurs and business people pay to what should be the performance of their lives. Oh, they crunch and crunch and crunch the numbers; they hire professionals to cook a film extolling the wondrous prospects of the new company. But the oral presentation on which, in the last analysis, everything depends, they either virtually wing or for polish entrust to the criticisms and suggestions of colleagues and subordinates. This is obtuse.

Go to professionals when you have an important oral presentation to make: before investment bankers, securities analysts, the SEC, stockholders, or in hot competition for a contract. And don't trust in-house advice either. Ask yourself: Has the self-proclaimed presentation "expert" ever got paid for giving a speech? Has he been tested in the open market? Does he possess any hard credentials as an expert?[10] What can he possibly know about writing and delivering a persuasive speech, a compelling presentation, except in the academic vacuum tube? Ask yourself further: Is this hired man going to tell me, a senior VP, that I sound like a pompous windbag, that I come off as arrogant, that I slur my words, that my jokes are awful, that I don't make my points clear, or that I have foul breath?

Go to the pros, always.

---

[10] A degree in communications from Podunk U., or even Northwestern, doesn't suffice. Can this expert in communications write his way out of a paper bag? Has any major magazine paid him $2000, $3000, $5000 for an article? What books does he have to his credit? And does his reputation as a speaker fill halls? Are civic clubs and business conventions willing to pay $3000, $5000, $10,000 to hear him talk? It beats understanding that big-time businesses, whose welfare depends on market valuations, ignore such credentials when creating in-house "communications" empires that are run (in my experience) by turf-protecting mediocrities of no known provenance. Help in an oral presentation should be outsourced always.

8. Gear the specifics of your presentation to the audience.

Size it up. If the primary decision-maker is a trader, emphasize the market aspects of the financing you seek, both with respect to a new (IPO) issue and any outstanding securities. If the primary decision-maker in the audience is an analyst, emphasize the fundamental strengths of your company.

9. Be sensitive to nuances of interest or concern in your audience, and be nimble: be prepared to adapt your presentation to those nuances, shortening this to emphasize that.

Be flexible in your presentation. Capitalize on opportunity when your instinct alerts you. Is the financial person in your audience evidencing unease in any way over your genre of company or business? If so, address those misgivings directly. If, on the other hand, you suspect that the investment banker is naturally inclined to favor the type of enterprise in which you are engaged, emphasize the distinctiveness of the terrain your company has staked out for itself, the niche it has captured and can handsomely exploit.

11. Develop a plan for discussing your company's competitive weaknesses.

Are you going to address your company's weaknesses in the main presentation or wait for the Q&A? I favor acknowledging them near the beginning of the pitch, then stating that they'll be dealt with in the questions and answers period. (Don't forget them!) Be candid, but dwelling on competitive disadvantages at the start detracts from what you want to stress: the strength of your position, your case, the company you hope to take public. The first ten minutes often tell the tale. You don't want niggling doubts getting in the way.

Remember always after the last question to sum up on a positive note. People who are practiced in debate (a neglected art inculcating the principles of negotiation and persuasion) automatically store in their minds those themes they want to return the audience's attention to and rivet the audience's attention upon. Most business people, having had little or no experience in verbal warfare, must be taught to do this.

12. Ask questions yourself to clear up any misunderstanding.

13. Allow ample time for Q&A.

Assuming you are given thirty minutes max with investors or analysts, reserve at least ten of those minutes for questions. If your total allotted time is one hour, allow up to thirty minutes for Q&A.

You want to make sure you've despatched doubts and nailed down your strengths. If you are able on your feet, here's your chance to shine. If you are naturally slow on the uptake or liable to confusion, invite a cool-minded partner to the stage or dais or lectern—the comptroller or finance officer perhaps. Hire professionals to drill you in the art of answering questions succinctly, completely, and well. Failing that, ask a tough litigator to coach you, or a seasoned and mean-spirited reporter.

14. Practice the Q&A diligently.

How ably one handles questions can be the most important and effective demonstration of management competence. The person who is authoritative on his feet impresses and instills confidence.

Men notoriously can't find anything in refrigerators. Some people of either sex can't find anything in their heads when they need to most. The whole shebang can depend on a strong reply. Listen hard. Remember: In debate, as in war, what *you* intend to say or do isn't the important thing; what *the enemy* does or says is what determines the outcome. Some questions may fall like down pillows into your lap, permitting you to respond just as you dreamed that fretful night before the meeting. Other questions may throw you for a loop. Forget the first, drill for the second. Rehearse the nastiest scenario that your fevered imagination can conjure. You may even raise the quotation on your stock by a point or two.

15. Always conclude by saying thank-you.

That tough, brilliant woman who midwives multibillion-dollar deals called me back to stress this. We had discussed other points on her short list. She wanted to be sure this one wasn't neglected, as so often the amenities are. Even in the snarling canyons of Wall Street, civility gains favor.

Thank-you.

❖   ❖   ❖

But we're not quite through. Robert Bedritis and Ward Cammack were emphatic in their injunctions concerning what not to do. These need little explication, so here they are:

1. Don't ramble. The typical stockbroker has an attention span of ten seconds.

2. Don't be mechanical spewing out the numbers; breathe life into them.

3. Don't fudge on facts; admit it when you don't know something and never forget to follow up with the missing information.

4. Don't be intimidated. Your audience is there to gather the facts, not your scalp.

5. Neither try too hard to impress. Quiet competence wins.

You're welcome, I'm sure.

TOASTS, RETIREMENT PARTIES

Toasts

Toasts differ in obligation, purpose, and function, depending upon the circumstances of the ceremony that they embellish, as noted below. In general, however:

1. The briefer the better.

2. The wittier the better.

3. The more anecdotal the better.

Sweat, Blood, Toil, and Tears: Surpassing Yourself

1. The briefer the better.

Unless you are the best man at the wedding, the father or mother of the bride, the ranking person other than the guest of honor, keep your toast under sixty seconds. That's plenty of time to be gracious; taking longer risks collaborating in a celebration that drags on too long. No one's toast—unless one is a phenomenon of wit (you'll have to be the judge of yourself)—should exceed three minutes—not even the groom's to the bride . . . unless he is being witty, which is sure to miff her.

2. The wittier the better.

Strive for incisive, revelatory wit. Never say anything touching on a debility in the subject's character, unless that fault is in the way of an endearing eccentricity. That a person is so absentminded that he commonly misplaces his car keys is okay, but that this same person absentmindedly sat on Aunt Eleanor's pet chihuahua, snuffing the poor brute's life out, is not okay.

In the effort to be amusing, some people unintentionally offend—even hurt—the person they are supposedly commending or expressing their appreciation for. It's bad form—it is caddish—verbally or in print, to disparage a person, unless he or she is a public figure or a celebrity, in which case the person is fair game. When toasting anyone, be especially sensitive to the cruelty that can adhere to wit.

3. The more anecdotal the better.

A toast that recounts some charming or amusing story about the subject is always flattering and in good form, so long as it isn't mawkish.

With anecdotes, be careful about tarrying in what professional comedians call the setup: taking too long arriving at the punch line. But if the setup includes revelatory insights about the person being honored, which, while leading to and preparing the punch line, are in themselves fun, take your time.

RETIREMENT PARTIES

As you may have gathered, I temperamentally detest the lachrymose, the abuse, by inordinate sentiment, of good taste (and also of one's privacy).

In the case of parties for a retiring employee or officer, however, Anglo-Saxon emotional reticence be damned. As always, when giving a talk, we must ask ourselves, *what is the point, the objective?* *We must (as always when speaking) make ourselves the humble servant of that objective*, which, in this case, is to make the occasion for the person retiring memorable. One is not out to please the crowd. One's purpose should be publicly to express the respect and affection that maybe in thirty or forty years of faithful service, the honored guest never knew he had earned, to the effect that his mind and heart will glow with the memory.

So pull out the stops. Do not be overlong, naturally, *but in this sole case,* err on the side of pardonable length, not brevity.

CHAPTER 4

SOCIAL EVENTS

BEARDING THE LIONS IN THEIR DEN

You must give a luncheon talk to the Lions, the Shriners, the Rotary, or in upscale circumstances, to the New York AC or the Union League Club.

1. *Keep it to twenty minutes, max.* People must get back to their shops and small businesses.

2. *Be graceful. Don't try to make a heavy point.* After a greasy-fry lunch at The Seafood Hut or Quincy's, nobody is in a mood to digest philosophy. (You'll eat well at the Union League Club or at the Petroleum Club in Dallas, but the fare they want from a speaker is no less light.)

3. *Make your talk topical . . . and keep it local.* Cover something that has occurred in the town or community, or something that has hit the city or state newspapers.

4. *If you're an out-of-towner, buy the local newspaper.* Find out what's going on, what people are preoccupied by or excited about: a basketball championship, a beauty pageant, a proposed school bond issue, a controversial variance in zoning. If you can work any of this into your talk, do; at the least, make graceful reference to it. This is being opportunistic in the right sense. You'll earn a heap of goodwill.

5. *In small towns avoid national topics, except for a glancing humorous allusion to something that is prominent that week in* People *magazine or* Entertainment Tonight. Remember that in towns like New York, Chicago, or San Francisco, city news *is* national news, the topic in which they are most interested. ♪*Give 'em what they like, and how they like it.*♪

6. *Be anecdotal.* A good story will please everybody and give the audience something to take back to work with them—something they can recount to their associates, customers, and friends.

7. *Try to be funny.* If you must, resort to a canned joke, but it is safer to dredge up an old one, dating twenty or thirty years back, than to risk a brand-new one. By the time you have heard the new joke, so has everybody else. Old jokes carry a certain charm. The graybeards in your audience may have completely forgotten it and will be nostalgically pleased by having you recall it to their memory; they'll start chuckling before you reach the punch line. Wink at them, encourage them, you're in this thing together. As for the younger people out there, you can safely bet the joke will be totally new to them. Oh, some young Americans find it difficult to laugh when listening to a speaker. They consider it indecorous.

8. *Be practical.* If you've just experienced something useful in your profession or business, by extrapolation, it may be useful to others in their professions or businesses.

9. *Avoid mention of sports.* Although your Rotarian, Lion, and Shriner audiences will in the majority be sports fans who play tennis or golf, who bowl, who attend high school basketball games, there's no imperative need for you to share, or to confess, their idiocy . . . even if it is the NY Athletic Club you're addressing (see below).

10. *Allow in your twenty minutes for five minutes of questions from the floor.* (See Chapter 2, Commandment 7, for how to handle Q&A sessions.)

Sweat, Blood, Toil, and Tears: Surpassing Expectations

1. Complex Topics

You may desire to introduce your neighbors, friends, fellow business people, or professionals to a practical new technique that they can profitably incorporate into their activities: a new software filing or accounting system, new marketing techniques through the Internet. Or you may wish to alert them to or warn them of legislation affecting individual and corporate taxes.

Such subjects are better reserved for a chamber of commerce luncheon meeting, or, if of sufficient sophistication, for such as the Union League Club, where the audience are expecting to receive instruction and to listen to a speech that may run over half an hour. Practical yet weighty topics of this nature require time and maximum attention for clear elucidation. The best you can offer at the Rotary luncheon is a survey of the advantages or disadvantages of the new system, the favorable or unfavorable consequences of pending legislation. Spare details. Tell results. And tell them where to find out more about the topic should they wish to. Here, handouts—an article, a survey, a chart, a technical analysis—are a good idea.

2. On Sports Heroes

Sports and athletes are adulated in American society, which should be your cue not to join the crowd (unless your sole desire is to ingratiate yourself in the lowest and most groveling manner, so that the audience will deem you a good joe, a regular fellow, a swell guy, and other such revolting characterizations of your person; which is to say, unless you desire to be unmemorable as a speaker).

If you feel you *must* make some concession to the middle-class mania that possesses this country and much of the world, don't fawn with the rest of them, set your audience back on their heels (see Chapter 2, Commandment 1). In Atlanta, tell 'em you hate the Braves, or in Green Bay, that football is the pastime of cretins.

Or say,

> Should you harbor any shred of respect for professional athletes, run to your psychiatrist right now to seek help for your attention deficit disorder or to your priest for the moral obloquy that clearly threatens your soul.

Continue:

> Sports stars are not heroes. They are in the main villains, and low-class villains at that. All sorts of virtues are ascribed to them. The truth is, beginning with John L. Sullivan and Jack Johnson in boxing (not to mention ear-eating Iron Mike Tyson); with Ty Cobb and Babe Ruth in baseball; with Nastase, Connors, and McEnroe in tennis; and culminating with the infamous O. J. Simpson in football; the superstars of sports[1] have been mean, bigoted, spiteful, vain, greedy, full of deceit, lustful, promiscuous, bad-tempered, boorish, and of violent, nay murderous and even cannibalistic, inclinations. They are not fit to grace a supper table with decent folk. They should be banned from most tables, and from the premises of schools. They are the worst rôle models for children imaginable. They ought to be contained in cages in a zoo for professional gladiators and let out only to ply their trades.

End:

> If you like and admire sports, there's something deeply the matter with you. I sure don't want to do business with you.

And then get out of town.[2]

The point being: Even when giving a talk of little consequence to you or to the audience, dig for something challenging to say. Adopting (for the sake of argument) the unpopular view about anything is one way of starting. Don't be foolhardy. If you are in Green Bay, it's folly to attack the Packers (as you discovered had you followed my earlier

---

[1] You might concede that golf is the noble exception.

[2] The writer of the above confesses (a) to have played football in high school and to be an ardent fan of the pros, (b) to watch golf assiduously, even though he cannot play the game, and (c) to an addiction for the (bloody) (and violent) "field sports" (shooting and hunting).

advice). But you might risk professing your loathing of cheese. Cheese smells. Cheese clots the arteries. People who make cheese tend to be smelly, fat, and prone to heart disease. Has any swain ever kissed the cheese festival belle and survived the fetid odors of her mouth? Has anyone in the room tried to wipe up crumbled cheese from a linen tablecloth or purge the refrigerator of the stink of a ripe Stilton or blue cheese? And so forth. Seek consciously to set yourself apart.

SPEAKING TO THE GARDEN OR LOCAL SOCIAL CLUB

1. *You may speak for forty-five minutes, though I don't like to myself.* The women—and the majority of your audience will be women—expect it. In the case of some traditional social clubs, they have come to spend the afternoon.

2. *Be graceful.* You may make a heavy point, but do so in style and in a light and friendly manner.

3. *You needn't keep your talk local, but references to the community are always appreciated.*

4. *Explain or set forth your topic in anecdotal fashion.* Telling a story helps people remember the subject matter.

5. *Make a special effort to be humorous if your topic is tough.* Don't ever make the mistake of being racy.

6. *Be practical.* As above. More and more of your traditional female audiences will be professional women (see below).

7. *Allow in your forty-five minutes for ten minutes of questions from the floor* (see Chapter 2, Commandment 7).

8. *Dress with extra—extreme—care.* <u>Men</u>: soberly. For a morning talk, 9 a.m., 10 a.m., choose a business suit. If it is a luncheon meeting or an afternoon function at which you speak, you may don a comfortable tweed sports jacket (over gray flannels or chinos), but favor a herringbone pattern to checks of any size or description and keep the colors subdued. *Be sure your shoes*

are polished to a high gloss. <u>Women</u>: also soberly, but smart. If God granted you the boon of great legs and a great body, resist flaunting either. And for pity's sake, keep that Harry Winston brooch in its box, or in the hotel safe. (For more on dress, see Chapter 21, Special Problems Generic to Women.)

9. <u>Men</u>: *Look like Vincent Price, dress like Vincent Price, sound like Vincent Price.*

Oh, if it's the Garden Club, learn the names of at least two houseplants and the Latin name for a variety of azalea or chrysanthemum.

Further Considerations

♪ *I left my heart in San Francisco* ♪

The rules above reflect a passing social phenomenon. Even in the Midwest, the stronghold of traditional women's clubs, these are fewer and fewer. The age of active members ranges from 45 to 85.

Count back to the formative years of your audience. A woman in her forties today was in her twenties during the 1970s; a woman in her fifties today was in her twenties during the 1960s; a woman in her sixties today was in her twenties during the 1950s. There will be a major difference in their responses. The educational background and career paths of women are quite different from what they were ten, twenty, thirty years ago.

Which is why men should be on guard. Do not take them lightly. Should you yet harbor a retrograde male tendency to condescend, discard it.

I must tell you a story. If any shred of male chauvinist piggism lingered in me from a childhood spent in the company of six tough, domineering, intellectually brilliant, and incorrigibly opinionated sisters, that shred was blown into the waters of San Francisco Bay.

It was the late 1960s. I'd been booked at a Junior League north of the city. Ordinary women's clubs were declining in membership even at that time, but they were still largely peopled by ladies—and I mean ladies—who dressed for meetings as though to greet Queen Elizabeth: whose beehives were blued and silvered and could be nestled in by wrens; who baked; who were selflessly active in a bewildering number of charities; who read romantic novels; and who were politely impressed by matters political, though not overly concerned with them. Helen Hokinson, the *New Yorker* cartoonist, had them down pat.

Some nine or ten months before I was scheduled to speak at this particular club, I received an exquisitely penned note inquiring of me what I intended to discourse on. I replied in suitably vague fashion (not being absolutely sure). Three weeks elapsed. In the mail arrived a second hand-penned note politely but firmly desiring particulars of my talk. Shrugging, I complied.

When I arrived in San Francisco in September of that year, a message awaited me at the desk of the Fairmont Hotel. I would be picked up at 8:00 sharp, because it was a two-hour drive from downtown to club headquarters in the hills above the city, the meeting was scheduled to begin at 11:00, and I would probably want a little rest before going on.

Two tall, handsome women in their early forties called for me next morning. Though somewhat reserved, they were solicitous, asking me whether I had slept well, what I preferred in the way of tea or coffee or Coke, and whether I would like a little time to myself before I went on. I was to speak for just under forty minutes, they informed me. There would be a question and answer period, which they hoped I would not object to. It was scheduled to last twenty minutes, but since lunch wasn't until half past noon, I wouldn't mind—would I?—should the questions continue a little after the hour.

No, of course not. They nodded. I had the distinct impression that they were observing me covertly out of the corners of their eyes, in the rearview mirror . . . studying me, for some reason. But I was graciously applauded by the audience upon being introduced, a brilliant array of smiles flashing up at me. Oh, those young women could not have been a more attractive bunch, nor more responsive. They laughed at my lances; they frowned becomingly at serious passages, as though concentrating hard on them. (Little did I suspect how intently they were concentrating on them.)

I got through my spiel. The first woman to ask a question stood up straight from her chair, gazed at me a second or so, and then declared in a loud, ringing voice, "Mr. Buckley, those statistics on urban crime you cited were interesting but out-of-date. Two new studies show . . ." The next stood up, pressing the attack. "Mr. Buckley, your assumptions are not only out-of-date and unsupported by the evidence, they are misconstrued. As Nathan Laser wrote in *The Public Interest* this past August . . ." A third came at me from an entirely different quarter. "Mr. Buckley, are you aware that you are routinely guilty of *ex post hoc, propter hoc* reasoning—the fallacy of the false cause? Don't you see that though most cocaine addicts may have tried marijuana and LSD, there's no justification in assuming from this coincidence that young people who smoke pot socially or experiment with other hallucino-genics are destined to end up on hard drugs . . ."

The assault was relentless, forty minutes of it. I realized then, as I was being turned on the spit and grilled first on one side, then on the other, how I had been bungeed. The moment these tough young women had pried from me the general lines of what I meant to say, they had divided themselves into committees, each devoted to a particular subtopic or angle. That spring and summer, they had studied up on the literature, determined to permit me to get away with not a single string of loose reasoning, false inference, or misconstrued, misstated, obso-lete, or wrong fact. Having roasted me, they skinned me alive, and then they consumed what was left.[3]

SPEAKING TO A "CELEBRITY SERIES" OR TO A KNIFE & FORK CLUB

One is invited to these luncheons and suppers because one has attained a measure of fame or notoriety, fleeting that it may be. One has swum the length of the Mississippi, upstream; one's album was mentioned by Chelsea on *Regis and Kathy Lee*; one has written a book accusing Martha Stewart of overcooking collard greens; one has unseated a female congresswoman from Watts whose mother is Mexican, whose father is of mixed African and Native Paiute American descent, and who was married by a female Episcopalian priest to her childhood sweetheart, who is also female.

---

[3] But they were the best fun audience I was privileged to have in all my years of lecturing. Few times have I felt so hon-ored as when I was invited back for a second appearance. Maybe their motive was to lick clean what remained of my bones. I didn't care; I was prepared to give battle and enjoyed myself hugely.

If you aren't enjoying your fifteen minutes of fame, skip this section; you won't be invited. And if you are truly famous or celebrated, skip it also; you are unlikely to stoop so low, because the stipends are generally insufficient to stock your wine cellar for a long weekend.

But assuming that you are an ordinary bloke (or female equivalent, whatever that may be) with some modest claim to public attention, and discover that you have been booked into Des Moines by the Hibernian Society or the Opinions, Unlimited lecture series, keep in mind that the primary function of these affairs is social, speckled with a slight case of *angst* respecting the economy, religion, the plight of the homeless, the (low) state of public morals, and so forth, but not so concerned that they desire their appetites to be ruined. In the case of the self-designated Celebrity Series clubs, *who* you are, not what you *say*, is the paramount interest.

For a Celebrity Series booking, the glitz, the glitter, and the glamour are everything: the sense that you are bringing to Mason City or Duluth a dash of cosmopolitan sophistication; that you are linking the audience to the global metropolitan world, which will never be truly to their taste, but about which they are curious, and ninety minutes of personal exposure to which (you will be addressed almost immediately by your first name) gives them nine months of something to talk about. The winters are long on the plains. *These are good people, mind. This is the salt of the earth.* These can be also excruciatingly dull and boring people in the phlegmatic Scandinavian way, the Midwestern, or Northwestern, or Pennsylvanian, or Ohio Valley, or upper New York State/New England way, bringing to mind at once the novels of Sinclair Lewis or Flaubert's *Madame Bovary* (you sympathize with her). But if you speak or act in any fashion deeply to shock them, you are a churl. If you are unable to respond to their essential goodness, narrow and provincial that it may be, you need to subject yourself to some soul-searching.

These audiences are not *averse* to talks touching on serious topics, but they do become uncomfortable with the serious vein if it is unleavened or (God forbid) apocalyptical. They are practical people and desire of the speaker clearly stated social or political problems (if this is the turf he brings with him) that are susceptible to commonsense repair. If it is useful (it may not be) to attempt a distinction between Celebrity Series affairs and Knife & Fork luncheons, the latter may prefer a talk on the future of Medicare (so long as it is neither too upsetting nor too ideologically partisan) to a talk on the language of the Polynesian tattoo; Knife & Forkers will opt for the weightier topic. But avoid philosophy.

1. *You may speak thirty or thirty-five minutes—a third more the length of a Rotary or Garden Club talk.* I recommend, preferring, twenty-five to thirty minutes of text, ten to fifteen minutes of Q&A.

2. *Keep your talk as accessible as possible.* Speak from personal experience. Interweave humor and anecdotes whose object is human understanding, not a punch line.

3. *When you inject humor, be warned that you may be talking before the most unresponsive audiences that can be conjured up in a speaker's nightmares.*

4. *References to Broadway hits, especially musicals, are not only safe, they are cunning.*

5. *Drop as many names as your text can reasonably bear,* without putting on the dog.

6. *If you are truly a sophisticate, be neither mean to your experience nor condescending to your audience:* speak with candor from your social, intellectual, and economic station.

7. *Assuming you're an out-of-towner, buy the local newspaper,* for the reasons mentioned in item 4 of the opening section of this chapter.

Sweat, Blood, Toil, and Tears: Surpassing Yourself

Just three of these rules require further comment.

3. When you inject humor, be warned that you may be talking before the most unresponsive audiences that can be conjured up in a speaker's nightmares.

Be tentative at the beginning. Test your audience out before you plunge too deeply into anecdotes that require ready wit or a measure of sophistication for the desired response. You will long to be in such urban centers as San Francisco, Los Angeles, Chicago, or New York. You will breathe deep relief to find yourself in the South or Southwest, or speaking before Jewish, Irish, and Latin audiences.

Neither assume too little, however. Who would expect to discover a lively audience in Michigan City? Well, you will, if you're invited by a certain synagogue. You'll be happily surprised by Milwaukee, Richmond, Louisville, and Cincinnati, to mention just a few medium-sized cities across the land where humor and panache thrive.

4. References to Broadway hits, especially musicals, are not only safe, they are cunning.

Almost everybody in the United States vacations every once in a while in the Big Apple. Broadway still beats crowding the sidewalks outside the *Today* studio in the hope of pressing Katie's or Matt's or Al's flesh. Mentioning *Cats*, or *Phantom of the Opera*, or *Chorus Line*, or *The Lion King* makes your audience feel a warm and fuzzy *in*ness and *with*-*it*ness. They have been there too!

6. If you are truly a sophisticate, be neither mean to your experience nor condescending to your audience: speak with candor from your social, intellectual, and economic station.

Do not be embarrassed about mentioning that you were at a reception with Deeda McCormick Blair (when the subject of Washington, D.C.'s municipal corruption came up); or that you happened to be at the Philadelphia Society meeting in Chicago, where a symposium under the direction of Milton Friedman was held on Chile's successful privatization of social security; or that you were on a panel at Aspen with, oh, Colin Powell, Peter Duchin, Mel Karmazin of Westinghouse Electric, and Madeleine Albright—". . . who's charming as well as toughminded . . ."—discussing the proper rôle of corporations in the political process; or even on a cruise up the Norwegian fjords on Steven Forbes's schooner, where you had the chance to corner Bill Gates about the increasing frustration individual users and small businesses experience with the relentless and unceasing innovations in computer hardware and software, rendering what one purchases obsolete before one has returned from the store, who replied that . . .

These are permissible. They are justified by your topic. But if you err, err favoring excess. Not for nothing are *¡HOLA!* and *People* magazines avidly read in the boondocks.

SPEAKING AFTER A BANQUET, OR COMMITTING SUICIDE WITH GOODWILL

This is the worst hour for being compelled to give any sort of speech. When one is obliged to deliver a serious talk on a subject that is too complex to despatch in less than fifty minutes, the event is forbidding. The reasons are so obvious they don't require review.

This "speaking occasion," as the jargon goes, comprehends at least three different functions. The second and third are serious, even deadly serious. The first is celebratory in nature.

Suppertime or After-Supper Entertainment

You are closing a successful company meeting during which good news prevailed. You are the featured speaker at the banquet following a fund drive that has smashed records. You are on the panel at the grand reception marking the fifth anniversary of the founding of a literary quarterly. You are the groom at the bridal supper party.

Hey, this is a *festive* occasion! Don't dare wax serious. Don't even think of it! The purpose of the event and your function are wrapped up in one mission: to amuse and entertain the audience.

1. Keep it crisp.

2. Be funny.

3. Make your humor *ad hominem.*

4. Never wound.

5. Refrain from slopping into sentimentality.

6. Don't take that third glass of champagne until after you have performed.

Sweat, Blood, Toil, and Tears:
Surpassing Yourself

1. Keep it crisp.

We have it on the authority of St. Ambrose: "Let us have a reason for beginning and let our end be within due limits. For a speech that is wearisome only stirs anger."

Which only goes to show that saints are not in all matters infallible, because a speech that is wearisome puts people to sleep long before their anger is stirred.

Addresses following supper banquets, depending on the length of the cocktail hour, the caloric scale of the fare, the wine (if you are lucky enough to be served drinkable wine), the lateness of the hour, and the grandness of the occasion, should be kept under thirty minutes. That's the star. All others slated to speak should harbor no greater ambition than to be footnotes to the festivities.

(Parenthetically, almost all introductions should be less than two minutes. If anyone requires more than two minutes to be introduced, why was he invited? He's a nobody.)

But if there are three lesser speakers on the card, you among them, find out how long the star intends to hold forth, keeping your spiel to one minute for every eight of his, and reducing that by thirty seconds for every speaker on the program beyond four. (This may sound silly, but half a minute too long can seem to the audience a paleontological age too long.) If the organizers have shown the stupefying bad judgment of packing the night's card with more than six or seven speakers, cut your contribution to a minute or less. Better yet, choke on your coffee when your name is announced, or fake a violent coughing spell, so that you are excused.

As the featured speaker, you do have a right to half an hour. But in the event the warm-up speakers hog the ring too long, show mercy: slash your address. You'll have gained the gratitude of maybe hundreds of weary guests in the hall, and you may even get invited back.

Corporate officers take note: Any after-supper program that exceeds an hour and a half, total, is twenty minutes too long.

2. Be funny.

Remember the rule about not starting with a joke? Go ahead, for this sort of occasion. Authentic humor—that which is derived out of your experience, or which is invented by you—is always preferable, but even a canned joke will do.

Keep it clean, for the love of Mike. Why risk offending anyone?

3. Make your humor *ad hominem*.

If free of malice and delivered lovingly, this can be the most delicious vein of humor. The foibles of individuals well-known to the crowd are mightily appreciated, and the target is flattered, or should be . . .

4. Never wound.

Permitting malice to seethe in your remarks about someone in the audience is wicked and unforgivable. Nothing can cut more deeply. Don't be a cur.

I was tempted once and sinned. The provocation was sufficient, a long weekend of poisonous and gratuitous affronts by the obnoxious fiancée of a boyhood chum.

After supper one evening, I gave a paraliptic toast whose cutting edge could not have been sharper. My message was delivered and received, everybody at the table and in the know laughed explosively, but our paths, my friend's and mine, have not crossed often the forty years that have meanwhile slipped by. And I regret that.

The Major Speech

You are giving the valedictory address. Or you have been requested to justify terminating the Veterans Administration. Or it has been your lot to be appointed to close the company meeting on a solemn note (you are announcing a radical change of direction that requires major restructuring and the dismissal of 12,000 employees).

Gravitas is expected of you. The audience are prepared for content that will challenge their minds and maybe not court their favor.

1. As much as possible, frame your reasoning or your ideological case in narrative and chronological terms.

2. Inject as much anecdotal material as clearly serves to advance or illuminate your argument.

3. Inject wit wherever possible, but beware of humor.

4. Reach for aphorisms and rhetorical resonance.

5. Be certain that you announce just where you are going right from the start, so that the audience know that you are progressing toward a clearly anticipated conclusion.

6. Absolutely plan your talk so that the first paragraph grasps the audience in an iron grip, boiling bubbles of concentration on their brows as their brains race to keep up with you.

Sweat, Blood, Toil, and Tears: Reaching into Your Deepest Self

1. As much as possible, frame your reasoning or your ideological case in narrative and chronological terms.

Say you are expounding the latest cosmological findings on the origin, state, and ultimate destiny of the universe.

Narrating how each astrophysical discovery came about tells of the triumphs and failures of human beings, which are of intrinsic interest to other people. Placing these discoveries (and their scientific discountenancing by subsequent discoveries) in their chronological order not only injects the excitement of drama but also provides the audience with a sense of the progression of your text. You may have begun with, say, Copernicus in 1543 and the publication of his *De revolutionibus orbium coelestium,* and ended with the NASA project known as MAP (Microwave Anisotropy Probe), which is scheduled to be launched in the year 2000. As you approach that date in your references, the audience know that you are building to a climax, coming to an end.

We human beings are able to endure almost anything so long as we are assured of a finiteness about it. We employ our special stratagems. For my matinal thirty-four minutes on the treadmill, which is sheerest torture to me, I have worked out a routine that requires my arising not later than 5:34 a.m. and incorporates watching a certain news program (no other will do), becoming irritated (I hope at least once), suffering through short stretches of boredom (basketball and baseball scores), speculating on the day ahead, planning to polish off this (or another) chapter, and saying my rosary. Everything serves like poles marking the furlongs: when I round the curve of the back stretch and head for home, I am sweat-drenched, no less exhausted, but I am sustained by a sense of imminent termination. A similar life raft must be provided to audiences.

3. Inject wit wherever possible . . . but beware of humor.

Wit is always a referent; humor is an egocentric rhetorical grace, demanding attention to itself for its sole sake.

A serious suppertime or evening lecture must absorb the listeners' minds. The talk should be so economically constructed, yet the content so challenging and dense, that audiences are from the nonce rapt. Appreciation of humor distracts, consuming attention. Wit, by contrast, sharpens the intellectual point. A burst of wit can make it memorable.

4. Reach for aphorisms and rhetorical resonance.

Keep ever present that the details of your reasoning will never stick to the minds of your audience. You set forth those details out of intellectual candor and in order rhetorically to prepare the audience for your conclusion; to prepare them to give credence to or to accept that conclusion.

You dutifully conduct them there, but they will not remember how you got from point A to points B, C, D, or E, what those points were (except imperfectly and often mistakenly), or how you leaped from them to your destination.

What the audience depend upon you for, and what you must try to provide, are those happy rhetorical encapsulations that *sing*, that adhere in the mind's memory: *If it doesn't fit, acquit . . . Liberty or Death . . . Blood, sweat, toil, and tears . . . What we have got to do is get the dope out of our veins and hope into our brains . . . He can run, but he can't hide.*

Such nuggets aren't easily come by. Every politician's speech strains for them, failing dismally almost always. (Hired gun Ted Sorensen could not resist embellishing the texts of JFK's speeches with inversions of subject and object, as in, *Ask not what your country can do for you,*

but ask what you can do for your country. That one worked.)
Nevertheless, cudgel your wits for the wit and grace of the born apho-
rist. Joseph Epstein, the brilliant former editor of *The Scholar*, wrote in
his 1993 collection of essays,[4]

> The aphorist is by nature, if not always by birth, aristocratic.
> He is a man who does not bother to argue or to explain; he
> asserts, and, if he has got it right, his assertion is sufficient unto
> the day. Implicit in the brevity of the aphorist's assertions is an
> impatience with logical proof. He also operates at a high level of
> generality. "Great thoughts are always general," wrote Dr.
> Johnson, "and consist in positions not limited by exceptions,
> and in descriptions not descending to minuteness."

Which may or may not help you. But studying the great ones can never
hurt. Mr. Epstein lists his favorites: La Rochefoucauld, La Bruyère,
Vauvenargues, Pascal, Joubert, Rivarol, G. C. Lichtenberg,
Schopenhauer, Nietzsche, Karl Kraus, and a "lone Romanian, a
contemporary named E. M. Cioran. William Hazlitt wrote aphorisms,
jolly dark ones too—'The youth is better than the old age of friendship'
and 'I believe in the theoretical benevolence and the practical malignity
of man'—but not enough of them are superior. Emerson," Epstein says
wonderfully, "is often included among the ranks of the great aphorists,
but, to my taste, he is too vatic, not to say uplifting, and I am prepared
to say boring. But then Emerson did not, strictly speaking, write aphorisms but instead in an aphoristic style, which allows anthologists to
pluck discrete aphorisms from the often heavy pudding of his prose."

Winston Churchill advocated vivid extrapolations for the same
purpose.[5]

> In spite of the argument of the cynic, the influence exer-
> cised over the human mind by apt analogies is and has always
> been immense. Whether they translate an established truth
> into simple language or whether they adventurously aspire to

---

[4] *Pertinent Papers*, New York, W. W. Norton.

[5] In an unpublished [!] essay entitled, "From the Canon: The Scaffolding of Rhetoric, 1897, 1997" (this can't be the
title placed on it by the author, obviously). A friend plucked it out of the Internet and sent it to me.

reveal the unknown, they are among the most formidable weapons of the rhetorician. The effect upon the most cultivated audience is electrical . . .

He proceeds to cite a few, one of which I like particularly: "A strong nation may no more be confiding of its liberties than a pure woman of her honour [sic] . . ."[6] It seems so quaint. Churchill continues:

> It is impossible to imagine any argument that could keep the field in the face of these or similar analogies. One such will make a speech or mar a measure.
>
> A tendency to wild extravagance of language—to language so wild that reason recoils—is evident in most perorations. The emotions of the speaker and the listeners are alike aroused and some expression must be found that will represent all they are feeling, this usually embodies in an extreme form the principle they are supporting. Thus Mr. Pitt, wishing to eulogize the freedom possessed by Englishmen: "The poorest man may in his cottage bid defiance to all the force of the Crown. It may be frail; its roof may shake: the wind may blow through it; the storms may enter, the rain may enter—but the King of England cannot enter! All his forces dare not cross the threshold of the tenement." (Earl of Chatham. Speech on the Excise Bill.) . . .
>
> The effect of such extravagances on a political struggle is tremendous. They become the watchwords of parties and the creeds of nationalities. But upon the audience the effect is to reduce pressure as when a safety valve is opened.

Whether by imagery, analogy, or aphorism, it is your obligation as a serious speaker arguing an issue of moment to boil down what you are saying to a ringing affirmation that the crowd will leave the hall buzzing about, one that reduces the whole complex argument to a thrilling image or a simple concept expressed in a few words. Strive for that, for the words that your audience will relish and repeat, for the words that may forever make your reputation and, as they are chiseled in the

---

[6] Churchill cites as the source: "Bishop of Derry, Albert Hall, 1892."

minds of the crowd, be one day chiseled on stone memorials to your memory. You are most likely going to fail, but the effort will meantime serve to clarify and refine your thinking, to the effect that the policy you seek to establish or the action you seek to elicit has that much better chance of acceptance.

6. **Absolutely plan your talk so that the first paragraph grasps the audience in an iron grip, boiling bubbles of concentration on their brows as their brains race to keep up with you.**

We discussed this in Chapter 2, Commandment 1.

Continue supposing you are giving that talk on the origins and end of the universe. You might open: "Nothing that the greatest scientific speculators and thinkers have discovered about existence since we lived in caves, and nothing that the most sophisticated Hubbell's telescope and state-of-the-art technology have verified since about these conceptual discoveries, is as protean and accurate as the first chapter of *Genesis*."

I am not arguing the merits; I'm simply illustrating how one might choose to begin that supper banquet lecture were one to hold the belief intimated and were one able to substantiate it. *Ça suffit*, as the French say.

The emphasis in this book up to this moment (where dealing with talks that are unrelated to business) has been to encourage you to captivate and entertain your audiences. That's what most of us are called upon to do most of the time. And in captivating and entertaining people, one persuades people in the smoothest and most painless fashion to one's point of view: by indirection; by subtly identifying their good feeling about one and their pleasurable recall of the good time one showed them with the case. (That is, merit becomes obscured by pleasure. Reason almost always surrenders to affinity.) But when it comes to what I dub a *very major deadly serious speech*, the emphasis, following on the gravity, shifts hard.

The Very Major Deadly Serious Speech

Here we chart new territory. The assumption shaping this advice is that your purpose runs fathoms deeper than ingratiation or entertainment.

You are accepting the Nobel Prize in a world that has become vulgar to the core. You seek to warn your audience of the imminence of a North Korean nuclear attack, or that China is planning an assault across the Taiwan Straits. You are arguing that the 1952/1965 laws governing immigration should be revoked if we'd prefer in the future to avoid civil disturbances after every municipal, county, state, and national election. You are calling for suspending the franchise of this generation of the American electorate on the grounds of imbecility and moral turpitude until they show otherwise (by demanding the impeachment of President William Clinton). You are announcing your unalterable opposition to the present chairman and his handpicked board of directors, whose policies you are convinced spell ruin for the company.

You aren't playing games.

1. *Dispense with anecdotal material.* Nothing should distract from your purpose.

2. *Reach for aphorisms and rhetorical resonance.* Yes. But be watchful that you do not overdo it. The gravity of your message should never be competed against.

3. *Convey necessary passion, but do not overlook the virtue of detachment, the more inherently passionate and serious your case may be.* Inexperienced speakers forget what a stunning effect detachment can have. Like the ham actor overdoing gesticulations and expressions, amateurs at the speaker's lectern feel compelled to overload.

The following paragraph is taken from *The History of Money*, by Jack Weatherford (1997, New York: Crown), Chapter 4, p. 64.

On Tuesday, May 12, 1310, French soldiers loaded fifty-four bound men onto carts and took them into the country outside of Paris, where they stripped off the men's clothes and tied them to stakes surrounded by piles of wood. As the prisoners vociferously screamed their innocence, the guards lit the wood beneath them. The flames crawled higher, singeing their hair and lapping at their flesh. The heat caused huge blisters to erupt and their skin to split open as their fat liquified and ran down their limbs in rivulets of flame. The roar of the flames gradually drowned out the screams of the burning men.

This is spare writing.[7] One is prepared to detest Philip the Fair of France, who thus destroys the Knights Templar, before reading a single word more. The amateur would have loaded this paragraph with emotional or sentimental adjectives, Mr. Weatherford permits the horror of the clinically noted details to accomplish what he intended in the imaginations of his readers. This is paraliptic argument at its best. (You'll enjoy his witty book.)

The speaker who is addressing an audience on a subject of the gravest moment or the first importance is best served by keeping his personal passion under tightest control . . . the tremor underfoot before the volcano erupts. Dread precedes terror. Apprehension caused by the speaker steadily piling evidence upon evidence builds to an explosive climax without his voice having been raised.

For more on this subject, see Chapter 22.

---

[7] One could quibble: The "vociferously" isn't strictly necessary.

CHAPTER 5

THE POLITICAL PITCH

INTRODUCTION

A certain ritualistic hypocrisy is required of anyone who is dragooned into a campaign. You must profess belief in the democratic system, even though your common sense tells you that it demands suspension of disbelief. You must put up with people whose company you would ordinarily despise. You must tolerate the professional henchmen—the campaign managers, press flacks, appointed spinmeisters, the speech writers—whose cynicism can cause you to pine for a monarchy.

The subject divides into two parts: (1) *personal preparation* permitting you to do a good job, and (2) *the pitch* to voters.

PERSONAL PREPARATION

Assuming You Are a Free Agent

1. Believe wholeheartedly in the person.

2. Believe wholeheartedly in that person's positions.

3. Believe that it will make a material difference to the city, county, state, or nation whether that person is elected.

Else, respecting any of the three conditions stated above, decline the invitation to speak.

It may be the case, however, that though you have serious reservations about the candidate, nonetheless the cause he champions seems to you to be so superordinating that you gulp hard and raise his banner. In this unhappy case you have to develop the agility of Catholics, who may personally despise their priest while baring their souls before him in confession and accepting the bread of life from him, because even the word of God is piteously vulnerable to the human agent. Remind yourself that for democracy to succeed, universal political virtue or wisdom among citizens is not necessary; one pins one's faith on the margin, the critical mass.

Assuming You Are Professionally Involved

Should you *not* admire and respect the candidate wholeheartedly or agree with all his or her positions or believe that he or she will make a farthing's amount of difference, yet are professionally obliged to serve the candidate in this or the other capacity, swallow hard, submit your scruples to the acids in your stomach, read up on ulcers, pray to the Lord for mercy, and somehow detach your soul from your professional obligations.

For our purposes respecting the duties you must discharge, I'll assume that you freely support the candidate in question, with few or no reservations that, in the balance, matter. This has been the happy case for me in the two major campaigns with which I was intimately involved, as co-chairman of the European Goldwater drive in the 1962 Presidential election (we won in our territory), and as a spokesman and on occasion surrogate for my brother James in the New York senatorial race of 1970.

THE PITCH

In preparing speeches or when helping to raise funds, the following precepts guided me:

The Long and the Short of It

1. Do not err on the side of adulation.

Say simply why you respect the candidate, what his virtues are. Don't waste time on his shortcomings; the other side will take care of that.

2. Select that attribute that stands out most in your candidate.

Perhaps it's his experience, his professional or business attainments, his voting record, his character. Don't try to cover too broad a spectrum. You'll bore the audience.

3. Find an anecdote that best characterizes your candidate.

You need only one good story that will stick in the popular imagination and be endlessly repeated, word of mouth and by the press: The exhausting night he spent rounding up fellow congressmen to save an important bill (*principle*), and his triumph (*effectiveness*); a private act of mercy by him in rescuing a constituent from the coils of bureaucracy (*compassion*); the scoundrel he grasped by the scruff of his special-interests neck and personally flung out of his office (*macho man/integrity*). Do your best to inject humor, pointing out his foibles (*human,* like the rest of us).

4. Don't attempt to stuff too many issues into your talk.

Pick out the two or three that at the moment seem to be the most prominent and of special concern to that particular audience. Boil them down to their essentials. Explain clearly why the well-being of the city, county, state, or country depends on the correct decision. Show why it is in the interest of the voters or the group whose support you are seeking that these positions carry.

5. Terminate with a detailed account of the process of a particular piece of legislation or a day in the candidate's life.

An hour-by-hour account that shows the difficulties he must deal with, the pressures withstand, the intellectual and moral judgment exercise, and maybe the compromise he is forced to accept. Don't lard your story with fawning fat. Tell it as a reporter might tell it. Let the audience infer what a special person your candidate is.

6. Now ask your audience whether he is worth their support.

. . . In campaign contributions, at the polls. Too many speakers in support of a candidate at the last moment fail to nail their purpose to the door.

✿   ✿   ✿

That's all you need to know, other than the name of the county chairman (very important!), his wife, their son or daughter, and the names of every last person who contributed in any way to the fund-raising event. Thank them all personally and publicly; pen a short note of appreciation to the county chairman, praising him beyond his just deserts. If all this sticks in the craw beyond bearing, quit.

PART 3

HOW EVEN A BUMBLER CAN LEARN TO BRING DOWN THE HOUSE IN A HURRY

CHAPTER 6

FINDING AN INTERESTING, BRILLIANT, AND ORIGINAL IDEA IN WHICH THE SPEAKER IS PASSIONATELY INVOLVED

Cut the whining.

In 1992, I invited the witty, erudite William F. Rickenbacker, Jr.—now deceased—to be a guest lecturer at a special Buckley School seminar. He wrote me a letter wondering out loud what he should speak on. Here are the choices he offered me:

- How I Spent My Summer
- What the North Wind Said
- Counselor Said I Couldn't Eat Dinner Till I Wrote Home
- Why I Hate My Sis
- Legalization of Crime: Pros and Cons
- Was Mozart Queer?
- The Bartender's Guide to the Upstairs Maid
- Are Lasers Protected under the Fourth Amendment?
- Public Speaking Minus One: A Tape Cassette of Wild but Intermittent Applause, with Stretches of Silence to Be Filled with Remarks by the Apprentice Orator

- Sexual Repression in Emily Dickinson's Punctuation
- Why I Am Running for President (*applause*)
- Why Dead White Males Don't Laugh
- Do Hydrogen and Oxygen Look Like Water? I Ask You!: Chemistry Disrobed and Shown to Be the Fraud It Is

You may never hope to be as funny as Bill Rickenbacker, but there are billions of ideas out there for the plucking.

Suppose you want to waste less and save energy while at the same time improving the quality of life. Draw up a short list. Start with abolishing the Department of Energy, which since its inception in 1977 at a cost of $300 billion, has produced not a drop of oil nor a cubic foot of natural gas nor an ounce of economy; make basketball courts one way; forbid photo albums of weddings and infants; limit State of the Nation addresses to twenty minutes (fewer follies advocated); raise the driver's license permit to age 17; invoke cloture on Capitol Hill after three months; abolish Mother's, Father's, Secretary's, President's, and all other "Days"; slap a $1.00 tariff on any fast-food carryout order (to be contributed to a municipal and county fund for local cleanup); shut down the U.N.; lower the height of the net on basketball courts to 5 feet, 3 inches; fine political parties for any poster left up or advertising uneffaced after an election; outlaw *I ♥ Anything* coffee mugs, sweatshirts, billboards; cut the NBA season to sixty days; promote gay marriages; (a) outlaw any commercial flight between points fewer than 250 miles distant from each other, (b) cease at once the construction of interstates, (c) devote all highway tax funds to the development of railway beds for trains of *très grande vitesse;* mass produce *I ♥ Celibacy* condoms; discontinue all narcissistic TV "awards" extravaganzas by the entertainment industry (utterly boring and self-congratulatory besides); hammer a bung into Barbra Streisand's mouth unless she opens it to sing; genetically select for and nutritionally foster the production of human beings fifty pounds lighter and one foot shorter; immanentize the eschaton speedily.

Any of the themes mentioned above would make a fun talk, maybe even a useful talk. The point: Don't at once reject ideas that sound zany to you at first or second thought. Explore them. Framing ideas in absurd, exaggerated, what the French call *outré* fashion may be just the juice you need to light a fire under your imagination.

Digging Deeper: Running with Novel Ideas

Take that rant on sports, which was started under Chapter 3, when discussing a talk before the Rotary. You've declared that sports stars are villainous human beings who should be caged rather than paraded before children as rôle models. *Push it further, dig for the reasons:* "And why is that?" you continue, rolling your thunder. "Why are superstars deplorable people? Because," you bellow, "the very game begets these vices. Sports in general and professional sports in exaggeration glorify egocentrism, wholesale narcissism, the competitive spirit carried to ruthless and even self-destructive excess (steroids), and viciousness of temperament. There is no room for charity or compassion in sports. The concept of fair play is for sissies and idiots. The supreme goal is to win. The Gipper may have felt differently way back in the age of innocence, but winning sums up the whole philosophy of Coach Vince Lombardi, who has been elevated to semidivine status. And to that end—winning—almost anything goes, short of actual homicide. Sports bring out the worst in everybody, player or spectator. Pat Conroy in *The Great Santini* exposes the essential viciousness of sports when the father in the novel browbeats his son into a potential life-crippling foul against the star player of an opposing basketball team. A high school championship was at stake. The Great Santini was no invention. He was Pat Conroy's father fictionalized. Been to a Little League game lately? Have you listened to the "moms" in the bleachers screaming and yelling in the most vulgar and violent language, spitting out obscenities? Have you watched them after the game (moms and dads) screaming at their weeping 10-year-old kid because he dropped an outfield fly or she swung at a high inside pitch—shoving them into the back seat of the car? A recent study shows that three men out of every twenty who attend an NHL hockey game come back home and commit high and aggrieved battery on their wives. More shocking yet, the study tells that three out of nine women who attend a wrestling match featuring Lillian Ellison, the "Fabulous Moolah," go home to beat their husbands. To a pulp! Everything to do with sports has been corrupted. It's not just wretched Tonya Harding's henchmen bashing in the knee of beautiful Nancy Kerrigan with a club. What about the judges in figure skating competitions? Hasn't bile soured your lips at the outrageously rigged scoring? Haven't you been disgusted at footage of rampaging British soccer "fans" before and after a World Cup match?

There you go! Let that lunker run your spool out. You can enlarge on this argument, fleshing it out with the lives and crimes of one superstar after another. You'll have a talk suitable for the Rotary.

CHAPTER 7

GETTING THE FACTS

... on the one hand, it is universally admitted and on the other hand, it is not true.

—Joseph Epstein, from *Partial Payments*, 1987

Should you be a professional who can expect always to speak about that which you know, (a) you are fortunate, (b) skip this chapter.

The following is for the occasional speaker, the person who happens to have spent three weeks hiking on the Himalayan slopes of Nepal this past summer and is asked by the local Odd Fellows Club to give a short talk about it, or for that odd fish, the generalist, who may be tapped for a talk on just about anything.

There are not a great many generalists on the professional speaking tour, or even around. (I was billed as a "social critic," whatever in the world that can be taken to mean, though I console myself in noting that Irving Kristol is similarly billed.) Back in the nineteenth century oratory was considered a big-time grace and big-time entertainment. The public paid to hear a famous orator speak because of his fame as an orator. No longer. Now the topic and expertise matter. We live in a Benthamite age. Most of us are tied to an occupation of some kind that endows us with a certain presumed authority in whatever it may be. Yet even for professionals, one is sometimes tapped for the disparate speaking chore, an introduction to someone else, a fund-raiser, a municipal ribbon-cutting ceremony, a graduation, a company picnic. If you are one of them, read on.

SELECTING THE GROUNDS

Talk about what you know and what you are best known for, whenever you can. Deviate from this rule at your peril.

Do Not Disappoint Expectations

If the reason you are asked to give a talk is that you have accomplished something in a particular field or are known as an authority on whatever, you upset audiences, courting their displeasure, should you choose an unrelated subject.

Martha Stewart is not invited for her opinion on the short stories of John Cheever. Audiences want to hear astronauts talk about space and space travel, not the baking of gingersnaps. From a lawyer, they expect either a heavy discourse on the Pernicious Anachronism of the Concept of a Jury of One's Peers in These Invidious Times or juicy inside gossip on famous litigations. A journalist is permitted latitude, but generally audiences expect a talk touching on politics or current sociological controversies. Specialists are much confined. A prominent author may be forever stuck to the topic of the book that made him famous. Only if you have achieved "celebrity" status may you safely hold forth on whatever you wish, because in your case audiences really don't give a hoot what you talk about, they just want to say that they have heard you speak or that, gasp, they actually sat on the dais next to you. A supernova like Oprah Winfrey can get away with dispensing *faux*-profound platitudes about the novels of (mostly black female) authors and the short stories of John Cheever and probably the philosophy of John Donne or the metaphysics of the cosmic superstring theory, not to mention gingersnaps and space travel. Should you not inhabit that sort of constellation, stick to your last where you are able, or to what comes closest to your last, requiring the least imagination and preparation.

Having selected your ground, dig for the facts.

KNOW THYSELF, KNOW THINE ENEMY

Beware of yourself and beware of others. Analyze your temperamental proclivities and your analytical weaknesses with merciless candor. When searching for the truth of a matter, contrive to know where the author of a book or article or study or opinion is coming from.

Sweat, Blood, Toil, and Tears: Surpassing Yourself

Everything in this state we call existence conspires to discipline and define us. When experience reinforces what our genes condition us to perceive, we live in a state of bliss. But when experience runs foul of the bias of our genes, we encounter dissonance. And when this dissonance becomes acute, we end up on a psychiatrist's couch.

To avoid this unhappy state, genes do their best to twist experience, bias to subvert reason, gut desire to deny, or to embellish, or even to falsify the facts.

Broadly speaking, there are two temperamental bents, two prevailing views: the liberal and the conservative. Our genes condition us to be the one or the other. There is the temperament that cautiously proceeds by casting an anchor to windward, the other that throws four sheets to the wind and piles on sail. I suspect the first temperament is the more reliable and successful in times of war, crisis, or economic depression, the second in times of peace and plenty. Which is a digression. The relevance of these ruminations is that when we seek the facts, we must be realistic about ourselves and our inmost biases and cautious about the agenda that may be screened behind the prose of others.

By all means, do your best to be fair-minded. But be realistic also: You will succeed in impartiality to a point; then your genes and the resolution of the war your genes may have waged with your experience will determine how you view the facts, how you weigh the reasoning. And everything you read on the subject you are investigating will be similarly colored. If you expect to discover and deliver the unvarnished truth, you are deluding yourself. Neither will you find it in others nor will you be able to expound it in defiance of your psychological constitution.

Therefore, guide by your biases, and discount the biases of others. This is the quickest way to dig down to that much of reality that you are willing yourself to countenance.

FINDING THE STRAIGHT POOP
(NOTHING BUT THE FACTS, MA'AM)

These reservations kept in mind, the straight scoop about anything can be the most difficult material to unearth, and it requires not only sifting through newspapers, periodicals, monographs, and books, but through intentional or unintentional distortion of fact, ingenuous or disingenuous reporting of fact, outright falsifications, and malicious interpretations. The task can appear so daunting, its very prospect numbs or overwhelms one.

This is one reason why it's so important to determine what one's angle of attack is going to be. That tends to narrow the compass. And like the word whose meaning was previously opaque to you that seems to pop up on pages everywhere once you have learned its definition, so having determined your angle of attack has the effect of popping to your notice those items in evidence or informed opinion that are useful to you. If your assigned topic is the liberation of women from oppression, for example, and assuming you are preparing a ten-minute or half-hour talk, not a 400-page tome, you begin by deciding whether you're going to discuss (1) women as the presumed prime agents in the rearing of children, (2) the imperviousness of that barrier to female advancement in business or the professions, dubbed the "glass ceiling," (3) the expanding rôle of women in politics, (4) the social and political peonage of women in Asia and the Orient, and how it's worse in Akron, or (5) the perpetual subservience that women are reduced to by Islam, the Boy Scouts, and *Hustler*.

Say you decide to speak on choice 1: women as mothers. And be fair-minded. You must hie yourself to your Christian church or Jewish synagogue for periodicals on this subject presenting the (predictable) orthodox view of Woman the Homemaker . . . and also to NOW (the National Organization for Women) for the Liberated Woman's view. You'd want to read (or skim) a book by Gloria Steinem and one by Elizabeth Fox-Genovese (*Feminism Isn't the Story of My Life*). Then you look up relevant recent articles in the weekly news magazines, *Cosmopolitan*, *Reflections* (published by the Independent Women's Forum). Tap into the "e-zines" of the Internet, *Salon*, *The Washington Weekly*, Pete DuPont's *Intellectual Capital* . . .

But that's much too laborious. Keep in mind whom you are talking to. Be not cynical, but practical. And honest with yourself. How much labor are you willing to devote to this obligation? Unless you insist on making a serious intellectual point that boasts of some originality and importance; unless you are planning to run for public office; unless you are preparing this talk in the context of assuming an important post that is in the public eye, subjecting everything you say to critical review; and unless you are speaking to a hall full of knowledgeable people on your particular subject; be satisfied with dipping into the vast seas of statements and counterstatements on such a subject as motherhood, selecting what you find convenient because it pleases your bias. (Which you must trust for essential decency and correctness. If *you* can't trust your biases, who may trust them?) One of the simplest dodges is to grab a recent article that has achieved a certain notoriety and comment on it. Use it as a scaffolding on which to hang your remarks. Or if, for some reason, you feel compelled to speak at Toastmasters for twenty minutes on the Bell Curve, do not, for Heaven's sake, plow through the (huge and heavy) book by Herrnstein and Murray, read a review or two of it.[1] Or a compendium of opinions, such as the one that was run by *National Review* on the subject when the book was fresh out. Be superficial. T'ain't worth it to attempt an exhaustive examination of anything before the majority of audiences and on a majority of occasions. Neither will you be understood, nor your effort appreciated. Your audiences are likely to be bored by scholarly labor. Please understand, I am writing a primer, not an essay on morals. If it consoles your conscience, be disgusted with yourself and ashamed; but by hewing to this advice, you will find what you need *sans* excessive labor (for which you do not have the time) and deliver yourself of a creditable talk for most purposes. And you will have learned the secret of success in democratic politics: fatuous certainty grounded in the shallowest of soils.

But should you insist . . .

Sweat, Blood, Toil, and Tears: Surpassing Yourself

Keep researching until the last minute, until your name is announced and you are compelled to mount the stage. Fight your prejudices as

---

[1]*The Bell Curve—Intelligence and Class Structure in American Life*, New York, Free Press, 1994.

fiercely as you do battle against sloth and ignorance. And be critical of your sources.

Back in 1988 I wrote on this topic:[2]

> Books, monographs, magazines, and newspapers can be pest-places of error that the magic of print perpetuates. (I used to believe anything I read in a library was true, or it wouldn't be there.) "My good friend Dr. Palache wrote a doctoral thesis about paralysis in paraplegics" won't do, because if it wasn't published, it was never subjected to broad, critical examination. "It was in the newspapers" likely may not do either, because newspapers are mine fields of misinformation that harried editors have no time to verify and correct. "I read it in *Time* or *Newsweek* or *U.S. News & World Report*" is safer, but a glance at the letters columns shows how often even these reputable journals, despite their elaborate infrastructure of researchers and copy editors, can make a hash of fact, and sometimes print fabulations as fact. To their shame, they are guilty also of shaping stories for politically sensational effect, a vice to which *Time* and *Newsweek* are notoriously prone. And even books from reputable publishing houses aren't totally safe. Whereas the factual content has probably been rigorously checked over a period of months, there is still no guarantee against error, and books about historical events, current issues, and political figures are almost always written not only by someone who has cultivated a strong perspective, which can have the effect of distorting evidence by selection, but sometimes also by a writer whose perspective has long deteriorated into bias, his bias into ideology, tingeing and distorting almost all evidentiary material.

Nothing has changed.

THE PERILS OF RESEARCH

There are other pitfalls associated with research.

---

[2]Whenever I quote myself in this chapter, I am quoting from *Speaking in Public: Buckley's Techniques for Winning Arguments and Getting Your Point Across* (New York: Harper & Row, 1988).

Dangers in the Attractive Anomaly

The piquant datum may be piquant because it is wrong, or deceiving. Avoid permitting your weakness for the fantastic or your esteem for the skewed perspective to do you in.

For too many years, I found it impossible to ascribe weaknesses of character to anyone who had a sense of humor. Several false (but funny) business partners cashed in on this badly mistaken assumption before I learned my lesson. Any statement or supposed fact that strikes your basic instincts as curious or dissonant should warn you that *it is probably not so or probably not as it seems.*

The Treacherous Quotation

There are few embarrassments quite so keen as having one's half-educated conceits pricked by authentic scholars. Make certain you get that quotation right, and make doubly certain that it actually represents what you purport it to mean. Often, passages taken out of context suggest something that is contradicted by the body of the text. "Reid Buckley advocates superficiality in speakers. Here's what he says: 'Be superficial. T'ain't worth it to attempt an exhaustive examination of anything before the majority of audiences and on a majority of occasions.' Those are his exact words, which he can't deny."

But you know I don't mean that!

Buy yourself a copy of Paul F. Boller Jr.'s and John George's *They Never Said It: A Book of Fake Quotes, Misquotes, & Misleading Attributions* . . . and bless their names in your prayers at night. Not everything has been covered in that most precious volume, but a lot that can cause you grief is there to save you from error.

Treacherous Generalizations

These can be insidious. (Again, buy that book by Boller and George!) "J. S. Mill is the apostle of liberty." True, but his dictums on what makes popular government possible would repeal the several promiscuous extensions of the franchise in our country since the 1960s. "Thomas Jefferson detested slavery." True, but he established a plantation that required increasing numbers of slaves to sustain. "In *Poor Richard*, Ben Franklin wrote precepts for the young to follow." True, but he was no model for the young to emulate. He defended venery as good for the health and led a debauched existence in England, frequenting Sir Francis Dashwood's "garden of lust" in Buckinghamshire, along with Lord Sandwich and other notorious rakes.

And so forth. You can't take it with you, nor have your cake and eat it, nor count your chickens before the eggs are well candled, because that may be a clutch of gators you are incubating. Generalizations that package folk wisdom can be trusted, but they are dull.

The Perniciousness of Received Wisdom

What we take for granted. What we have always assumed. What may have been ignorantly and wrongly told to us by our teachers. This is the most difficult and elusive of misinformation to identify and then dislodge from our minds. There is no easy solution (though it helps to buy that book by Boller and George!).

Sweat, Blood, Toil, and Tears: Surpassing Yourself

Take that so-called apostle of free trade, Adam Smith.

Well, he did fervently espouse it, but in Book 4, Chapter 2, pages 430–431 of his *Wealth of Nations*, Smith subordinated what he called the "opulence" that a people enjoy from the untrammeled commerce of goods across borders to considerations of defense, advocating industrial self-sufficiency and approving (reluctantly) retaliatory duties in certain cases. This argument, Pat Buchanan or Roger Milliken would happily seize upon in their objections to NAFTA.

In your research, it may be useful to follow the four laws or prescriptions for logic advocated by Descartes in his *Discourse on Method*, Part I, the first of which is

> . . . never to accept anything as true if I did not clearly know it to be so; that is, carefully to avoid precipitate conclusions and preconceptions, and to include nothing more in my judgment than was presented clearly and distinctly to my mind, so that I had no reason to doubt it.

Be skeptical, not trusting.

Making Doubly Sure the Authority One Cites Actually Supports One's Case

This is another peril that defies a simple prescription. Depending on how deeply and truthfully you determine to plumb a subject, you must be willing to devote the hours of scholarly work that are required. Which is why I recommend that when you decide to speak on topics with which you have little acquaintance, which is a bad idea, or when you happen to be assigned such topics, you keep it light: you do not pretend to speak as an authority.

Sweat, Blood, Toil, and Tears: Surpassing Yourself

"If J. S. Mill was not the radical libertarian we had assumed and Adam Smith not the uncompromising free trader, surely we can trust other received premises, such as what we have always known about the great Prussian Karl von Clausewitz's (1780–1831) preference for offense in war over defense. This example is particularly interesting, for being so deceptive, because so much is true about Clausewitz. He did prefer a pugnacious attitude to a static attitude; nevertheless, it is more accurate to say that he favored an opportunistically offensive spirit, while recognizing that the strategic advantages lie with the defense."

This is the kind of tangle that speakers get tripped by. Almost nothing can be trusted to be as it seems or as we are comfortably accustomed to assuming it is, and we are required again and again to verify even what we hold to be certitudes so consecrated by use that they sound platitudinous. We can start with the self-evident: *Good taste runs in the blood.* Wrong. Good taste can be neither inherited nor bought. *Britons are boors, the French rude.* Wrong. Either couldn't be nicer. *New York taxicab drivers are amusing grouches who give you the straight scoop from the street.* Wrong. New York taxicab drivers no longer exist. They are Egyptian or Persian or !Kung or Kakwakus or Yanomamos from the Amazon (or some place). They can't give you the straight scoop about anything, speaking no word of English, and as far as being streetwise is concerned, they have to be directed to Times Square.

Even what purports to be sacred writ cannot be uncritically accepted by anyone researching a speech. In our Advanced Seminar (for graduates), we have routinely assigned a moving speech by Chief

Seattle of the Duwamish Indians, which he delivered to the governor of Washington territory in 1854. It goes, in part:

> How can you buy or sell the sky? The land? The idea is strange to us . . . Every part of this earth is sacred to my people. Every shining pine needle, every sandy shore, every mist in the dark woods, every meadow, every humming insect. All are holy in the memory and experience of my people . . . Will you teach your children what we have taught our children? That the earth is our mother? What befalls the earth befalls all the sons of earth. This we know: the earth does not belong to man, man belongs to the earth. All things are connected like the blood that unites us all. Man does not weave the web of life, he is merely a strand in it. Whatever he does to the web, he does to himself.

Hearing these noble words recited by a talented student, my faculty and I could become quite weepy. How filled with goodness! How tragically prescient! Vice President-to-be Al Gore was apparently affected in much the same way, because in his treatise on the ecology, *Earth in Balance*, he quotes the whole speech. It is a favorite of environmentalists, intrinsic to whose creed is that "Native" Americans (native noble savage non-European Americans) lived in a state of symbiotic bliss with nature.

Alas, Al Gore and Reid Buckley and the hard-bitten faculty of The Buckley School are mightily deceived. Chief Seattle never uttered the words. Moreover, it's doubtful he harbored any such sentiments in his noble Rousseauian soul. As British zoologist Matt Ridley tells us in *The Origins of Virtue* (Viking, New York, 1997):

> Nobody knew [what the chief] said that day. The only report, made thirty years later, was that he praised the generosity of the great white chief . . . The entire "speech" is a work of modern fiction. It was written [in 1971] for an ABC television drama by a screenwriter and professor of film, Ted Perry [talented guy!] . . . Though many environmentalists . . . like to pretend otherwise, Chief Seattle was no treehugger. Among the few things we do know about him are that he was a slave owner and had killed almost all his enemies . . .

Chief Seattle is as fit to be placed in the pantheon of environmentalist prophets as Chief Powhatan (Walt Disney's *Pocahontas* notwithstanding) in the pantheon of the peace-loving aboriginals.

Getting back to Clausewitz, human blood may be spilled on account of such misattributions of sentiment and slavish subjection to them. Danton's *"l'audace, et toujours de l'audace"* is the spirit that precipitated the slaughter of the Charge of the Light Brigade, and maybe Pickett's charge at Gettysburg, and also the hideous *danse macabre* of trench warfare during World War I, where in the single extended battle of Verdun, more than 800,000 young French, English, Americans, and Germans were slaughtered. To the great fourth-century B.C. Chinese strategist, Sun Tzu, the pinnacle of military genius was the psychological maneuvering of the enemy into surrender, without a pitched battle having been fought nor a drop of blood shed. His prudence is recommended to the neophyte speaker. Make few assertions. Check those you do make. If you are wandering afield from that homely backyard which you know, oh, be cautious!

Citations from Authority That Do Not Ring True

"When you quote anybody, do not only check to be positive that your citation is accurate and that it fairly and completely represents the position of the source, try to make sure also that what you quote isn't rubbish. That is, that the great man wasn't nodding. If, upon analysis, you personally decide—pay no attention to established opinion or to what you think you ought to think—the generalization is stupid, or fatuous, or just wrong, you may wonder whether it is accurately attributed to the otherwise sensible fellow."

You have probably had flung at you ad nauseam the assertion, "Though I disagree with what you just said, I'll fight to the death for your right to say it," which pious liberal sentiment is attributed to Voltaire. Only, Voltaire never said any such dumb thing. (He said other dumb things.) The Bible never claimed that cleanliness is next to godliness, George Washington never could not tell a lie over chopped cherry trees, it is a *foolish* consistency that is the hobgoblin of little minds, Barry Goldwater not once recommended that we resort to nuclear weapons in Vietnam, and Lord Acton never wrote that power corrupts absolutely.

The Coiled Viper of Subtle Distinctions

Collect pet dictums and aphorisms, be prepared to defend them, but don't let them dictate to you. They do not substitute for thought, nor, often, do they represent the whole of the thought.

If only for this reason, toss out your Bartlett. Such *aperçus* stolen from those pages and sprinkled into the text, are not only cheaply come by, they are cheating—and can be deceiving.

Sweat, Blood, Toil, and Tears: Surpassing Yourself

Take Clausewitz's celebrated dictum: "War is nothing else than the continuation of state policy by different means." Do a job on that.

Once shot, twice warned. As the saying goes, there is no education in believing Bill Clinton twice. (Hamlet had it easy in his "To be, or not to be"; we are all still wondering what is, is, or when.) You are wondering: Am I being set up again? Did Clausewhatsis make this statement, is it correctly quoted, and is its sense a fair representation of what he intended?

The answer to all three misdoubts is yes: (1) the words are his, (2) you are not being sandbagged. (That's the correct sense of what Clausewitz wrote.) Nevertheless, (3) the aphorism is frequently incorrectly interpreted that Clausewitz *proposes* war as an *extension* of policy. This imputed sense is false. Clausewitz wrote further on (in his magnum opus, *On War*), more elaborately, of his proposition,

> War is nothing else than a *continuation* [emphasis added] of political transactions intermingled with different means. We say intermingled with different means in order to state at the same time that these political transactions are not stopped by the war itself, are not changed into something totally different but substantially continue, whatever the means applied may be . . . How could it be otherwise?

He continues by asking,

> Do the political relations between different peoples and governments ever cease when the exchange of diplomatic notes

has ceased? Is not war only a different method of expressing their thoughts in writing and language?

He terminates with a memorable phrase: "War admittedly has its own grammar but not its own logic."

All of which is nice, and philosophically interesting in a very Germanic way, but the distinctions are next to impossible—in my opinion—to impress upon the comprehension of the run of American audiences. It is not, I hasten to add, because we are egregiously a dull-witted people, but because (1) not since maybe the Founding have Americans been trained to the fine distinctions, failing consequently to understand them when they are drawn, and (2) in common with most other civilized folk, our capacity for audile understanding is not as keen as in (wholly) illiterate societies.

When a saying strikes your fancy, annotate chapter and verse. *Read the book*, or a standard authority on the book. Be certain you have the quotation correctly rendered and do everything possible to make sure that you are using it appropriately. Moses himself might have made a mishmash of the Ten Commandments had the Lord not provided him with stone tablets, nicely chiseled.

CHAPTER 8

SEEKING INSPIRATION

INTRODUCTION[1]

There is, of course, the Internet.

As Yogi Berra said, "You can observe a lot by watching." An NPR broadcast informs me that websites are growing at a rate of 60 percent every six months, extrapolating from which there may be five million of them in cyberspace by the time this book lights up your day.

I believe it. I can believe anything at all about the Internet except that it is able to make our Vice President interesting. The Internet partakes of the attributes of the Lord God, according to St. Anselm. It is that than which nothing greater can be imagined. It is a source of facts and information and thus, for the speaker, of ideas than which nothing less costly and more munificent can be imagined. Should you be at a loss for a topic for next week's meeting of the Hibernian Society, or even the Royal Order of the Garter, surf it, cruise it, loll and wallow in it.

The ticket is to be opportunistic, to seize on fresh ideas. I imagine everybody has his favorite source. One of mine is the *Natural History* magazine, which I enjoyed twenty years ago more than I do now. Almost every issue contains nuggets. One dandy issue[2] featured an anthropological hypothesis by Stephen Jay Gould on the genealogy of prehistorical man. It seems that Homo sapiens probably coexisted with *Neanderthalensis* and another species, *Homo Heidelbergensis* (a beer

[1]Almost everything in this chapter has been borrowed from *Speaking in Public*, Chapter 3, "Where to Go Looking for What You Need and Discovering Fresh Material . . ."

[2]April of 1997.

drinker and a brawler, no doubt). We bipeds did not replace each other in neat, deterministic, survival-of-the-fittest succession, he argues. Rather did modern man emerge as a "branching bush." That's nice . . . and a little sad too, to contemplate that we outthought, outcompeted, maybe murdered and in other historically inscrutable ways elbowed our close cousins out of existence.

The descent of man is rich fodder for the speaker hungrily in search of a topic. The magazine carried two other articles that provoked the imagination. The first, entitled

The statement below is true

Folklore is invariably false

The statement above is folklore

—by Roger L. Welsch—began marvelously:

> I once sat in an audience of folklorists listening to a friend's scholarly paper about the abundance of treasure legends in the American West. This distinguished researcher cited narratives of hidden troves from Aztec treasures plundered by conquistadors, contemporary [stories of gold] discovered and lost by prospectors, chests of loot hidden by thieves, shipments of bullion lost in storms, personal riches buried by spiteful owners. Next he regaled us with observations about people who devote their lives to searching for lost and hidden treasures, companies that make their own fortunes selling equipment to fortune seekers, and a world of research techniques centering on antique maps and stories that might lead the clever analyst or decoder to fabulous wealth. "Why," he asked, "are we so captivated by the notion of lost and hidden treasures? What is it within us that so fascinates us about such a folklore?"

I wish I had been at that lecture, and don't you? Why indeed are we spellbound by the glittering prospect of stumbling upon an Aladdin's cave? It's not the wealth alone, considered in terms of acquisitive value. Jewels and gold are special; one doesn't thrill in quite the same way when kicking up coal. Treasure Island is a never-failing topic for audiences of all age levels. And the authority of the oral tradition contains rich lodes for the mining as we ponder how much of our civilization depends upon it, beginning with the Old and New Testaments.

The very next article, "The Flower of Frozen Deserts," by Eric Hansen, is an intriguing offbeat account of the ice cream whipped up in Turkey, not out of curds and whey, but out of orchids. The dessert is called *salepli dondruma*, and the best ingredients (finest tubers) are found along the mountainous edges of the Anatolian plateau. The properties of this delicacy are wonderful. It can ". . . heal the spleen, prevent cholera and tuberculosis, facilitate childbirth, stop hands and feet from shaking, and improve one's sex life." Oh, and the frozen stuff can also be used as a jump rope.

All three of these articles are fun, fascinating, and fecund for the imagination and in themselves would make marvelous topics for a Civic Club, a Rotary meeting, or a Knife & Fork luncheon.

Which brings me back to . . .

PERSONAL EXPERIENCE IS THE MOTHER LODE

Odd, peculiar, singular, inexplicable, revelatory personal experiences never fail to intrigue audiences, assuming that they are truly odd, peculiar, singular, inexplicable, or revelatory, and that they are well-told. Most of us think of ourselves as leading humdrum existences. We undervalue our experiences because they are so familiar to us or because we have told them so often to family and friends. But these are the anecdotes that strike responsive chords, that are most authoritative and carry the highest veracity, that are original, and whose suggestiveness requires no more than the ruminative mental exertion of the speaker to develop.

Once when he was visiting me in Madrid, the late Russell Kirk, author of seminal books, regaled my wife and me with stories about his maiden aunts, both long dead, who resented his modernization of the family house in Mecosta, Michigan, tormenting him by extinguishing the lights. This usually happened when he had company. He would patiently take a flashlight down to the cellar, pry open the power box's door—to have the bulb dangling from its long cord in the cellar's ceiling shine tremulously back on before he had examined or touched a fuse.

This happened sundry times. His aunts insisted, he said, that he put himself to the trouble of half-stumbling down the narrow cellar stairs in the dark, groping his way to the power box, before relenting in their protest against modernity.

We were at a restaurant in the ancient part of Madrid when he told us this story—at a long table in a cramped ell, at the end of which was a small casement window facing on the street. He told us other tales. Poltergeists pestered him regularly, and not only in Mecosta, he said. They had followed him to Europe. Oh, yes, they had traveled across the seas, manifesting themselves in Edinburgh and Geneva. At that moment—as he uttered those words—there came a sharp, hard rapping, three times, startling my wife and me, but apparently not Russell Kirk, who simply shut his mouth and gazed in the direction of the sound. I leaned my upper torso toward the window and pulled aside the barred shutter to look out; to see that the street here plunged down from the restaurant building at a sharp angle, that the drop between window and sidewalk was twelve feet at least. There was nobody down there in the ill-illuminated street. There was no possibility that anyone could have reached up to rap on the window pane. When—astonished, incredulous, skin prickling on the nape of my neck—I looked back at Russell Kirk, he was gazing at me with a smug smile on his round face.

Ghosts are good stuff, like buried treasure. You may have to dig for both into your past. I hadn't thought of this story in years, until writing this chapter, and I've never told it in a lecture. One day I'll find occasion for it.

Sweat, Blood, Toil and, Tears: Surpassing Yourself

Which does not require that you be a born raconteur or short story writer.

Okay, such natural graces help. But if you are not marvelously gifted in this fashion, the way to achieve what you want is (1) to tie your experiences to a narrative line or to an intellectual point, and (2) to concentrate not on how best to tell the episode but how best it fits into your theme or how, in itself, it makes, suggests, or illuminates the point. Ask, Why has this story or incident stuck in my memory? What is its meaning? That the incident with Russell Kirk happened and is inexplicable in ordinary terms (as far as we could tell) does not of itself qualify it for use. One must make the connections. What does your experience tell you about yourself, life, the human condition? Why is it significant . . . or as haphazard and emptily boring as the relation of a dream, best stuffed in a drawer with the socks?

Which can be an obstacle. On the tongues of some people, personal experiences are best forgot among the socks. The danger of relying on them as a talk's main bill of fare is that, at the mercy of a second-rate intelligence and a third-rate sensibility, they are likely to be rendered in shallow, trite, mundane, sentimental, credulous, often sanctimonious, and irredeemably bourgeois terms. They become smug, dull, and embarrassing. Should you fear that this may be the case with you, then you must borrow.

PILFERING FROM OTHERS

Appropriate the ideas of an entire article, as suggested above in the introduction to this chapter. Or hang your talk on the ideas engaged by an article or study or book. Further develop what the author tells; adduce more evidence in its favor; take issue with it. A book that is high in the bestseller lists or a study, poll, survey, or report by a government commission that has provoked hot controversy is a natural, assuming that you boast some background on the subject and are able with some authority to comment on it.

Sweat, Blood, Toil, and Tears: Surpassing Yourself

Don't imagine for one minute that riding on the back of somebody else's thinking is beneath dignity. One of the wisest (and liveliest) intelligences I've ever known, Sophie Wilkins, translator of the plays of Friedrich von Schiller and longtime editor for a distinguished publishing house, put it bluntly in a New York taxicab one afternoon while we were discussing the fiction of Gore Vidal (which I despise): "Amateurs invent," she chided me, "professionals steal." This is in itself a hoary writer's adage. There is no such thing as an original thought since God created the world, so quit fretting.

But you do have an obligation to be honest. Declare outright, "What I'm about to say, I owe [entirely?] [in a major way?] to Larry King, the unabridged story of whose intellectual pilgrimage was published in the May 3 issue of *People*, on page 16."[3] Or, "I am basing my entire talk this afternoon on the account that appeared in *The Theophysicist Gazette* on how Shirley MacLaine discovered the attar of the essence of transcorporal existence, as told to Elizabeth Taylor." And never appropriate the words of anyone without citing them as a quotation or paraphrase without crediting the source.

WHERE TO HIE FOR INSPIRATION

Which I've suggested in the introduction also: to the Internet, to little-read or offbeat periodicals, to the newsletters of hobbyists. I never knew what a pontil rod was, nor could I have imagined how those exquisite complex canes of brilliantly enameled glass were produced in paperweights, until I read a monograph about antique millefiori weights by Baccarat. Do you know how to tell a bead drilled by the pre-Columbian Incas from a counterfeit, or an unfiltered 1990s Californian red from the antiseptic stuff vatted in the 1970s and 1980s? What use is such trivial knowledge? It depends on the individual. For me, the canes, the beads, the wine become metaphors for integrity. What you devour need not be appetizing. Anything that is odd, quirky, absurd, strange, and revolting in a brilliant way is also wonderful.

Browse through bookstores. Collect curiosities. Develop and indulge your intellectual yen in as wide a spectrum of interests as possible. I have on my shelves titles on heraldry, Scottish tartans, wind instruments, seashells, herpetology, English double-barreled shotguns, wildflowers, numismatics, sexual deviancies, metaphysics, and sundry other exotic and arcane subjects. They range from Kraft-Ebbing to Thomas Aquinas. From an old engraving belonging to my wife, I learned that Louis XIV's bird dogs—Spanish setters—were called Bonne, Ponne, and Nonne, for which marvelous information I have yet to discover use, though I am sanguine that some day I will.[4] At various

---

[3]Truly!

[4]Just did!

times in my life, I've studied or dallied with or developed a passion for football, boxing, ornithology, the keeping and propagation of exotic fishes, horse-jumping, steer-riding, Civil War histories, fishing, hunting, retriever-dog-training, the fastidious consumption of fine wines, mountain-climbing, bullfighting (very small bulls), post-Impressionist paintings, indoor plants, farming, forestry, practical ecology, Cherokee paint stones, "found" sculptures, particle physics, speculations on the ontological destiny of the universe, and so forth. Browsing through the literature of these subjects has been fun and has provided me with inexhaustible springs of reference.

Everything under the sun becomes useful, is fodder; the more hobbies or intellectual interests one pursues, the richer the mountain. *Even a boring person can be the source of an intriguing subject.* Cultivate bores. (Nobody else does, poor people.) I learned from one how to arrange the silverware for a banquet of eleven courses, including two fish and a fowl. I learned from another the difference between *that* and *which*. Don't neglect the works of fanatics and monomaniacs, either. Their obsessions can be fascinating. Almost any biography by a candidate for national office who lost is an example. (One reads without believing.) The sheer ego of some people is instructive and fertile with insights about the human species, at least for me. Life is a hard teacher. From age 5 to age 9, I determined that I should be Pope and wore a halo fashioned from the cane fastening of asparagus bunches. When it was revealed to me that only Italians get elected Pope, I fell into a deep depression from which I was rescued by my decision to become President. When it was revealed to me (by an envious school chum) that only natural-born citizens of the United States are eligible to be elected President, disqualifying me because I was born in Paris, my depression was profound—until I discovered that all along I had wanted to be a writer. Which, for lack of anything better, is what I have done with myself, writing about religion and politics and forlorn hopes since. The point being: One's lifetime dilettantism can be a San Luis Potosí of purest silver, an inexhaustible trove.

Be warned of two major dangers, both of which involve excessive and uncritical enthusiasm. There are glamorous causes that are hyper-inflated, and there are good causes that are wretchedly argued.

Delving Deeper

Glamorous Causes That Are Hyperinflated

Try not to be sucked in by glitz. The more the "right sort" approve of a cause, the more suspicious we should be. Christie's auction of the late Princess Diana's gowns in the last week of June (1997) was the last word, but is it a subject for a Garden Club talk? A "cheering, chortling" throng of 1100 attended the event, according to *People*, among whom were the likes of Henry Kissinger, Lord Hindlip (whose name must be taken on faith), Tomasso Buti (identified as the owner of the Fashion Cafes in New York and London—a cousin, one supposes, of Buti Buti Gala), designer Pat Kerr, and glittering others. The royal wrappings fetched "a tidy $5.76 million," which, we are told (and here's where caution must be exercised), were "destined for AIDS and breast-cancer charities."

Main Street cries, Enough already. AIDS is Hollywood chic, not a subject to tickle Peoria with. There is resentment out there in the boondocks. The likes of Elizabeth Taylor and Barbra Streisand expend hysterical energies on raising money to combat this single disease, which, if examined objectively, is a largely self-inflicted malady peculiar to a minuscule portion of the populace. Look, one's heart goes out to human beings stricken by AIDS, but given the relative incidence of the virus compared to cancer and heart conditions,[5] the disproportionate national effort being lavished on it is so preposterous that one wonders how Princess Di's gowns weren't reduced to stitches, and Lord Hindlip, for shame, did not develop a harelip. Keep your sense of proportion.

The Right Cause Badly Advocated

The perspective will differ according to your politics. You have the ACLU-types who litigate to outlaw a yuletide crêche in a public park because they fear an implied infringement on the First Amendment.

---

[5]In 1995, 38,000 people were fated to die of AIDS as against 575,000 Americans who fell to cancer and 925,000 who died from heart disease.

You have right-wing gun-nuts who perceive a threat to the Second Amendment in any legislation curbing the sale of weapons, though the ones in question are designed for the sole purpose of mowing people down. Or how about fanatical "pro-choicers," who ride roughshod over the right of peaceable assembly in seeking to outlaw public demonstrations against abortion clinics, and their counterparts, fanatical "pro-lifers," who bomb those clinics and assassinate doctors associated with them. The totalitarian temptation to which righteousness is prone. The absence of tolerance and charity.

Be cautious, when happening upon an article or book that seems to proclaim everything you believe, that it does not advocate measures in promoting the cause with which you would take exception.

Good causes may suffer not only from bad actions on their behalf but also from bad argumentation and poor writing. In this case, the reputation of the writer is no guarantee. A speaker seeking ideas must be on his guard against permitting the style in which an argument may be expressed to damage its authority.

Veteran journalist Georgie Anne Geyer wrote a book called *Americans No More*, which was published in 1996 by Atlantic Monthly Press. I was asked to review it. Now, I was sympathetic to her argument: the decline, debasement, and dissolution of citizenship in our country over the past generation and our potential disintegration into hostile factions rooted in ethnic- and economic-group interest. But oh! how wretchedly written her polemic is. I was careful to draw the distinction between the soundness of her contentions and the value of her evidence for them, both which I praised, and her style of expression, which I lambasted:

> Ms. Geyer is prolix. She piles example on example with the effect of smothering the point she is making. A hundred pages should have been, could have been easily, edited out of this book. Her allusions are sometimes so esoteric that a po' country boy like me fails to make the connection when (p. 325) she pins down her argument by saying, "And at that moment I thought of my respected friend Askar Akaev, the president of faraway Kirgizstan, who essentially told me the same thing." On top of which, Ms. Geyer is an atrocious

writer. I mean bad. Three times, she misuses the word *fissi-parous*, signifying reproduction by fission, when she wishes to convey splintering into hostile parts. She cannot leave well enough alone: all her sources are introduced as "fine," "wise," "penetrating," "brilliant," "seminal." The only buttering she missed are "condign" and "mordant." She is enamored of apocalyptical adjectives. Everything is dramatic, incredible, terrifying, tragic, diabolical. From p. 21 alone: "Indeed, I was in India that hot, ominous summer . . ." (When was an Indian summer cool, or *un*ominous?) "Those events had their zenith [one attains or rises to one's zenith], though surely not their end [she means limit], in the Armageddonesque [*aaargh*] explosion of hatred that shook India to [guess where?] its ethnic roots." The lady can be rhapsodic: "With its glorious green mountains and legendary cedar groves . . . descending to the azure [what else? you got it] blue of the Mediterranean." "That summer in Korea I was invited to the July Fourth party at the luxurious Korean-style American embassy residence, which is one of the most beautiful in the world. But when I entered, I stood there, stunned. The beautiful red, white, and blue tables were filled to [guess what?] overflowing with rich and tasty food . . ." (Thank heaven they weren't overflowing with fried locusts.) The breathless, hyperbolic style achieves a kind of zenith, or end, on p. 328: "I got some *valuable* insights into the cause of that state of *constant dread* when last in *lovely* Finland, from the *famous and multi-talented* young artist Bjorn Weckstrom. I had stopped by his *beautiful* studio . . . and soon noticed, in addition to the *gorgeous* jewelry, *exquisite* sculptures, and *fine* drawings . . ." (Italics mine, enthusiasm hers.)

Ms. Geyer is the Martha Stewart of journalism. Be sure you are not so enthralled by your enthusiasm for a point of view that you ignore either its inherent weaknesses and contradictions or what may be the unfortunate style in which it is expressed. Many a sound argument has been devastated in its expression. The purpose of the Inquisition, keep always in mind, was loving.

Sweat, Blood, Toil, and Tears: Surpassing Yourself

EXPANDING ONE'S CULTURAL BASE

For most of us, speaking in public is an occasional and infrequent chore. It is something we are now and then called upon to do because of our position in society or business or profession. It is not our main business. We don't believe that our reputations will stand or fall on how well we acquit ourselves on the stump. And we are wrong.

Our reputations may be dangling on the brink. Our main business may, in fact, be—is probably dependent upon—our powers of persuasion. If we graduate to this understanding of the importance of public speaking, we will exert ourselves more than we may be inclined to by aggressively expanding our general knowledge and doing what we can to repair the deficiencies of our education.

Which is the rub, and the shame, and the disgrace. Just as almost nobody under 70 in this country is able to write a decent paragraph of English prose, so almost nobody under 70 in this country has received a respectable education in the liberal arts, or in the humane letters, which is the only education worthy of the name. Everything else is an acquired trade. We suffer from inflated self-esteem and portentous terminology. A college linebacker with a neck the size of a watermelon whom I met on a plane told me that he was studying "distributive economics." "Oh," said I, "and what is that?" "Retail selling." That's not an education; that's fraud. A surgeon is no more than a glorified mechanic. A psychologist is often no more than an infantile fantasist; an economist a bean counter crossed with an astrologist; a graduate in "communication skills" a tongue-tied, slack-minded practitioner of obscurantism; and a sociologist the dullest fellow in his class posturing as a seer through the rendering (in impenetrable prose) of tendentious numerical data putatively reflecting human reality.

If one is serious, one must get serious. One must study. Captains of industry, eminent professionals, and those on their way up are often culturally as the baboon on Petrus Camper's scale.[6] (I only became

---

[6] A nineteenth-century phrenologist much in vogue, who deduced from the angle of the face a scale of relative intelligence: greater than 70 percent, the angle, the higher; lower than 70 percent, the lower. Quite spurious.

aware of the existence of Camper thanks to Stephen Jay Gould.) That's low. (Wall Streeters drop off the charts.) As a nation, we have become cultural boors, and it is questionable—it has been questioned for years—whether it is taxonomically admissible to style ourselves a civilized people. It's not less than tragic that until 1945 or 1950, one could assume that any American from the most basic literate background was versed in our cultural heritage, which nourished the imaginative faculties, because if he didn't pick it up at school, he picked most of it up at home; and that until maybe as late as the early 1960s, even illiterate households in this country were familiar with the fundamental document of our civilization, the Good Book.

This is no longer the case. And it's a shame, because many of the more ambitious readers of this primer, through no fault of their own, must put themselves to a pile of catching up. A person aspiring to become well-furnished in his imagination, and thus better than an apprentice speaker, simply must fill those gaps in his cultural knowledge that he may discover. *Do not count on your business or profession to assist you, or even to be sympathetic with your aspirations.* Corporate America still believes that what you need is yet another course on management or marketing. Though it's no secret that the majority of CEOs of the Fortune 500 companies are graduates of liberal arts colleges, notably the Ivy League,[7] Corporate America is mired in late nineteenth-century utilitarian thinking. Corporate America is abysmally ignorant of the process of thinking, of what actually constitutes the workings of the brain and what produces original thought. Corporate America still subscribes to the myth of "cool" and "dispassionate" reasoning, which is a superstition, which does not exist. Corporate America has never heard of Phineas Gage. Corporate America is unaware of the work of Antonio Damasio and a slew of other neurologists, who have rediscovered what classical philosophy knew instinctually, namely, that *nihil est in intellectu quod prius non fuerit in sensu*—nothing is in the intellect that was not first in the senses. The act of cogitation depends on the messages that the brain receives in a continuous stream from the senses, which include the skin, the organs, and the bloodstream. The brain is a receiver, a storer, an editor, and a

---

[7] I have this from my friend Joe Williams, Yale graduate and recently retired CEO of The Williams Companies. I haven't checked it out.

shuffler of everything about the outside world that becomes known to it through the senses. The brain deals in concrete images. Nothing is abstractly thought or "reasoned" in the sense of *ex nihilo* by the brain; nothing originates in the brain. The most complex abstractions of which our minds are capable are produced by synaptic correlations of proto-types in which hundreds of millions of neurons collaborate. (Hear that sizzling!) The inspired hypothesis, the epiphany, and the stroke of genius occur to the mind through the instantaneous cross-referencing of hundreds of thousands or even millions of electromagnetically stored bytes of data that have been resting for weeks, months, or years in that powerhouse of brain matter at the front of the skull—that bulge of our transcending humanity, the advantage that Homo sapiens had over *Neanderthalensis* and *Heidelbergensis*—resonating with potential, waiting for liberation. The conclusion from which is evident to every-body except Corporate America and, alas, the educational establish-ment (ignorance plays no favorites); namely, that the broader and more disparate, eclectic, and unorthodox a person's cultural background and experience are, the better, the more rigorously, the more fruitfully and originally will he think. It is the ratiocinative equivalent of hybrid vigor. No, we do not need yet another crash course on cost computing; our brains hunger for poetry, music, art, mathematics, philosophy, and sweet science. When one speaks of cultural deprivation, one is in fact speaking of the regimented starvation of the brain, which is being denied the nutrition that it cries for.

But Corporate America is like the medieval Church in denial of Galileo. If the results don't show up in the next quarter's financials (round which event their universes spin every ninety days), Corporate America wants no part of Copernicus. You are on your own. Happily, the chore is pleasurable. A nice thing, too, is that since all of the foun-dation stones of our culture are universal in character, perusal of any one of them, say, the *Iliad*, say *Hamlet*, say *Moby Dick*, will almost certainly provide the public speaker with insights for his very next talk, at the least aphorisms. The reading of a single great epic poem or play or novel will at once enrich the speaker's text. It will feed and may even suggest the next twenty texts. There are no shortcuts, however. Though T. H. White's King Arthur is terrific, Sir Thomas Mallory's is the source. It is never too late to start.

PART 4

PUTTING THE DAMN THING DOWN ON PAPER

INTRODUCTION: BUSINESS PROSE

I tell them: When you walk into the Buckley School, you enter a different world.

I tell them: You have left Wall Street, Main Street, Company Street behind. We don't have any use for and we do not tolerate either business babble or professional obfuscation. Corporate prose is the pits. It is uncivilized. It is characterized by a half-educated inflation of language. It is full of conceit, the enemy of clear sense. Where Shakespeare, in *Hamlet*, lugs the guts across the floor, American business "implements the removal of the remains from the premises."

I tell them: I haven't read your papers, but I will . . . and I don't want to hear about a corporate "philosophy." Clever ways of making money may be wonderful; they are not a philosophy. Using that honorable term to describe the method by which a company rides herd on costs, seeks out new business, and turns a profit is not only impertinent, it is vain, arrogant, and stupid. Nor is there such a thing as a "paradigm" in connection with business. A paradigm is a complicated intellectual term proper to cosmology and theology, not money-making. It was first given currency in this country (to my knowledge) back in the 1950s, by philosopher-historian Eric Voegelin, in connection with the modern gnostic heresy of attempting to immanentize the eschaton, which isn't exactly the business of business, which doesn't know what in blazes an eschaton is, or the meaning of immanentizing. What business babble wants to say when appropriating the word "paradigm" is the limits or confines or even parameters of a subject. Say it that way, then.

I warn them: There is jargon in business and professional babble that is unacceptable not only here at The Buckley School but in civilized company. Even the SEC has laid down the law to Wall Street and to Corporate America across the land. It has issued a directive demanding that reports to stockholders and to the Securities Exchange Commission be written in plain, simple English using the active tense and personal pronouns. The SEC has served notice that it will no longer tolerate corporate mumbo jumbo. No longer will business be able to hide behind thickets of turgid syntax. No longer will "It is thought" or "It is considered" or "It is proposed" be allowed to protect the chairman or president or reporting officer from responsibility for what he is saying or what he is proposing. This means that American business—you—must slough off the prose habits of the past half century, which are designed to cloud meaning and avoid responsibility. Do not use the word "empower" when all you are doing is permitting. Do not use the word "meaningful" when you have no idea exactly what you do mean. Do not use the words "significant" or "critical" in conjunction with this or that measure of performance when you haven't the least notion what exactly is significant or critical about it.

I beg them: Stop trying to be fancy. Do not use "implementation." Say get going, set up, put in place.[1] Do not use the word "proactive." What's the antonym of "proactive"? "Antiactive?" "Prostatic?" As in cancer of the prostasis? What the devil do you mean by that barbarian term? That

---

[1] An implement is a tool, a utensil, an instrument. The verb form derives from the Latin *implementum*, the action of filling up. The five-syllable "implementation" not only is pretentious, it produces that ugly, mushy, *ashun* sound.

you're all for getting things done? That you will take the initiative? Say that, then. Stamp "proactive" out from your prose, if you are guilty of it.

I entreat them: And stamp out almost all words, beloved of business, containing the ugly *ashun* sound. They're like stuffing your mouth with marshmallows or filling it with peanut butter. They are an agglutination of gluey and mostly unchewable syllables conducing to the gumming up and ultimate obliteration of meaning, as in, "The procrastination of middle management descended like an ominous obnubilation over the ranks, bringing about an infestation of prostatic inertia in the work force, whose consequence was delayed implementation of production processes incurring a precipitation of complaints." Just say that lazy middle management destroyed morale and gummed up the works, making customers furious.

I tell them: When Commodore Vanderbilt got back from his extended European tour, he discovered that two of his partners had been playing him false. He wrote them: "Sir, I find that you have been cheating me. I will not sue, because the law is too slow. I will ruin you." That's twenty-one one-syllable words and two words of two syllables each, for a total of twenty-three chilling bullets of doom. He did indeed ruin them, within the year.

I implore them: We want you to write like that: tough, chiseled, simple prose. The language of Caesar, who crossed Rubicons, who came, saw, conquered. You want to write in that clear, vivid, declarative style, not only to avoid my wrath, but to rejoin the human race.

*   *   *

We become fast friends. Now I tell, beg, entreat, and implore you. Refer to Chapter 3, the section called "Beseeching the August Indulgence and Favor of Your Superiors." Read what they ask for in a report or speech from a subordinate. They don't want the kind of prose I deplore above. Business and professional writing is an affront to the language only because subordinate officers and younger professionals who are unsure of themselves think their superiors desire such excrescences. Believe me, they don't.

CHAPTER 9

ORGANIZING THE WRITTEN ARTICLE OR SPEECH[1]

ORGANIZING YOUR CONCEPTION, THINKING, AND RESEARCH

Dear God in Heaven, how do I begin?

Let not that cry of anguish paralyze your will. When painters confront the terrible challenge of a blank expanse of canvas, the only way they can master their fears is to grab a brush sopping with paint and slash across it, or so I've heard.

You're not ready to throw ink on the blank canvas of your mind, however. Not yet. You don't even know in which direction to hurl it. Your paralysis isn't in the execution, it's in the conception.

Four simple prescriptions will help.

Establish Your Point of View

This may be the most difficult and time-consuming factor in the organization of a talk or an essay, and it is the most necessary. Nothing works until, first, one's angle of attack has been decided.

It's your first order of business. Only when you've got clear in your mind where you are heading, setting the whole tone of what is to follow, are you prepared to jot down the first sentence or paragraph.

---

[1]This is almost all filched from *Sex, Power, and Pericles: Principles of Advanced Public Speaking*.

125

Only when you've decided where you want to go can the research commence.

Sweat, Blood, Toil, and Tears: Surpassing Yourself

You need to define what your perspective is going to be (not to be confused with what your conclusion may end up being) before you can begin looking up facts and materials reflecting on the topic or shaping what you wish to say about it. That perspective becomes your editor, nudging you in the right direction.

Selecting the angle of attack is no cinch. But—valiant soul!—should you decide that you'll exhaustively read all the available literature on, say, free will before putting thought to test, pen to paper, bully for you, we'll see you in about forty years.

There's ground between intellectual integrity and inflated ambition, and that's being practical. Before the first page of research is scanned, the writer must have formed some idea of what aspect, facet, or byway of a subject he wishes to consider. Which means that some arbitrary anterior mental editing must take place, and that, of course, invites the prospect that you may set off on the wrong track, the research you *do* undertake exposing (after many hours, weeks, or months) the fallacy of your operating assumptions. Take comfort in this: Just as one's first impression of a person often turns out to be, for good or ill, correct, so one's first reaction to a topic is often the useful reaction. Guide by your instinct. Change or modify that gut opinion only under the pressure of evidence.

Buck up. The likelihood is that you have been ruminating on your topic subconsciously for years, which you only discover when you sit down formally to contemplate it. *We can never imagine how much we know about anything until we set ourselves to writing about it.* Compelling yourself to the task of constructing an essay calls upon all those random thoughts and impressions that maybe for years have accumulated in your brain and been given storage in its recesses. Writing liberates what has been locked up in the mind. You can go to your death without realizing that when it comes to potlatches, cross-stitching, gingersnaps, basement construction, selecting fine paintings in an auction, or the Rime of *The Ancient Mariner*, you are a seer.

Refrain from parroting old arguments.

> Your point of view is the attacking edge. This edge must
> be not only sound on evidence, but also original.

Most any opinion heard on the evening news, or read in *Time* or *Newsweek, Readers' Digest, The New York Times, The Washington Post, The Christian Science Monitor, The Los Angeles Times, The New York Review of Books, Rolling Stone, The New Republic, National Review* and the *American Spectator* (now that these two have become mainstream journals of reference), *The Wall Street Journal*, and, of course, *USA Today*, is already tired or soon destined to be.

Read widely.

> Establishing your point of view requires wide reading
> on all sides of the issue within the parameters of the
> issue. Surprised?

People resist this second subprescription. Executives and professionals (doctors, lawyers, architects) do not have the time for copious reading, even in the literature of their particular fields. Too bad. Shut up. Only a lot of reading prevents a person from making a fool of himself, becoming a parrot of pop opinion, or being dull. (For more, see Chapter 6.)

It's long been my opinion that when a building is completed, the architect should be required to stand on the highest sill. If the crowd below give him a thumbs down, he should be required to jump. The world would be saved repeated visual ravages by the same culprit.

The penalty for being dull as a writer or speaker should be a draught of hemlock. Your audience will to Lethe-wards have sunk[2] in any event.

Winnow

Out of the material you use, separate those matters that are germane (indispensably related) from those that are merely accidental.

---

[2] Cf. *Ode to a Nightingale*, John Keats.

1. Not everything can be covered in any one speech.

2. It is best to establish one solid point well.

3. The depth with which one point can be treated depends on how much time (space) one has. List the subpoints in descending order of priority. Lop off the least important, entrancing though they may be.

The political scientist Willmoore Kendall once rebuked me, saying, "A person cannot make more than one point in 1500 words." He was a master stylist and polemicist. His *obiter dictum* is probably true for a political article; it is certainly true for a speech.

Sweat, Blood, Toil, and Tears: Surpassing Yourself

At my school, we pound on this theme in the critiques that we meticulously work up on each of our students after they have attended the Executive Seminar in Communication Skills. We wrote one fellow:

> Conferee must get to the point. He must remember that audiences are as a rule obtuse. He may be speaking at the Cosmos Club in Washington before a roomful of Nobel Prize laureates; in the aggregate no better than an audience of high school kids will they keep up with a talk that is clumsily circumlocutious and hence difficult to follow.

The repercussions of packing too much into a short talk can be worse: one may incur hostility . . .

> When a speaker delivers a complicated text or one with transitions that are a bit of a stretch, or spouts off information that seems superfluous, his audience may decide that communication isn't his primary objective. He only wants to show off his knowledge, like the professor who is impatient with his dullard students. Their opinions, their support, aren't Mr. BigEgo's concern. Speakers must strive, above all, to be succinct. There should not be a soul in the audience who misses

the point or who doubts the direction of the talk. A speaker's goal must be crystal clear from the beginning.

Argue to the Core

You have established your point of view and decided what is germane. Now ensure two things:

1. The drift of the argument should progress logically and coherently either to or from the main contention.

2. Sift argumentation to make doubly certain that only what is germane and necessary to the point is there. Do not permit fortuitous (accidental, happening by chance) evidence or reasoning to slip in.

Some people are easily distracted by tempting detours or matters of tangential interest. Resist this.

Resist also the anecdote, amusing or simply expository, that occurs to the mind in conjunction with one's argument but that is not essential to it. *Reject any anecdote that does not actually advance the argument.* By which I mean that upon the termination of the anecdote, the reader or listener must view the point you are making from a more complete vantage, so that you can proceed to examine the same point from another perspective or to the next point, secure in the knowledge that your audience (thanks to the anecdote) have filled in the exposition *whose place was taken by the anecdote.* If exposition of the argument does not suffer when the anecdote is left untold, don't tell it. (Lacking which justification was why I left untold the delicious anecdote that occurred to me earlier in the book.)

Sweat, Blood, Toil, and Tears: Surpassing Yourself

Our critiques are littered with admonitions to this effect:

Conferee must not allow himself to go off on tangents. That's a mortal sin of indulgence that no speaker or writer may commit without incurring the fires of damnation.

Again:

> Conferee *overloads listeners with information*. He must
> reduce and simplify the content of his talks. His objective
> should be to leave his audience with one or two compelling
> ideas. They should never feel swamped by his verbiage. In *The
> Elements of Style*, William Strunk Jr. tells us: "The surest way to
> arouse and hold the attention of the reader [listener] is by being
> specific, definite, and concrete. The greatest writers—Homer,
> Dante, Shakespeare—are effective largely because they deal
> in particulars and report the details *that matter*. [Emphasis
> added] Their words call up pictures."

You are not Descartes nor Stephen Weinberg, frantic to discover
T.O.E. (the Theory of Everything). Your object in a talk is not to explain
the universe. The late (d. 1990) Juan Antonio Vallejo Nágera, one of
twentieth-century Spain's fabulous men of letters, wrote a tract on
public speaking (*Hablar en Público*) that became a runaway bestseller
because it is full of wit, wisdom, and solid good sense. "Apprentice
orators speak too long," he notes. (Great orators never attempt to say
too much.) We must kill those precious darlings. "If you have any
doubts about whether you ought to include [an anecdote; phrase; expla-
nation; line of argument, etc.] . . ., suppress it. If you yourself, who are
the father of the baby . . . maintain doubts as to whether it is oppor-
tune [or necessary], you can have no idea of the . . . doubts the [audi-
ence] is going to have . . ."

Vallejo gives the theme another couple of whacks. "There exist
magnificent orators from whom we flee," he declares. At public functions of all kinds, "there appears that fellow whom we all know 'who
speaks very well,' but who insists on demonstrating this for too long and
with excessive frequency . . . There's a terrible phrase one hears from
those who comment on a public ceremony. 'How was it?' 'Fine, fine . . .
but a little long.'" And: ". . . at the conclusion of an especially well done
lecture there will always be a simpleton who says to you: 'You were very
brief; the audience was left thirsting for more. What a shame!' What
this fellow doesn't [have the least notion of] is that in his [lectures] the
audience is always left thirsting for less. And this is truly a shame [*y eso
es una verdadera pena*]."

If you are a good speaker, and full of achievement, heed Vallejo. The coldest ring in Dante's hell is reserved for the bore, whatever you may have heard. In Heaven, God flees from the company of Hubert Humphrey. As you should flee from the example of William Clinton—that superb public speaker—who bombs every time he delivers an oration. Lincoln's Gettysburg Address was neither too long nor too short.

Fourth and last,

Do Not Worry about a Conclusion

If the first three steps are followed rigorously, your conclusion will suggest itself.

The conclusion is not to be confused with the point of view or the angle of attack. It is through exploring the point of view that one arrives at the conclusion.

1. One doesn't realize how much or how little one knows about a subject until one starts developing it.

2. The meticulous hard labor of constructing solid argumentation tends to ignite the imagination and often reveals to ourselves the interesting, original, or sophisticated insight that we never knew was there.

Neophytes try too hard and fret too much. That an interesting and original conclusion will suggest itself is guaranteed by two matters of fact.

First, we are, each of us, unique. There is no clone; nobody else on this earth possesses our peculiar genetical ingredients. These alone endow us with a unique intellectual perspective that is further refined by unique sensory, emotional, and psychological reactions to an experience or thought. Second, our experiences, though they cannot be guaranteed to be unique with the same mathematical certainty as our genes, are, nevertheless, almost certainly so. The combination of experience + DNA is the absolute warrant that what we end up thinking about any subject, assuming we have examined it rigorously, will be original. Unless . . .

Sweat, Blood, Toil, and Tears: Surpassing Yourself

Unless, unless, unless we betray ourselves!

Unless we are untrue to ourselves.

Unless we permit ourselves to think or write or speak received wisdom, *de rigueur* thought, what we kind of imagine our boss or the crowd would like to hear, because in our earnestness and desire to please, we believe (mistakenly) that this is the correct thing to do.

It is what sycophants, flatterers, wimps, yes-men, of neither character nor spine, speak and write. People who serve up what they imagine their superiors, peers, subordinates, or the Beltway *approve* reading or hearing will be neither heard nor read.

To your own self be true, or you'll be true not even to yourself. Dear God, I know how hard the saying is. My heart goes out to the hundreds and hundreds of junior executives who have come through my school, some of whom live in the most awful state of anxiety. It's a wonder they are functional. Many will never be more than that: functional; functionaries. They as little dare to shuck the prescribed patterns of thought encouraged by their corporate culture as to rid their talks of charts and other visual aids that conspire to put audiences to sleep. It's as though they are on toboggans, whizzing down the chute, from which they dare escape only by risking life and limb. Every now and then, the velocity of their thought hurtles them with centrifugal force up on the boarded rim of a curve, photographers, like scuba divers, flipping over backward to escape their suddenly perilous approach. But they never do go over that edge. They think within rigid parameters, deeply grooved. They think in compact set-phrases that have been rendered meaningless and that interfere with original thought, impair and militate against original thought, but that are acceptable to the culture. They write and speak in jargon that lulls their listeners into the complacence of knowing that nothing unsafe or unacceptable or subversive of the corporate creed is going to be uttered. People at Coca-Cola live, breathe, dress, drink, and think in red and white. The cultures of Gillette, DuPont, Eastman Kodak and other long-established, successful, and paternalistic companies are as pervasive . . . and dangerous to the person who is trying to think his way through the barriers to originality that deference to custom has long implanted.

Don't misunderstand me. Those cultures worked. They wouldn't have been enshrined had they not succeeded in the marketplace. But the danger lies in becoming wedded to whatever triumphed in the past or continues comfortably to serve the present. Eastman Kodak has undergone an agonizing fifteen years attempting to revamp the culture that is now its albatross.

I'll speak of jargon further, and more kindly, in the next chapter, but meantime, know that it is the enemy of hard thought. It is a substitute for thought. Jargon packages propositions, each of which may be questionable, in what philosopher-historian Eric Voegelin brilliantly labeled as a "compact" statement that has become acceptable from usage: that is, a statement that is so often flung about that it resists analysis and is virtually meaningless. This is why I object so strenuously to such awful corporatese as *paradigm, empower, meaningful*, and *proactive* (see Chapter 10). They remind me of the walls of the Milliken & Company headquarters in Spartanburg, which are festooned with hortatory aphorisms in bas relief. One glances at the first three or four, ignoring the rest. I wager not one employee (excuse me, the jargon is "associate") . . . not a Milliken associate in a thousand, has paused truly to read and ponder a single one of them.

Take the currently fashionable "family values." The phrase gives people a warm and fuzzy feeling—which is treacherous, as Vice President Dan Quayle discovered in the spring of 1992, when he lashed out at *Murphy Brown*. (He was essentially correct, but his focus was off.) Because to the margin that "family values" is differentiated, people may disagree violently. They may go for one another's throats. I'm all for family values, please understand, *my* family's values. What are our Western-oriented, Christian-based family values to a Muslim? To a Masai warrior? To a single mother subsisting in a ghetto? The irony, of course, is this: Only to the degree that such a term becomes emptied of meaning from repetition, from supine and uncritical reception, is it acceptable. If a writer or speaker desires to become renowned for cant, all either has to do is study the catchphrases and received opinions currently favored in newspapers and weekly news magazines, the clichés. Anything the Establishment—your boss, your department chief, the chairman of the board—has pronounced its approval of is no longer interesting. Alfred North Whitehead tells us, "When a matter ceases to be a subject of controversy, it ceases to be a subject of interest." The virtue of being dull is that you run no risk. The virtue of running risks is that you liberate yourself from thralldom.

ORGANIZING THE WRITING OF YOUR ESSAY OR SPEECH

The better you have your conception and thoughts organized, the easier is it to transcribe this hard labor into language. Nevertheless—sorry—it's never easy.

The First Paragraph[3]

Content

The opening paragraph should *announce the major themes.*

It should engage the mind in the manner that the mind prefers to be engaged, satisfying first the question, *"Why should I listen to you?"*; second, *"Tell me in short, sweet, succinct language what this is all about; then, prithee, proceed—quickly—to spell it out."*

The conclusion of the essay or speech should be foreshadowed in the first paragraph, though not fully revealed. *It should be cunningly suggested.*[4] The mind should be tickled, or tantalized, by the possibilities contained in the opening blast, in which (in the mind's excitement which) a willingness to suspend outright rejection is incited, though skepticism may yet reign.

In a word, the first paragraph should be *pregnant* with the succeeding, second paragraph.

Verbal Strategy or Style

The language of the first paragraph should seize the interest of the reader through its audacity.

---

[3]Here we are abandoning our division of the topics between statement (the quick fix) and further discussion or elaboration (surpassing oneself) because it's not useful in this context. See the chart on page 134 for quick reference.

[4]Example: "Though no one in his right mind will advocate return to lynch law, the atrocity that took place in Jasper, Texas, causes one's blood to howl for sudden, swift, and merciless retribution." Is the writer, in fact, going to advocate lynching those three degenerate white supremacists? The reader is going to have to find out. (The planted intimation, however, is that no, in his conclusion, the writer will renounce vigilante action . . . but can one be sure?)

The Quickest Fix of All: Writing a Speech

OPENING PARAGRAPH

CONTENT:	1. Announce major theme.
	2. Engage curiosity and attention of reader.
	3. Foreshadow conclusion.
	4. Should be pregnant with the second paragraph.
STYLE:	Seize interest of reader through audacity, originality, and freshness.

PARAGRAPH 2:

CONTENT:	1. Broaden and reflect upon themes announced in first paragraph.
	2. Briefly introduce subtopics that will be developed in the body of the essay.
	3. State those subtopics, from first to least important.
	4. Terminate with a rhetorical summation.
STYLE:	Less bold or contentious, yet virile, vivid and audacious.

PARAGRAPH 3:

CONTENT:	1. Develop the last proposition stated in the second paragraph (this may require breaking up into four or five bunches of prose).
	2. Final sentence should suggest the next proposition to be examined (which should be the penultimate proposition set forth in the second paragraph).
Style:	1. Lively, vigorous.
	2. Must be the faithful servant of the exposition, never distracting from it.

↓ Paragraph continuing development of third paragraph . . . ↓

↓ Paragraph continuing development of third paragraph, etc. . . . . ↓

SUCCEEDING PARAGRAPHS:

CONTENT:	1. Follow prescriptions for paragraph 3.
	2. Knock off the subtopics one by one.
STYLE:	1. Sentences will be denser, longer, packed with more information and careful reasoning.
	2. Thoughts should defy breeziness, though never be excessively wordy.
	3. Resist the Orotund Temptation, the Rodomontadian Temptation, the Shallow Temptation.

CONCLUSION:

Content:	1. Should finally arrive at the conclusion suggested in the first paragraph.
	2. Should culminate the whole intellectual endeavor.
Style:	Majestic, triumphant.

Ideally, it should appear to say what it does not actually or fully mean, beguiling, by gulling, the reader, or, alternatively, clash candidly and directly with accepted opinion on a subject, thus challenging the reader. (See Chapter 2, Commandment 1.) Think of the opening discordant seven blasts of Beethoven's *Eroica*, or the portentous, mind-riveting syncopation of the first stentorian trumpetings in Beethoven's *Fifth*.

The first paragraph's final sentence should be in the way of a minor rhetorical summation or encapsulation, setting the stage for the second paragraph.

The Second Paragraph

Content

This paragraph should broaden and broadly reflect upon the theme(s) announced in the first paragraph.

It should continue to hold the attention of the mind in the manner that the human brain prefers to have its attention held: *"Say that again; elaborate on that first statement. What do you mean by it? What is it that you are getting at?"* These questions should be satisfied by the second, follow-up paragraph, which should advance the argument from the high audacious ground of its announcement to the less lofty terrain on which it will actually be fought (ratiocinated, reasoned).

This means that the fuller restatement in the second paragraph of the themes announced in the first paragraph must suggest the subtopics or minor themes that are to be comprehended in the body of the essay in support or in elaboration of the major contention.

Those subtopics should be arranged from first, or maximum, to last, or least, importance, that is, *in inverse order to their separate consideration.* That is, the last proposition advanced or contemplated in the second paragraph should be the subject of the third paragraph. *The final sentence of this second paragraph should be a full rhetorical summation.* (See below.)

Style

The language in the second paragraph may be less bold or contentious but no less virile, vivid, and audacious. (See Chapter 2, Commandment 2.)

The last sentence in that paragraph should be an eloquent rhetorical flourish encapsulating the adumbrated (foreshadowed) themes, sufficient unto itself and wholly satisfying to the mind and soul of the reader, yet at the same time alerting the careful reader that the writer is about to broaden his argument and maybe embark on a different (and surprising) course. Lincoln accomplishes this superbly in his *Gettysburg Address*, where, having reviewed for his audience the ostensible reason for the ceremony (the country was engaged in "a great civil war . . . ,"; they were standing on "a great battlefield of that war . . . ,"; of which they were dedicating "a small portion . . ."), he polished off that segment of his talk with the solemn phrase, "It is wholly fitting and proper that we should do this"—from which, after a long pause (the reader pauses, savoring the statement), he launched into his electrifying appeal for the Union to rediscover its purpose, so that the men there buried should not have died in vain.[5]

The Third Paragraph

Content

The third paragraph should pick up the last proposition of the second paragraph and at once explore, ventilate, elaborate on, and examine it, arriving at a conclusion respecting that proposition.

This may require two or three or four or five bunches (paragraphs) of prose, depending on the subject of the essay and the space (scope) allowed. (These paragraphs become chapters in a book-length treatment.) But space and attention devoted to this sole point should be kept in balance with the space and attention that will be dedicated to other propositions that are to be examined and from which a conclusion is to be drawn.

Everything that is ventilated concerning this sole point should advance the major argument of the essay. Seductive bypaths, though they may be in themselves pertinent and directly relevant to the proposition under consideration in the third paragraph, should be sternly rejected; *only that aspect of this particular proposition that advances or is critically pertinent to the major theme should be entertained* (unless

---

[5]For a thorough rhetorical examination of that magical oration, see *Sex, Power, and Pericles.*

you are writing a book). The mind of the reader must never be permitted impatience: *"But the writer is tarrying too long on this minor matter. The writer has permitted himself to become enraptured by detail. When are we getting back to the point announced in the first paragraph?"*

The final sentence of the third paragraph should suggest the next proposition that will come under examination, and that should be the penultimate proposition set forth in the second paragraph. This is both rhetorically and ratiocinatively satisfying to the human mind. And this is another reason why the writer should not have taken too long exploring the proposition of the third paragraph, inasmuch as the reader will forget the order of the propositions as set forth in the second paragraph.

Style

Though a writer must always seek to be lively and vigorous, beginning with the third paragraph, when he is seriously analyzing his propositions, *his language should never detract from the act of reasoning*. It should not call attention to itself. It should be the faithful servant of the thinking in the paragraph, taking second place to it.[6]

Succeeding Paragraphs

Content

Follow the suggestions for the third paragraph. Each successive theme to be considered should receive greater weight, deeper reflection.

Style

By now, the style should be stately, rhythmic. The sentences will be longer, because they are packed with more information, with more carefully reasoned propositions. The thoughts being written should *defy* breezy, succinct wording, though there should never be excessive wording or structure that is unnecessarily complicated. *The Orotund Temptation and the Rodomontadian Temptation must be mightily resisted, as should be the Shallow Temptation.*

---

[6]Even in the first and second paragraphs, style, through its very zest, by calling attention to itself, should focus attention on content.

Conclusion

Content

It should be intellectually thunderous. *It should contain within itself the surprising conclusion that is discreetly suggested in the first paragraph,* rendered inevitable, or at the least acceptable, by the strong strokes that the major theme has been dealt in the intervening paragraphs. *This last paragraph should culminate the whole intellectual endeavor.*

Style

It may be majestic. It may even be triumphant.

❖   ❖   ❖

That's it for organization. In essence, be soritical. The formal prescriptions set forth above for writing your speech admit variation. Treat them as a guide. You are now ready to start framing your thoughts in one of the grandeurs of God's creation, which is the English language. The Lord's Word is accessible in any of the hundreds of tongues used by mankind, but He thinks in the English of King James.

CHAPTER 10

HOW TO WRITE . . . BRILLIANTLY[1]

> A scrupulous writer, in every sentence that he writes, will ask himself at least four questions, thus: What am I trying to say? What words will express it? What image or idiom will make it clearer? Is this image fresh enough to have an effect?
>
> —George Orwell

It takes twelve years to produce a writer.

This seems to be the consensus of professionals. But don't be discouraged. Many successful writers never develop the exquisite ear of masters and never do learn the craft.

But what about you? You are an electrical engineer by trade, a surgeon, a forensic psychiatrist, a business consultant, a home appliances salesman, a retail buyer, an executive, a civil servant, a schoolteacher presiding daily over a class of seventy-five students who at any given moment may (erupt into) hem. Twelve years? You don't have twelve minutes!

Nevertheless, what good is it to conceive delicious thoughts or to discover the mysteries of the universe (among the latest of which is that the law laid down back in the final century B.C. by Titus Lucretius, that you can't expect anything out of nothing, known as *ex nihilo, nihil,* is the bunk[2]) . . . where was I? Oh, what good is acquiring all the cosmological

---

[1]Some of what follows is plundered from *Sex, Power, and Pericles: Principles of Advanced Public Speaking.*

[2]The whole universe issued out of nothing, they are telling us now . . .

wisdom and insight of our modern physicists on top of all the knowledge and wisdom of the ancients if one cannot express oneself lucidly, gracefully, and with a touch of class?

So something must be done. You are obliged to deliver a speech. Somehow, it must be written. As day follows night, a poor, dull, cloddish text will produce a poor, dull, cloddish talk. What in the world can you do?

Well . . .

1. Never resort to a speech-writing service.

2. Free yourself of the circadian rhythm.

3. Resolve never to be a bore.

4. Avoid lachrymose subjects.

5. Set your thoughts down in the simplest language possible.

6. Scrutinize your text to make sure that you have not muddled concepts that don't fit in the same paragraph.

7. Make certain that the line and development of your logic are clear and unconfused from paragraph to paragraph.

8. Check sentences and every paragraph for non sequiturs.

9. Check them for sense.

10. Check them for nonsense.

11. Place any word over four syllables under suspicion.

12. Place under suspicion all sentences longer than twenty-five words.

13. Sniff each verb for its lettucelike crispness and freshness.

14. Weed out tired and worn images, clichés—whatever may smack of received wisdom or trite wit.

15. Scrape tired formulations to the silverbright; wherever possible, insert fresh images, metaphors, apposite analogies.

16. Judge whether you cannot say anything that you say in your text more compactly and (or) in more vivid and original fashion.

17. Test each paragraph (a) for the possible reduction of one of its parts into a witty phrase, (b) for the insertion of illumi-

nating wit, or (c) for revision of the thought into wittily conceived articulation. (Whew!)

18. Abolish the third person and passive voice; prune intransitive verbs where possible.

19. Consider whether what you have set down in the form of exposition cannot be better or mere helpfully explained by anecdote.

20. Meantime, begin devoting an hour two evenings each week to relevant readings of William Buckley, Reid Buckley, and Christopher Buckley, not to mention other Buckleys.

Getting down to devils in the details . . .

Sweat, Blood, Toil, and Tears: Surpassing Yourself

1. Never resort to a speech-writing service.

Packaged brilliance is an illusion.

There are services on the market with billings such as Words to Order, Inc., or Talks Unlimited, Ltd. (I invent the names.) These are not scams, exactly. They are factories. And judging from what occasionally gets dumped on my desk, their product is awful.

I dislike knocking any outfit trying to make an honest buck off foolish expectations, but the fancy prospectus of one such bureau advertises just about everything that is dreadful in canned talks. You want humor? They got it for you: a million and one jokes in their database to fit every occasion. Example:

[Do you wish to make] a humorous point about the "national debt"?

> *The incredible thing about the federal debt is that we actually got into this terrible shape by buying from the lowest bidder.*

Wow.[3] Are your sides aching? Mine are like to split. The attribution is to Robert Orben. Here's another from the same outfit:

---

[3]Trust me, I have not made up any of these examples.

Would you prefer to come off as clever? . . . perhaps you want to make an historical point about these "changing times," we might provide you with material such as this:

> *The earth was formed 4.6 billion years ago. In the first 4599 million years nothing much happened. In the next million, man invented use for his arms, legs and his cave. In the 100,000 years that followed, he invented language, tools, the wheel, fire, primitive warfare and agriculture. 5000 years later, he had invented recorded history, chariots and the Dark Ages. The next 500, he invented gunpowder, printing, the steam engine, and the industrial revolution. But in the last 100 years, he invented everything else.*

The attribution here (for shame) is to the *Encyclopaedia Britannica*. But how about a dose of profundity? Here's

[an] informational point about the "importance of learning":

> *John Pierce was a renowned scientist who worked for AT&T's prestigious Bell Laboratories. He was known to many as the father of satellite communications because of his work on the Telstar in the 1960s. "Knowledge," said Pierce, "sharpens our vision. Skill makes us effective. But it is the consciousness of ignorance, the consciousness of not understanding, and the curiosity about that which lies beyond that are essential to our progress." John Pierce's goal was to broaden his ignorance. To avoid at all cost "final wisdom" in which we think we know beyond doubt what is right, what is wrong, what is good, what is bad, where the world and the country are headed, where they should be headed.*

That's not bad in itself, if you ignore the moral relativism, but it is simply too long for a speech. Quotations should be crisp. Brevity is not only wit; it's comprehended. But suppose your immediate need is neither to sound the tocsins of solemnity nor to tickle the audience's ribs. None of that. You wish to make

[a] motivational point about "winning":

> *When you are not practicing, remember, someone somewhere is practicing, and when you meet him he will win.*

You must agree that this is priceless. (The attribution, if memory does not deceive, is to Bill Bradley, former Princeton and NBA star, onetime Senator from New Jersey, now practicing slam dunks for the Presidency.) Maybe not as pithy nor as funky as Satchel Page on the same theme ("Never look back. Someone may be catching up to you."), but *good*. The service offers other such gems . . .

For example, if you want to make the point that "performance is a marathon and not a sprint," we might provide you with a quote [they mean quotation[4]] from Harold Geneen, former CEO of ITT:

> *Performance is not limited to one quarter or a year's earnings statement. Performance is an attitude that is built into a company and its people for the long haul. It is something that says a company can repeat what it did last year and continue to grow year after year. It is a positive attitude toward growth and achievement over time.*

One is stupefied by the wisdom to wit herein above; one is also impelled into postprandial stupor, whether one has lunched heavily or not.

The nuggets of wisdom or humor or clever philosophical profundity that this speech-writing service can dredge up for you out of its database are extraordinary. Let's merely touch on what's so bad, wrong, and pathetic about these wares and why you should eschew having anything to do with providers of same.

Take the "funny" about the national debt, which for some reason, speaking about the debt, is put between quotation marks, as though it doesn't exist. All right, so it's not a howler. Well, yes, that's the first thing wrong with it. Unless your funny is truly funny, don't utter it. Second, don't use any quip that, like this one, is already stale. By the time goodies get into the vats of these services, they are bound to taste like a ship's biscuit after it's been around the Horn. Third, invent your own. Borrowing humor, unless you have the knack of improving on the original through your raconteurial zest and imagination, is worse than

---

[4]On the subject of which, never introduce a quotation by saying, "Thomas Jefferson has provided us with this quotation," or, "I have here a quotation from Thomas Edison." Jefferson and Edison *wrote* or *spoke* what you are about to *quote*. *They* wrote it; *you* quote it. (You turn their words into a quotation by the act of quoting them.)

"borrowing" a match: you appropriate under false pretenses what was probably expendable in the first place.

Respecting the reduction on "changing times" that was lifted from the *Encyclopaedia Britannica*, that's the first mistake: use nothing from the *Britannica*. Speak no quotation from *Bartlett's*. Absolutely renounce a thesaurus. These are crips. They sound so. They betray the shallowness of your mind and the paucity of your culture. But if you are driven to a common source book because you are unable to think for yourself and haven't read a book through since *The Hobbit*, avoid choosing an *illiterate* sample, for Heaven's sake. In this proudly presented nugget, we are told that man "invented use for his arms, legs and his cave." Ignore the asymmetry of the syntax. Invented? That's the wrong word, egregiously so. Man was *born* with the use of his arms and legs, and man found or took advantage of the shelter of the cave. Man did "invent" language, okay; he did "make use" of tools, which in the beginning were probably a serendipitous discovery, as in the way chimpanzees use twigs to fish out termite larvae and other delicious grubs or the way bonobos use sex to sublimate aggression. The wheel was an invention proper, and so, we may guess, was the *making* or *causation* of fire, not the element itself. But primitive warfare and agriculture? Warfare man engaged in from the first snarl; he didn't have to "invent" the ugly and violent passions. Survival took care of that. Agriculture, like tools, falls under the category of discovery. And what's this about *inventing* the Dark Ages! (Inventing a hindsight!) Not only is the reduction illiterate, it is stupid. Even worse is the canned wisdom these services offer. It takes a truly original, profound, and philosophical mind to recognize a truly philosophical, profound, and original thought. One is not likely to find such rare breeds in a commercial service. What one does get is middlebrow commonplaces. The sample attributed to Senator Bradley shrieks of middlebrow; the sample attributed to Mr. Geneen is quite ordinary as far as business advice goes, old as the hill, and also dull. The speaker should, anyhow, avoid dressing himself in borrowed clothes (as we know from Chapter 1, Cardinal Sins 6 and 7).

Avoid trying to purchase authority on the cheap. Either select a skilled professional speechwriter who knows you inside and out to be your Cyrano, or do it the hard way: write your speeches yourself.

2. Free yourself of the circadian rhythm.

Many of the most sublime thoughts occur when one is deep in slumber. Many of the stupidest thoughts, too, occur in the hours of dark, in the stillness of bed. Succubus, incubus . . . visitation of the Muse? You won't ever know which it is unless you resolve to sit up, switch on the bedside lamp, and trudge blear-eyed and nasty-mouthed to legal pad and pencil, or to laptop.

Don't struggle against nocturnal intrusions of the work in progress—if you hope to get any rest at all. Come dawn, and breakfast, and the long gray day in the office, your spirit will be nagged by the sublimity (or was it stupidity?) that your subconscious plucked at by the tail but that you, slothful fellow, lazy dame, declined to rouse yourself to jot down.

Nighttime is when your written piece is marinating in the mind. Free yourself of the circadian imperative. There is no difference between 3 a.m. and 7 a.m. except that in the latter case you must be up; in the former, you needn't be.

3. Resolve never to be a bore.

We've stressed brevity in this book. No matter how spellbinding the topic and how fascinating the mind elucidating it, a monologue becomes tedious after fifty or sixty minutes. Be brief!

The other prime ingredients of *boring* are (1) saying trite things and (2) saying anything tritely. Combine them—saying trite things tritely— and you achieve oblivion. (See below, point 12.)

4. Avoid lachrymose subjects.

Don't ask anyone to feel your pain. If you are Alfred Lord Tennyson, you may get away with *Tears, Idle Tears*, but even though you may be Alfred Lord Tennyson, you just do get away with *Break, Break, Break*—and there are critics who challenge that he did.

Flee from the lachrymose: Mother, children, pets. If you bedew your keyboard with tears, you will assuredly bore your audience to tears, and have them squirming miserably in their seats in the anguish produced by your sentimentality.

5. Set your thoughts down in the simplest language possible.

Why is this injunction so difficult for people trained in business and the law to accept?

Do they feel unprotected when they see the sense of what they have written so nakedly transparent? Is an essential disingenuousness in their innermost character thus—to them—revealed, rendering them vulnerable? And do they deceive themselves into imagining that the shallowness of their minds and spirits is obscured by a heavy, multi-syllabic style?

Some people tend to think that in the minds of readers, simplicity of expression in the writer betrays simplicity of feeling or thought. Which is wrong. Read the Sermon on the Mount. Model your writing on that spare, luminous language.

This is the place to speak in defense of jargon. I quote myself:

> You have heard about this, and it makes you uncomfortable because you know you are guilty of it. There's the plague of business or professional jargon: HiTekspeech, call it. Medicine, rocket science, the computer industry (hardware and soft), the military of course, government, particle physicists, lawyers, undertakers, building engineers . . . [you name it]: all have developed an encoded language that is incomprehensible to the layman, but that may be necessary and unavoidable when Hughes is talking to Boeing, or Digital Computer to Microsoft, or a professor in medical school to his students, or Stephen Hawking to Steven Weinberg, or Lee Iaccoca to God. The language may be ugly, or abstruse, but it is clearly symbolized to those audiences, and the information communicated by the jargon or acronym cannot be as instantly or economically communicated by a paraphrase. Snob, posh, RSVP, *i.e.*, ETA, asap, snafu, and *aka* are examples; so are software, default (position or mode), GOP, Parkinson's Law, the Peter Principle, Rusher's Law of the Gap, *pi*, and $E = mc^2$. These have passed into general understanding.
>
> So use your particular HiTekspeech without compunction or embarrassment when conversing with fellow wonks; but when speaking to me, or to the general public, spare us, spare

us! Descend from Olympus: we are lowly mortals, of limited wattage. Shed on us thy light, but as though to little children.[5]

In his wonderful collection of essays,[6] Joseph Epstein reminds us of the obloquy with which unnecessary polysyllabic writing has always been greeted. "Even though Gowers [Sir Ernest, of *Plain Words, Their ABC* fame] was a more understated man than Fowler [of *Modern English Usage* fame], he could turn out a more than fair imitation of the master in his best whiplash mode, as in this passage from an article he added entitled 'Abstractitus':

> A writer uses abstract words because his thoughts are cloudy; the habit of using them clouds his thoughts still further; he may end by concealing his meaning not only from his readers but also from himself, and writing such sentences as, *The actualization of the motivation of the forces must to a great extent be a matter of personal angularity.*

Intellectuals, who should know better, sin—often. On page 257 of that same collection, Epstein skewers Lionel Trilling for academic mush. "In Trilling's essay [an introduction to a 1952 edition of George Orwell's *Homage to Catalonia*] there follows a paragraph of extraordinary qualifications that begins, 'Or could do if we but made up our mind to it,' which suggests most of us cannot; and here one senses how Lionel Trilling, that academic Demosthenes, his mouth filled not with pebbles but perpetual qualifications and hesitations, must have achingly envied Orwell's plainspokenness and readiness to act on his views."

6. Scrutinize your text to make sure that you have not muddled concepts that don't fit in the same paragraph.

7. Make certain that the line and development of your logic are clear and unconfused from paragraph to paragraph.

Studying the principles of organization set forth in Chapter 9 should help here.

---

[5] Lifted from *Sex, Power, and Pericles.*

[6] Joseph Epstein, *Pertinent Players*, New York, Norton, 1993, p. 58.

Thoughts, no matter how intricate, must be joined with the simple inevitability and satisfaction that can define beauty. Some mathematical formulas achieve that perfection, I'm given to understand (I cannot understand the math). An astrophysical cosmologist like Alan H. Guth can thrill to the concept of a vacuum fluctuation as that creative anomaly that brought forth out of nothing the colossal mass and matter of the universe, and be stunned by the vertiginous beauty of this unimaginable event. We cry *eureka* when a paragraph is perfectly reasoned, our souls responding.

No less must we aspire to.

8. Check sentences and every paragraph for non sequiturs.

It's amazing how often and how subtly this mismeshing of thoughts occurs. Some things *seem* to follow when put down, but upon examination clearly do not. Paragraph by paragraph, scan the logical sequence.

On the other hand, wit frequents non sequitors, and genius resides in them.

9. Check them for sense.

10. Check them for nonsense.

Make these two separate steps.

Things may follow logically yet make no sense. Things may seem so—may seem right and proper—yet be preposterous. Oil is heavier than water. Evidently, the sun revolves around the earth. Congress will spend less than the projected budget increase on a certain program; therefore, thrifty Congress has cut spending.

Sometimes, there is no help for the anomaly. The "profit *and* loss" financial statement bears a nonsensical title, but there it is.

11. Place any word over four syllables under suspicion.

That word, derived from the Latin or from German, is almost always inferior to the shorter synonym that owes its origin to the Anglo-Saxon. The more syllables packed into a word, the more likely is it to be slurred, its meaning mistook.

12. Place under suspicion all sentences longer than twenty-five words.

First, such sentences are generally difficult to understand because vast plains intervene between subject and predicate. Second, extended sentences are often loaded with modifiers and discursive relative clauses that confuse the hearer as the main drift trickles erratically into the eardrums. Third, long sentences are the devil to utter.

Kathleen Parker, the columnist, always enjoins her students to read their texts aloud; if one gasps for breath upon verbalizing a sentence, so will the audience strain and gasp for relief as they do their best to comprehend it. Break it up. We are not accustomed to the fastidious, attenuated style of a Henry James. Only the most seasoned writer is able to construct a sentence exploring the full implications of a complex line of reasoning in all their diversity and richness without muting the thrust of the principal argument; and only the most accomplished orator is able to deliver such a sentence with such articulated brilliance that it will be comprehended in all its parts, each as it is issued forth, without the audience losing the sense of the whole.

13. Sniff each verb for its lettucelike crispness and freshness.

Be particular. Words fall in and out of favor. A rediscovered word enjoys a vogue, and it's fun to use for a while. But though it may be a good word, short and pungent (or short and mordant) (or short and trenchant), it will inevitably wilt on the stem of long exposure. I want to shriek now when I hear a bourgeois Southern matron say "tacky" or "tad." Once-fun phrases suffer similar fates. "Make my day" has been pillaged of its irony by repetition. During his second Presidential campaign, Reagan did to death "You ain't seen nothin' yet" (his adherents had in fact seen the best of him).[7]

In connection with which, just as you should shun that atrocious word *insightful*,[8] so fly from *meaningful*. I truly detest this expression, which, from abuse, has become meaningratherless—I'm always

---

[7] Some marvelous reductions are inexplicably shortlived. I regret the passing of, "It's plastic," which has not survived the 1960s of its invention. Attach the noun to a personal pronoun and one achieves shattering dismissal of the person.

[8] As fastidious a prose stylist as Senator "Pat" Moynihan is guilty of it!

reminded of liberal-minded women giving me meaningful looks while they pause meaningfully and place a hand on my knee meaningfully, while leaning meaningfully forward in their chairs toward me—it don't mean a thing.

Earnestness is a disease.

Other words become preferred because of the temptation in many writers to put on the dog, calling attention to themselves instead of keeping themselves strictly in the background, in service to the sense of what they are saying. Back in 1954, I was publicly humiliated by a tall, imposing, senior editor of *Time* magazine, the featured speaker in a lecture series, because I had asked a question from the floor, using the word *exacerbate*. What, he demanded to know—sneering—did that mean? He had never heard of the word; he doubted anyone in the audience had heard of the word. I was young, and fond of wielding vocabulary I had freshly discovered. But I suspect from my memory of his supercilious tone that I had used the word correctly, to describe the mealymouthed, pusillanimous[9] policy he was endorsing in response to the latest Soviet provocation. It was easier to attack the callow youth for his pretentiousness than to answer his question.

Since that time, *exacerbate* has become a bane. It is used promiscuously as a substitute for *worsen* or *make worse*, instead of in its strict sense, which is to make more violent, bitter, or severe. (My point to the *Time* editor—a jackass by nearly the same name—had been that to respond to Soviet bluster with another pointless U.N. resolution was to feed the totalitarian temperament, encouraging Nikita Khrushchev to act more outrageously.)

14. Weed out tired and worn images, clichés—whatever may smack of received wisdom or trite wit.

15. Scrape tired formulations to the silverbright; wherever possible, insert fresh images, metaphors, apposite analogies.

Imagery suffers from too frequent use also. If you don't take my word (my word!) for that, you are whistling Dixie. Few attitudes are so self-

---

[9]Two favorite epithets hurled by militant anticommunists at the time, which also speedily suffered from overuse. I'm certain I used them.

defeating as spitting into the wind. One can fashion prose that is as limp as old lettuce and falls flat as a pancake, even while enunciating truths that are tough as nails.

As for worn concepts, truisms, aperçus, and plodding, plebeian composition, try testing your text, paragraph by paragraph, in this manner. Ask, Is there a way of saying what I just said *quicker*? Compress: Prune the adjectives; drop the relative clauses; abolish sentences, when you spot one that is redundant. *Nevertheless, keep in mind that the speech cannot be as tightly written as the essay.* Some things—subtle concepts especially—require repetition or analogical elaboration for them to sink into the minds of the audience.

Having achieved compression, seek out the tried-and-true in your text. Toss out the tried, sometimes the true as well. Tried + true = trite. Too often. The verity is commonplace. Keep in mind the sense of *tried* as that whose feet have (fat has) been put to the flame, that which has been refined, as in whale blubber → whale oil, and which, therefore, from usage, has become unremarkable. A penny saved is a penny earned, though to be penny-wise can be poundingly (that's my headache) foolish. (There are trieds-and-falses also: ♪ . . . *the rain in Spain falls mainly in the play-yun.*♪) (It falls hardly ever on the play-yun.)

Then there are those verities that can't be avoided: *It can never be repeated too often that dishonesty is poor practice.* Oh, how true! And how tritely expressed. Sir Walter Scott said it better: *Oh what a wicked web men weave / When first they practice to deceive.* How about: *The trouble with being dishonest is that one ultimately cheats oneself of the trust and respect of everyone.* A touch labored. Or: *The person who shortchanges truth all the time runs out of credit.* Better. Or: *When Bill Clinton speaks with perfect candor, one gets the clearest understanding of Heisenberg's Uncertainty Principle: namely, if one ascertains Mr. Clinton's position, one can't judge his momentum; and if one is alerted to his momentum, one can't tell what his position may be.* Which is too long, but funny.

The ultimate test of tried + true = trite is this: Have I heard it somewhere before, expressed in just this way? The cliché has its place, but resorted to without a fight indicates sloth on the part of the writer and will induce torpor in the audience.

16. Judge whether you cannot say anything that you say in your text more compactly and (or) in more vivid and original fashion.

17. Test each paragraph (a) for the possible reduction of one of its parts into a witty phrase, (b) for the insertion of illuminating wit, or (c) for revision of the thought into wittily conceived articulation. (Whew!)

Endeavor yet once more to eliminate wordiness and tighten your sentence structure. Test whether some more zestful or stylish manner of saying the same thing occurs to you. Having smoothed the syntax, play with it—for startling or original effect. Stand back from what you have written, viewing it from a different plane, in skewed perspective, with a grin and a catawampus eye. (The universe, after all, is not isotropic, as Einstein believed.) Contemplate how ridiculous the cab of a trailer truck looks without its van. Contemplate the first human couple copulating on a gravity-free surface, such as the moon. Have fun! Experiment. Of a posturing left- or rightwinger: *Insufficient is the wit for the evil thereof.* To a sanctimonious envirofreak: *What's sauce for the goose is sauce for the whooping crane.*

You may fail, and some texts can resist the witty reduction or irreverent invention. Yet do try.

18. Abolish the third person and passive voice; prune intransitive verbs where possible.

What one must strive for in the written or spoken word is immediacy, intimate rapport, directness, concreteness. One must grip the audience with simple language, framed in the most intimate terms, and with images that cause what one is saying to leap into the mind's eye. The third person and passive voice put one's syntax at a remove. The writer or speaker is at a remove. Intransitive verbs can have the same effect, distancing writer or speaker from his audience.

19. Consider whether what you have set down in the form of exposition cannot be better or more helpfully explained by anecdote.

Anecdote cannot substitute for reasoning, nor should it merely ornament a text. But narrative entertains—everyone likes to listen to a story—and anecdote, by its implications, can illuminate the reasoning. A good story can make the point more memorably than explication of it.

Remember: If you have to explain the moral or point of your story, it's no good, it's not doing the job, drop it.

20. Meantime, begin devoting an hour two evenings each week to relevant readings of William Buckley, Reid Buckley, and Christopher Buckley, not to mention other Buckleys.

Well, of course, I am being facetious, but I am not. We write well, as a tribe. Christopher's wit is superb. For anyone engaged in the task of articulating difficult concepts, Bill's joyous, richly baroque language is a wonder (his stylistic master is neither Albert J. Nock nor Willmoore Kendall nor Cardinal John Henry Newman; it is Johann Sebastian Bach).

There are books you can profitably peruse. They will help you write better. My *Speaking in Public* and *Sex, Power, and Pericles* I believe I've mentioned, though modesty stains my cheeks crimson. There's the collection of my brother Bill's obiter dicta on the English language, *The Right Word*, put together by his longtime editor, Sam Vaughan. Christopher Buckley's *Wry Martinis* is a scintillating demonstration of classy style and hilarious humor. Essays and the books by Florence King gladden the heart with their inspired expuspilitations of contemporary American stuffed-shirted solemnities, from feminism to cuckoo environmentalism. James Thurber, Bob Newman, William Safire, Joseph Epstein, and John Leo—among so many others—write deliciously about writing.

There are four indispensable manuals for people who can do without the ultimate authority of a Fowler: *The Elements of Style,* by William Strunk Jr., with revisions, an introduction and a new chapter on writing by E. B. White (The Macmillan Company, New York, 1959); *Plain Words, Their ABC*, by Sir Ernest Gowers (Alfred A. Knopf, New York, 1954); *The Writer's Art*, by James J. Kilpatrick (Andres & McMeel, Kansas City, 1984); and *The Art of Persuasion*, by Linda Bridges and the late William F. Rickenbacker (National Review Press, New York, 1991).

These are all in print. Three of the four are short (the exception is *The Writer's Art*). They are entertaining and to the point. *The Art of Persuasion* is the most difficult of these manuals. Just as you and I keep the Kilpatrick book by our bedside tables, beside our Bibles, or should, so James Jackson keeps the Bridges-Rickenbacker book. That's quite a compliment from a redoubtable stylist.

*　*　*

A last word on this topic: Cultured folk have lamented for a generation the illiteracy that—like a malaise, or the pall of approaching night— has descended on our country, beginning with the like, uh, you know, uh 1960s.

The telephone replaced letter-writing; television has expelled reading. And now the computer . . .

May bring literacy back, hurrah! More and more people are infatuated by e-mail. Nothing yet in terms of epistolary art has emerged from this new medium of expression, but at least, young people are writing *to* each other instead of merely yapping *at* each other. At least, in the privacy of their studies or offices, they are sitting down alone, thinking, concentrating, pondering, editing their thoughts, and composing those sentences that best express them. The nature of the medium is slapdash and inelegant. But it is intimate, immediate, militates, I think, against pretentiousness, and likely (I hazard) will develop style and eloquence. The word processor not only is a boon to professional writers, it makes acquiring the craft of writing that much simpler. Spelling is no longer a problem, or shouldn't be. Revisions are a snap. More: An obstacle to the development of lean, compactly stated prose has been removed.

Like apprentice speakers, apprentice writers tend to want to say too much, to leave nothing out. In the days of pen and ink and the typewriter, they were reluctant to exercise this restraint because it was such a lot of manual as well as mental trouble to formulate one's thoughts in writing, and the idea of suppressing or yanking anything hurt. Self-editing required scratching out laboriously constructed phrases and sentences, on which one might have lavished hours of energy, suffering through hours and even days of frustration. Each revision in the days before word processing required scribbling the page anew, or retyping. The fresh clean sheets of paper made neat piles; trashed sheets were crumpled and tossed at the wastebasket (rarely—in the heat of fury— into the wastebasket). My 11-year-old daughter, when we were living in Spain, was asked by the nuns at her Sacred Heart convent school what her father did for a living. She replied, "Oh, he crushes paper into balls—two wastebaskets full a day." Those inspirations that did not quite jell were lost, probably forever. Those subtle nuances and graceful sidelights were gone, thrown out, consumed in the incinerator.

That was then. Now those nuggets that do not quite fit, or that are redundant, or that unnecessarily string out the theme can easily be saved and stored for future use. They are no longer doomed to oblivion. The reluctance to cut, to compress, to discipline oneself—the biggest impediment in acquiring the exacting craft of writing—is relieved.

For the purpose of speech-writing, keep those nuggets handy, stored in bins, such as Humor.1, Humor.2, Humor.3, or Outrag.1 (for outrageousness), Outrag.2, Outrag.3, and so forth. These can be called in when you have developed a popular basic text that needs modifying depending on the audience, or when you are asked to deliver that text or speak on the same topic so often that your eyes bulge and your mind goes blank with tedium. (See Chapter 20, for more on this subject.) To your relief, you can summon the material stored in those bins, refreshing and varying the text while making it more suitable to next week's audience. This is one of the supreme gifts of the word processor to writer and speaker.

A warning: Amateurs tend to pile example on example, quotation on quotation, anecdote on anecdote. They begin with a good speech that is twenty-five minutes long. Before one can say Boutros Boutros-Ghali, however, they have culled interesting passages from some magazine or book here, new empirical evidence from a survey there. *They never substitute.* They won't exercise the discrimination to weigh the new against the old. They won't sacrifice. They keep adding. And the speech bloats to thirty-five minutes, then to forty minutes. Nothing truly new has been injected. Simply, the dead horse is thrashed and thrashed and thrashed until deafening boredom sets in.

Florence King faxed me a letter back in August of 1994 in which she said, "I . . . then had to do the final revisions and copyediting of my anthology . . . As usual, when I start out to revise, I end up more or less rewriting: 'Polish, repolish, every color lay / Sometimes add, but oftener take away,' said Boileau-Despréaux,[10] and I always do his bidding."

As any writer should do hers.

---

[10]Nicolas Boileau-Despréaux (1636–1711), French critic and poet.

PART 5

THE MECHANICS

CHAPTER 11

PRESENTING YOURSELF AND EYE CONTACT

PRESENTING YOURSELF

You must do it alone.

There is no support, no staff, no comforting infrastructure. As a speaker, you are on your own.

Even CEOs—maybe especially people of high rank in business or the professions—don't like it. (It's one reason they hunger so for visual aids and resist so fiercely my unalterable opposition to them, their insecurities demanding a life raft.) There are exceptions: a Keough of Coca-Cola, an Iacocca of Chrysler Motors (both now retired), gloried in public speaking. For most people, being called upon to perform on a stage, where one is frighteningly, awesomely, singularly by oneself, or even at a country club banquet table, surrounded by sympathetic friends and acquaintances, is a terrible prospect.

Again, you are referred to Chapter 20 for more on stage fright. This section is about what you must do to make the singularity of your lonesome presence attractive and impressive to a crowd.

1. <u>Men</u>: Get a haircut. <u>Women</u>: Have your hair done.

2. <u>Men</u>: If you sport a beard, have it trimmed close; if you sport a mustache, ditto.

3. Scrupulously check clothing for cleanliness and freshness.

4. <u>Women</u>: Guide on modesty. <u>Women</u> and <u>Men</u>: Guide on conservative attire.

5. Beware of certain colors and patterns in your clothing.

6. Leave your jewelry at home or in the hotel's safety-deposit box.

7. Take command of the lectern and of the audience.

8. Express your presence through your posture.

9. Make the most of your gorgeous self.

10. Make the most of your ungainly self.

11. Cling to, keep foremost in your mind, your purpose.

Sweat, Blood, Toil, and Tears: Surpassing Yourself

1. <u>Men</u>: Get a haircut. <u>Women</u>: Have your hair done.

Where concerning women, I'm driven to suppose there's a mystique about washing one's hair or having it tended to. Raised amidst six sisters, my childhood seems to reverberate with cries of distress about needing to wash or needing to have hair dressed and cries of satisfaction from having just done either. Men feel better after a haircut also. A pedicure, a massage, a sauna, a brisk five-klick run: Anything that promotes well-being and the glow of good health feels and looks good from the stage. A speaker's interior confidence happily affects both his performance and initial audience reaction.

2. <u>Men</u>: If you sport a beard, have it trimmed close; if you sport a mustache, ditto.

I used to wear a full Garibaldian mustache and beard, of whose fiery bristles I was well content—until one morning, after a talk in Denver, a sponsor complained, "You know, I make it a practice to sit toward the back of the theater always; and from my position, I found it hard to read your expression and at times to understand what you were saying."

I shaved it all off. Facial expression radiates from around the lips and zygomatic muscles. If these are obscured, a person sitting anywhere in the audience will find it difficult to read our meaning. Theaters and lecture halls ordinarily ascend from the stage. A person seated toward the rear may have a view of nothing but hair of head, white of brow, tip of nose, and bush.

If you cannot bear to scrape your facial efflorescence off to the skin, clip the beard close and in Mephistophelian style, exposing as much of the region around the cheeks and mouth as possible. Those of you who boast mustachios worthy of a Pancho Villa or Jerry Colonna, trim at least a quarter inch back from the rim of the upper lip and down from the rim of the lower lip.

You'll look neater from the audience, and you'll be more prepossessing. Besides, it's nice to be understood.

3. Scrupulously check clothing for cleanliness and freshness.

4. <u>Women</u>: Guide on modesty. <u>Women</u> and <u>Men</u>: Guide on conservative attire.

A speaker can be undone when suddenly discovering a soup stain on his tie or a stain on her blouse.

For the audience, fresh, clean, spruce clothing—a well-pressed pair of trousers, a handsome suit or skirt—creates good vibes. They infer the person up there is confident and fittingly respecting both of himself and of them. It was considered smart at one time, or "cool," or "with-it," for an academic type to deliver his lecture in Levis and sneakers (sometimes with a tweed sport coat flung on top as a condescension). This became fashionable in the 1960s, when the flower folk of Barbaria threw down the gates of decorum on their way to smashing through the portcullis of sexual restraint. Particle physicists, mathematicians, rock stars, Episcopalian clergymen, Bill Gates, and congeries of other wonks, gurus, gee-whizzes of Hi-Tek, and also nobodies and weirdos, continue to affect proletarian dress before audiences.

Let them. Don't you. Swinishness belongs in the sty. If they enjoy billowing forth foul garlic-laden breath from the charnel pits of their entrails; or displaying teeth so stained they look as though they'd been dug up; or eating at the banquet table in a tank top with rank hairy underarms and blackened fingernails; or slopping their ties in the soup (and maybe sucking them afterward); or supporting their *isms* with no bras, when gravity summons both to the navel; or looking crushed and crumpled like balls of wastepaper, and then flattened out without the help of an iron; or in other manner as though they'd rather not be where they are and despise the audience for gathering to hear them, never mind. They belong to the dregs of civility. You needn't.[1]

Just as a good hot shower makes one feel good, so do irreproachable duds. Again, self-confidence is aided. Be stylish, but be conservative.

Oh, modesty. It all depends on your purpose. Diana Dors, England's answer to Marilyn Monroe, quite won my heart that day (in the 1950s) that she landed in New York on the *Queen Elizabeth*. She had on a tight-waisted frock whose V-neck plunged below critical mass or margins of belief. Reporters flocked to her as bees to honey, crossing their mikes in front of her. "Take them away, boys!" she quipped cheerfully. "You're hiding what I'm selling."

Just so.

5. Beware of certain colors and patterns in your clothing.

6. Leave your jewelry at home or in the hotel's safety deposit box.

Anything busy distracts attention: a ski sweater, large checks on a sport coat, bold patterns.

Men: If you are told you'll be filmed or if you suspect you may be televised, make sure your shirt is a soft pastel, preferably light blue, and solid, not striped. A dazzling white shirt dazzles the camera, which can't adjust to the stripes either, producing a moiré effect. Neckties are newly colorful and fun, but don't permit them to monopolize attention, and watch out for those metallic silvery threads that are woven into some ties, which shimmer on film. If you work in an office, your complexion is almost certain to be of a gray or ghastly pallor, which in

---

[1]One of the (minor) discontents of the great New Critic, Cleanth Brooks, leading to his retirement as an active teacher from Yale, was his growing disgust with the deterioration in student manners. "I dress always in suit and tie [he was in fact a natty dresser] out of respect for them," he complained to me one day in his mild, sorrowful manner. "I think they could show at least as much respect for me by attending class in *clean* blue jeans and *washed* shirts that I can't smell."

the crucial beginning—when you make your first impression—can be off-putting to an audience. They desire the semblance of good health; which means that male speakers must submit to makeup, whether they like it or not.

Oh, and don't flash that solid gold Rolex or knock the lectern with its solid gold wristband.

<u>Women</u>: The smart black suit can be too stark, contrasting too vividly with the face. Women should check out backgrounds too, when possible: backdrop curtains come often in sapphire or butterfly blue, and dresses approximating those hues may merge into them, causing hands and face to appear disembodied. Women have special problems in their dress. If they are too modish, they'll be resented by their own sex in the audience. Neither must they allow themselves to appear drab. The balance is fine and difficult. Innate good taste can't be taught, but if you, as a female speaker, harbor any doubt about your judgment in these matters, consult with a sister.

Jewelry is a distraction and a detriment to the female speaker on almost all occasions (like deep cleavages and exposed bosoms, diamonds are great on Oscar and Emmy nights). Audience attention, ideally, must be concentrated on the speaker's mouth and the pearls of wit, the gems of wisdom, issuing from it. Glittering bracelets interfere. There's also—as with men and their wristwatches—the danger of clattering them against the lectern, these sharp sounds transmitting across the public address system.

<u>Both women and men</u>: Dress as smartly as you know how, avoiding the garish, the too daring, the mod, and the bizarre. Speaking is a lot like show biz. Clowns are expected to dress like clowns, leading men and women like leading men and women. People who pretend to authority must project substance in their dress. (That's you up there on the stage. In the act of getting up there, you are assuming authority, either personally or speaking for the company, the professional association, or the cause.)

7. Take command of the lectern and of the audience.

When you are announced, walk briskly to the lectern from the wings of the stage.

Don't acknowledge applause that may greet your name or your entrance. You haven't yet earned the crowd's approbation. That's in the balance. That's in doubt. Go directly to the lectern, and square yourself behind it, taking possession of it. Adjust the mike, the shade of the lamp. Don't yet acknowledge or thank the chairman, either. There's no hurry at this critical point. This is when the crowd sits bated with expectation. Prolong those few seconds of suspense. Gaze down at your text, whether you need to or not. There's no hurry! Then, perhaps abruptly, lift your chin, bring your body erect, sweep the auditorium with the most penetrating gaze you are able to summon, permitting a smile to flourish on your lips, *as if reluctantly*, and in a good loud voice, launch.

In bullfighting, the adage goes: *domar, mandar, templar*. The first business of the matador, when the gates of the toril are swung back and the bull comes careening out of darkness into the blinding sun of the arena, snorting and filled with murderous fury, is to dominate the animal. *Domar*. (The audience is your bull, your black beast, with which you are going to lock in a death's grip.) Following which, the matador's business is to command the bull, obliging it to charge and bend to his will. *Mandar*. (The audience is your foil, on whom you will exert all the art you possess, to the limits of your intellectual capacity and your passion.) And then, once the bull is dominated and placed morally under command, the matador's job is to gentle it, placate it, encourage it, engage it in a mutual act of surrender to the art, until he and the beast become one spectacle, one drama. *Templar*. (You must pacify and gain the willing acquiescence of your audience, incorporating them into your design, the moral force to which you have subjugated them, making them partners in your performance, willing participants.)

Do I overdramatize for your taste? Then you are not serious. Your purpose as a public speaker is frivolous. You are permitting your hands to wilt from the wrists (see Chapter 15).

These prescriptions are not easy; they are, nevertheless, the goal. And a lot depends on those first few seconds when you fill the stage with your presence.

8. Express your presence through your posture.

You must not slouch. You must keep your body kinetically erect.

A vital force must be centered in your being. The audience must feel from the instant the speaker takes the stage that a combustible store of energy is being kept by him in hold, creating a current of energy that transmits *to* the audience, in turn creating a current of communication in response *from* the audience.

The attitude of the body is what produces this effect, which is why the speaker's weight should favor the balls of his feet, why the knees should be limber, and why that weight must be evenly distributed between the feet. Never relapse on a hip, right or left. Never slump. Never grasp the lectern as though for support or lodge an elbow on its surface so heavily that someone in the front row is consumed with the desire to slap it off, just to see whether the whole scaffolding of the speaker's body may not follow it to the floor. You are to be reckoned with. You must establish this apprehension in the audience from the start.

9. Make the most of your gorgeous self.

I'll not drop the name, but this is who she is.

She was born in Small Town, New York. Blessed with beauty and a knockout figure, she was modeling clothes for Hattie Carnegie by the time she was 18. She caught Bill Casey's eye, and she enrolled in the OSS. This was 1942. She conducted undercover missions in Franco Spain; and in Málaga, she was tossed into jail. Another romantic character from those times, Barnaby Conrad, then our consul in Lisbon, used his influence to set her free. She married a handsome young Spanish count from one of the oldest and richest aristocratic lines. She conceived and bore three sons. She remained flawlessly beautiful. (Not many women liked her.) For twenty or thirty years, she was perennially on the ten-best-dressed list. She became an international figure. She met and knew everybody: in society, in government, in the film and theater worlds. Among her intimate friends and acquaintances were the Duke and Duchess of Windsor, Ava Gardner, "Ceezee" and Winsted Guest, Truman Capote, Grace Kelly and Prince Ranier, Audrey Hepburn, James Mason, Paul Getty. The years rolled off her seamlessly. She kept fit, rising early in the mornings for a two-hour gallop. In her mid-fifties, she could don a bikini and cause men to drool, women to become sullen. She was the true and original barefoot contessa (Ava Gardner starred in an undistinguished movie of that name), longtime

European editor and correspondent of *Vogue*, and as a maven of fashion, always brilliantly dressed in sequins and furs, pearls and rhinestones, or simple unadorned black dresses at big bucks a throw. In her sixties, she wrote an account about her youthful experiences as a World War II spy, which purported to be biographical and, thanks partly to her indefatigable promotion, sold dazzlingly. In her seventies, rumor spread through the capital cities of Madrid, Paris, London, Athens, and New York that she had indeed made, *must* have made, had *had* to have made a Faustian pact with the devil, because she was still outrageously, infuriatingly, flagrantly, unbelievably, and incontestably beautiful, with a figure that moved with sovereign independence under whatever garb she had on, its integrity intact.

The point is, God blessed her, and she took advantage of His gifts. The speaker has the right to do the same, but like this extraordinary woman (who remains deeply modest about her achievements), without claiming any personal credit for it.

Some people are youthful, lithe, tall, fit, glowing with health, rich, charming, handsome, and beautiful. Flashing eyes. Radiant hair. A voice like whisky mellowed fifty years in a charcoal barrel. Exploit these physical advantages.[2] It is legitimate to do so. Your mission is to captivate and entrance your audience; your design may be to change the world. Whatever: In those first few moments on stage, if you are able to cast a spell by your physical presence alone, do not hesitate.

Though keep in mind: Handsome is as handsome does. Unless you also possess the inner tension and dynamism, the magnetic force, you'll pall before ten minutes are up. At my school, we've had outstandingly virile and handsome men, women of remarkable beauty. A few relied on these physical attributes (as, I suspect, they had accustomed themselves to doing most of their adult lives), instead of merely being opportunistic about them. These didn't make it.

10. Make the most of your ungainly self.

By contrast, hundreds and hundreds have become speakers of extraordinary power because by their intelligence, temperament, and art, they are transfigured.

---

[2]My first agent, William Colston Leigh, took me aside one day, saying speculatively, "Reid, you're good . . . but you're not as good as Vincent Price. Try to be more like him, won't you?" Which would have required a pact with Mephistopheles that it is unlikely he'd be able to deliver on.

. . . As fat old Pastora Imperio was that afternoon in my apartment (see Chapter 15) when she showed me how women should use their arms and hands. Under the magic of her art, she radiated the illusion of youth and beauty. I've read that Sarah Bernhardt was supremely able to cast this spell (as a one-legged woman in her sixties, she was accepting young men into her bed). A Spanish friend and performer who has since died, Gabriela Ortega, was tall, ill-proportioned, heavy-hipped, and heavingly bosomed, with a masculine jaw and a long, arbitrary nose. She did possess wonderful eyes—big, dark, heavily lashed black orbs set in alabaster whites. The attribute that best served her, however, and on which she fashioned a stage career, was her voice: a deep contralto, richly toned, wonderfully cadenced. She would recite poetry to Flamenco beat, stomping floorboards so hard with her heavy-heeled red shoes that the dust rose from them. Declaiming Garcia Lorca's "Five o'Clock in the Afternoon," the melodramatic account of a bullfighter's death, Ortega shivered the timbers of cabaret or theater, entrancing her audience. She became majestic, tragic, even good-looking.

If you develop the intensity of desire and acquire elements of the craft of public speaking, don't be discouraged by the face or body the Lord, in His mysterious dispensation of favors, allotted to you. A recent graduate (who, like Ortega, possesses a pipe organ for a voice) took me aside at the conclusion of the seminar and asked me whether his weight was not an impediment to his success as a speaker.

I stepped back from him, of a sudden freshly aware. It's my guess that he stands 6 feet, 5 inches tall, while supporting 375 or maybe even 400 pounds. Three days earlier, I had been impressed by that tremendous bulk first thing; he had only to enter the building. But the whole hour of the final exercise, in which he excelled, earning the silver medal (our highest award), I had been utterly unaware of his obesity.

I told him that for his health, sure, he should reduce. It hardly mattered to his speaking. His passion is so brilliant, his voice so powerful, his intelligence so keen, that art overwhelms reality.

It can for you also. Which is yet another reason why you must . . .

11. Cling to, keep foremost in your mind, your purpose.

There's a reason that put you on that stage. Either you were forced to stride out upon it, or you wished to.

In the first case, it is because there was no alternative. Your boss said bluntly, "You give that welcoming address, Al, old fella . . . and you tell the stockholders their dividend is going to be cut."

Your purpose in this case may be as sufficient as desiring to be kept in your boss's employ. This may not be a noble or glorious goal, but it should do. You must walk out there and give it your best. Psyche yourself to the necessity. If you can't cut that, you can't cut anything.

The second case should be easier. You are speaking because you feel a deep commitment to what you are going to say. Hew hard and tight to that purpose. Desire will imbue your presence and your words with passion.

Which is why the subject of establishing instant eye contact with your audience has been left for now, last.

EYE CONTACT

We tell people you can speak just fine without establishing eye contact, but no way can you communicate without it. And no way will you persuade anyone to your point of view.

But if you establish eye contact with as few as ten people in a crowd of one hundred, you will have won the whole audience (or the better part of it).

1. Never permit yourself to conceive of an audience as a sea of anonymous faces.

2. Individualize the audience.

3. Concentrate on five, six, seven—as many individuals as time permits—and cement intimate personal relations with them.

Sweat, Blood, Toil, and Tears: Surpassing Yourself

1. Never permit yourself to conceive of an audience as a sea of anonymous faces.

They are persons.

2. Individualize the audience.

Seek them out as such: that plump, beaming, grandmotherly woman fifth row center, with shining white hair. That young fellow ten rows up from her, to the left, who may be a student. That serious-looking middle-aged man in the business suit, across and to the right. Accountant? Banker? Doctor?

As fast as possible, familiarize yourself with them—as persons. (What's to be afraid of?)

3. Concentrate on five, six, seven—as many individuals as time permits—and cement intimate personal relations with them.

Hard, fast, individual eye contact. Any seasoned hunter will tell you, if you shoot into the flock, you won't hit a thing.

The speaker cannot simply surf the audience, but must single people out. He mustn't gaze vaguely at the crowd, turning his head left-right, left-right, like a spectator at a tennis match. That's no good at all.

We tell (and tell and tell) our students:

> A speaker must implant listeners with the impression that they are of supreme importance to him; that he desperately desires to win them to his side. In order to accomplish this he must quarter the crowd into zones, selecting a friendly looking individual here, another there, on whom to focus his attention, taking the measure of each person he engages in this personal contact just as that person takes the measure of him. What is it that we seek of people? Candor and good will. What is it the members of the audience seek of the speaker? The same. The speaker must probe into each selected individual's soul, eliciting the sparkle of lively intelligence signaling that he or she is truly listening, truly absorbing.[3]

---

[3] A personal critique is written upon request for each student attending the Executive Seminar in Communication Skills, which he receives with the videotape of his performances. Each of the exercises in which he participated is freshly analyzed, the good and the bad, with specific recommendations for improvement. These critiques run between fifteen and thirty pages, single-spaced. Coupled with the video, they are a nifty learning tool for years to come.

This personal eye-bonding with individuals in the dim hall is what humanizes the crowd and establishes a dialogue with everybody out there. As the speaker fastens his attention on this man or that woman, a half dozen others in the vicinity get the impression that it is they on whom he is individually concentrating, an impression that spreads throughout the audience, until the entire crowd becomes as one, reacts as one. They are all individuals who, each in his or her way, must be worked by the speaker. Peering into the faces assembled before one in this discrete manner, with this design, *and with this desire* (a) virtually eliminates the least possibility of stage fright, and (b) identifies the speaker with the audience, the audience with the speaker, and in the process, the audience with the case the speaker is trying to make. *One must be fiercely determined to accomplish this personal engagement*, which is how the supremacy of the speaker's will over his audience is established. One's eye-bonding must be of the intensity that Homer describes when he sings of the "eagle's" gaze of his heroes, which lesser mortals were unable to withstand.

My constant stress on marshaling and exerting moral will by eye contact and by body language in order to exert dominion over the audience may once again strike the reader as overly dramatic, but this is what happens, *this is the only way it happens*, this is the magnetic field of persuasion. This is how the small presence on the vast stage in a large theater grows in magnitude, how art transcends physical limitations, transfiguring the speaker.[4]

---

[4]A note on eyeballing in close proximity to the other person. An Argentine by birth, Roberto Garcia Carbonell is a professor in the Polytechnic Universities of Madrid and Valencia. His book, *Everybody Can Speak Well (Todos Pueden Hablar Bien*, Madrid: Editorial EDAF, S.A.), has interesting things to say about eye contact. [All capitalizations are his.]

> Since childhood [he writes] we are inculcated with an elementary norm of good manners that consists in "looking cleanly into the eyes of others." . . . But is it possible to look cleanly [at others] in this fashion? Obviously NOT . . . [We either concentrate on a single eye] or "jump" intermittently from eye to eye.
>
> So o.k. . . . How should one look [at one's target], then? Why, by directing one's gaze at the SPACE BETWEEN THE EYEBROWS [*ENTRECEJO*] of the person . . . The not insignificant problem being: NOT TO BLINK during these moments. And not only avoid blinking, but projecting one's gaze in a manner demonstrating affection and sweetness . . .

CHAPTER 12

THE VOICE: TRAINING THE TONGUE

INTRODUCTION: YOUR NATIVE ACCENT, POETRY[1]

The sounds that issue from our mouths either attract or repel the attention of our audiences.

They are the prime prehistorical means of communication. And though the voice may have been tumbled from its pinnacle since the advent of the Gutenberg press (c. 1436) and the universal advance of literacy, it is second in formal learning only to the all-absorbing eye and remains first in primary communication—in our daily social and business intercourse and in the lecture hall.

The man at the lectern may be tall, virile, fit, blessed with an imperial gaze and a mind of the first magnitude, but should a thin, high, reedy voice emerge from his mouth when he opens it, he had might as well hand his text out to the audience, sit down, and let them peruse it. The woman at the lectern may be as arresting as Pallas Athena to regard, her shield blazoned with accomplishments and her brow noble

---

[1] Parts of this taken from *Speaking in Public*, Chapter 10; then from *Sex, Power, and Pericles*, Part 2, Chapters 2 and 3.

with brain power, but should a high, shrill screech issue from her mouth, she had might as well sit down next to the hunk and play draughts with him while someone else reads her remarks. He who does not have the courage of his convictions is a sad case, to be pitied; she who does not possess the voice with which to enunciate her convictions is lost and often deprecated.

Athletes in particular tend to disappoint, even shock, the hearer. There can be an unsettling dissonance between brawn and sound box. The high intonations of the "Golden Bear" ill befit his historical stature (in golf). Muhammad Ali's voice in its prime was charming but also thin and high. Female gymnasts and figure skaters seem prone not only to teeny little-girl squeaks but also to a flat nasal twang that is gratingly Midwestern. A rich and powerful voice is a boon; a voice that neither shocks nor offends can be acquired. Ross Perot will never become President.

THE VOICE

Whatever sounds they may be that issue from your chest, pleasing or displeasing, *hie thee to a speech instructor.* Or to a speech pathologist, should your problems be physiological. This may be the best investment you have made after buying this book.

For advice as to the first, call your fine arts center, your local music school, your actor's studio, or your summer stock theater organization. Someone will know of a 5-foot 10-inch, 260-pound ex-diva with bellows for lungs and voluminous pillows for paps, which can be intimidating, but whose voice is capable of bringing down church steeples at two hundred meters—and who can teach you how to do it. For the pathologist, consult your doctor.

Sweat, Blood, Toil, and Tears: Surpassing Yourself

There are gifts of God for which we may take no credit but for which we should be grateful . . . and of which, as speakers, it is legitimate for us to take advantage.

Among these gifts may be our voices. Should you, man, be blessed with a deep, resounding baritone, fall on your knees, thank your stars, and *cultivate it*; should you, woman, be blessed with a full throaty caramel contralto, which you are able to project to the furthest corners of the lecture hall, fall on your knees, thank your stars, and cultivate it.

Nothing is ever so wonderful that it cannot be perfected; nothing is ever so desperately bad that it cannot be helped. No matter how good your voice is, take it to a *speech instructor*. (Conversely, if your voice is an affliction to you: if, man, it should be pitched too low and be scratchy or *buzz-zzz-zzz* like the engine of a badly tuned car after it's switched off; if, woman, it should be papery, or when heightened in volume, screech like the bats of Carlsbad rushing out into the twilight; take it to a *speech pathologist*.)

A speech instructor can show you in a few hours how to make of your natural endowments a wondrous instrument that delights the ear and may even thrill the hall. A pathologist may be able to correct those abuses of your vocal cords that have become vicious.

Repeating: *your voice is the passport to the understanding of your audience.* Its power and beauty may gain immediate admittance for you; its faults may close the gates. *But do not fall in love with it!*

That's so dreadful, and so obvious: when speakers are enraptured with what comes forth from that layered gristle of muscle tissue that we romanticize with the name of "vocal cords" or "pipes." They stand with an ear half-cocked to the magniloquent sounds they are producing, self-satisfaction crinkling the corners of their eyes, choosing ever-rounder-voweled and ever-swankier and more lusciously syllabled words, filling the auditorium with the orotund resonances of their conceit. It's as though they are standing beside themselves, listening and approving.

Don't be that way. Even though you may be able to coax rich sonorities and brilliant cadenzas from your chest, *do not rely on this to maintain your audiences' attention for more than three minutes.* If your voice is an affront to the ear, it will alienate audiences, that's for certain. But though it be as smooth as honey and as intoxicating as mead, it will captivate audiences only for the briefest while. *The mind*—content—*is what counts.* The intelligence of the speaker is what keeps people riveted to his words. It is the mind that distinguishes between Brahms and Claude Debussy; it is the mind that distinguishes between Benny Goodman and André Kostelanitz, Nat King Cole and Lawrence Welk.

TRAINING THE TONGUE

1. Be sure you *pronounce* the word correctly.

2. Be sure you *articulate* your words clearly.

3. Be sure you *enunciate* your vowels and give plosive power to your consonants.

4. Be sure your *diction* is crisp.

> ♪*Whether you whisper soft*
> *Or whether you loudly call . . .*
> *Distinctly, distinctly speak*
> *. . . Or do not speak at all!*♪

Concisely stated: Maybe nothing puts an audience off more than a speaker who mispronounces and muffles and slurs and shuffles through or hurries or flings his words off to the wings of the stage. It is irritating in the extreme. The audience are disgusted.

Pronunciation

Correctly to pronounce your words is elemental. You'll find in Appendix B a list of commonly mispronounced words that I have lifted (now twice) from Professor Paul Soper's *Basic Public Speaking.*

These are a wonderful guide. Check yourself out on that list. You will be surprised by the faults you commit without ever having been conscious of them. But there is more to say about pronunciation, *including when the accepted practice should be violated.*

Sweat, Blood, Toil, and Tears: Surpassing Yourself

Some words seem to be misbegotten when spoken from the podium, their arrangement of syllables inviting confusion. *These must be intentionally mispronounced* (according to standard practice) *in order for them to be understood.*

Take the word *era.* If you utter it from the stage or even across the air waves after the approved American manner, *ehruh,* you will incur what's known as amphilogistic misunderstanding,[2] as in, "The sinking of the Armada in 1588 culminated a great era for Spain." The audience will hear *error*. The *r* sound commencing the second syllable of the word dominates the aspirated *h* sound concluding the first syllable of the word. Yes, the Armada sure was a colossal mistake. For this reason, I always pronounce era after the British fashion, *ihruh*. There's no mistaking the meaning then.

The proper pronunciation of *c-o-m-b-a-t-a-n-t* is cómbatant, not combátant, but nine gets you ten that if you utter the word as it ought to be uttered the audience will hear *competent*, as in, "That bunch of noncompetent troops stood idly by while the battle raged." Similarly, there aren't ten people in a thousand who will comprehend you unless you screw your features into an unsightly knot when you speak of a *grimáss*, notwithstanding that this is the (hideous) correct pronunciation of *g-r-i-m-a-c-e*; and since Daffy Duck in the famous cartoon found Bugs Bunny *despícable*, this (incorrect) emphasis of syllables is what people both prefer and comprehend. Maybe that shouldn't be so, but it would be *impíous* in this great democracy to set ourselves against the popular will.

Some words in combination are the devil to say. As a lector in my church, I cannot for the life of me pronounce *the Thessalonians* without taking a gulp between the definite article and the noun. And some words are plain malicious, as though possessed of an intention to convey the wrong meaning. *Eschew* is often taken to signify *espouse*; I don't know why. The phrase *What a day!* is fraught with amphibolous potential. A circuit court judge I know, when charging juries, *never* uses the word *credibílity*, because (he tells me) somehow they hear *créditabílity*, and their minds leap from that nuance to irrelevant considerations of the accused's credit standing. Why should this be? Maybe because the teaching of good English in our schools has fallen into *decáydence*.[3]

---

[2]An *amphilogism*, stemming from the root *amphi*, meaning on both sides, is defined by Webster as an ambiguous mode of speech, an equivocation. It is closely related to an *amphibology*, deriving from the Greek *amphibolous*, meaning doubtful. It's defined as (1) double or doubtful meaning, an ambiguity, (2) a sentence capable of double meaning owing to doubtful syntax, as in "the Duke yet lives that Henry shall depose."

[3]*Decadence* stems (through the French) from the Latin *cadens*, which means to fall. *Decade*, for example, stems from the Latin *decas*, which means the number ten.

Articulation

To . . . *artículate*. What a rugged, terrific word. Mouth it out in your mind. Stretch and purse your lips, move that lower jaw on its hinges: *arrrtículate*. Four vowels: *a, i, u,* the long a. But it has six consonants, five of them rocklike: *r, t, k, q, l, t.*

To articulate is to utter one's words distinctly so that they are intelligible, each syllable clearly demarcated. One may pronounce correctly, yet articulate poorly. Words of seven syllables can elide or jam together into five syllables, which should teach you a lesson about choosing monstrosities.

Remember, *sense rides on the back of sound*. Sense must travel; it must leap across what can be the awesome space between one person and another, one understanding and another's, one universe of self-consciousness and another's. Stars can be trillions of light years distant from each other, but maybe nothing is so distant from anything else in this universe as the expressed thought of person *A* from the understanding of person *B*. This is because, among other reasons, it requires person *B* to extract himself from the total self-absorption in which we normally abide. It requires a suppression of the ego, the most powerful magnetic field in nature, which is the shield that the speaker must somehow smash through.

Sense needs all the help it can get. The words on the back of which it travels must be articulated as though chiseled with the tongue. Try these exercises.

1. Speak tongue twisters and jawbreakers aloud to yourself.
   Such as
   > *Peter Piper picked a peck of pickled peppers* . . .
   >   or
   > *Why wouldst thou rude on me Thy wring-world right foot rock?*[4]

―――――――――🎗―――――――――
Sweat, Blood, Toil, and Tears: Surpassing Yourself

There are dozens of them, of graduated difficulty. Say them aloud to yourself, *distinctly*. Say them faster and faster to yourself, as fast as you

―――――――――
[4]There are choice ones in Spanish: *Un tigre, dos tigres, tres tigres*. And a lalapalooza: *El cielo está enladrillado. Quien lo desenladrilla? El desenladrillador quien lo desenladrillare muy desenladrillador será*. Thanks are owed to Sra. Dña. Rosario Hornedo.

can get your tongue and jaw moving, *always distinctly. Keep in mind that good articulation depends on hitting those hard and soft consonants well.* The *P*s and *T*s and *B*s and *D*s must come forth explosively and with imperial distinctness, so that the differences between them are unambiguous to the audience.

Recite doggerel at maximum speed into a recorder. Play the tape back to yourself. *Are* you being distinct? Are your words absolutely clear to you? When do the syllables begin to collide or mush? When do you begin skipping and eliding? *There's your maximum speaking velocity.* (Knowing this becomes important when encountering loudspeaker problems. See "Volume and Dynamics" below.)

2. Speak tongue twisters aloud to a child or—better—a patient adult.

Sweat, Blood, Toil, and Tears: Surpassing Yourself

Have your devoted widowed mother begin at, say, twenty feet from you. Then, upon each recitation of a series of tongue twisters, have her move another several feet distant from you; and another; and another; each time, as you lengthen the distance, increasing the velocity with which you deliver what you say.

Ask your mother at what point your words begin to slur, become indistinct, or try her attention to comprehend. *There you have the maximum distance at which you are understandable at that velocity* (without the aid of loudspeakers).

Enunciation

To enunciate is to articulate with distinctness, but I associate the word with the vowels particularly.

Pay attention to them. Many people speak with lazy lips and an indolent lower jaw, incompletely formulating the vowels. *A* must stretch the lips in a grimace, even though it may be unsightly. *E* must raise the upper lip almost painfully, while lapping the lower lip over the teeth of the lower jaw, tightening the nostrils as if in a fastidious sniff. *I* must drop the lower jaw, lifting the upper jaw and that portion of the lip between the eyeteeth in rabbity fashion, bugging the eyeballs a little. *O* must purse the lips into a tight round sphincter, forming a little hole through which the vowel is to be projected. *U* must extend the lips in round tubular fashion. And *Y* must stretch the lips wide at the corners, while lower jaw descends from upper jaw.

1. Practice enunciating *A*, *E*, *I*, *O*, *U*, and *Y* in the fashion described above while staring at yourself in the mirror.

Exaggerate, so that you truly feel your lips stretch and your jaw distend. When you begin to feel unutterably silly, stop. But recall what you did from time to time, and should you suspect that you are reverting to the bad old lazy ways, check yourself out against the mirror once again.

2. Develop a sensual appreciation for language and the lusciousness of the vowel sounds.

This is not falling in love with the sound of your voice. But do become intoxicated with the glories of the English language and make yourself its vassal, taking a solemn oath never wilfully to dishonor it. You would never smear a prized mahogany tabletop with tar, nor dash ink across the canvas of a master. So must you treat language, avoiding sloppiness while enunciating the vowels and those nasal atonalities that scrinch their sound. Conceive of the vowels as a fine wine. *They must be rinsed in the mouth, chewed, in order to be enunciated properly*. Roll them under the tender sides of your tongue, slurping them deep into its recesses where your wisdom teeth once were; taste their astringency and acidity as well as their sweetness. E*nunz*sceeate them![5]

Diction

One's diction is good when words are pronounced correctly and with scrupulous distinctness, the consonants articulated, the vowels enunciated.

Good diction is pleasing. It relaxes the audience. It is a gateway into their understanding.

How to acquire decent diction fast? A cinch: *Declaim poetry*. (See below.)

The Power of the Pause

Few sounds produce such extraordinary effect as that of the sudden cessation of sound, dropping on an audience like perfect silence at the base of a waterfall.

---

[5] For instruction at the feet of a master, buy yourself the Capitol CD recordings (CDP 7943172) of Frank Sinatra's greatest songs, and harken to (emulating) the magic that he extrudes from the vowels.

As though the spigot has been turned off.

It can occur between syllables, in the midst of a phrase, after a colon or full stop, between paragraphs, at the conclusion of a dramatic passage, or at the commencement of a new line of reasoning. Pause. *Stop*. Permit that caesura in the flow of the talk to sink on the audience until silence establishes a perfect reign, ruptured only by the cough of someone way back in the fortieth row or a rattling in the throat of someone up in the box seats. The rest of the audience is held in suspense.

Then resume. *Learn to relish the silence*. Become comfortable with it. It's the amateur who hurries. The amateur runs through applause, through laughter, through the dramatic potential of what he has to say. This is a question of timing—timing in the delivery of your text. What you say must be apportioned to the audience, here and there temporarily denied to the audience. Suspense is what holds people in their seats. What is coming next? When will the speaker let drop the other shoe, the last syllable? What [grand] [funny] [foreboding] [terrible] thing is he about to enunciate?

Artful use of silence is essential to the speaker's craft.

Modulation/Inflection

This art, all speakers must cultivate. We must acquire the same identification of the words we use to express what we are saying with what we hold to be the truth of what we say, honoring the expression of it only less than the truth itself. It is love of and respect for language, the only medium by which we are capable of explicitly conveying truth, that conduces to beauty in its utterance, that bestows on truth the form revealing truth in all its power. This is the understanding that totally escaped the revisionists who, during the 1960s and 1970s, ravaged the Book of Common Prayer and the Roman Catholic liturgy; that when one says, "This is the lamb of God who takes away the sin of the world," it is not the same thing at all as saying, "Behold the lamb of God, behold Him who taketh away the sins of the world." And when one says, "I tell you solemnly," it is not the same thing at all as, nor an acceptable substitution for, "Amen, amen, I say unto you . . ." The authority of truth is vitiated in the vulgarized form, losing power and vitality. Truth is damaged.

Therefore, if you have something to say in which you believe with all your heart and soul and might, and wish to say it memorably, and hope to gain the rapt attention of your audience to what you say, do not drone your words monochromatically, boringly, energy and vitality and desire and joy absent, but charge and animate your voice with the gift for modulation that we inherit with our tongues, pitching and inflecting the words in such manner that when you speak the truths, you aspire to music.

Read poetry out loud every night for a week. If the very idea embarrasses you, lock yourself into the shower stall, or into the basement, or in the garage, where you won't be disturbed. If necessary, build a tree house. (Should your children snigger at you, hurl a baseball bat at them; if your spouse convulses with laughter, tell *her* that her bosom is sagging, *him* that his stomach resembles a collapsed pig's bladder.) *Never mind who overhears you.* Good poetry compels one, through its internal rhythms and exacting arrangement of words, to articulate, to modulate, to inflect.

Then, having declaimed to yourself all week—and maybe even to your children and spouse, who, you may be surprised to discover, enjoy listening to you (good poetry decently spoken captures the soul)—read that Saturday morn the text of the speech you plan to deliver at Tuesday's luncheon meeting of the Young Presidents Club. If the thoughts you express now strike you as so lackluster that you yourself are unable to summon any compelling interest in them, rethink them, redraft them. Or if the language with which you set out your thoughts now strikes you as so drab that you are unable to imbue it (when reading it out loud) with the color and passion and sensuous tension of the poetry you have been declaiming, rewrite it. (You should have time between now and church on Sunday.) A couple of lapidary sentences can save a text; a single brilliant paragraph can make it memorable; a concluding page in which sense and form are wonderfully joined can transform a ho-hum "motivational" meeting into a thrilling event. Treat yourself to that possibility.

Now: When the thinking has been strengthened and made supple, when the language has been reformed the more lucidly and brilliantly to expound that thinking, *speak it aloud to yourself with the same respect and devotion that your reading of poetry teaches you.* You have plenty of time before lunch, golf, fishing, chess, or weeding the garden. Relish your words, articulate them with pleasure; explore the registers of which your voice is capable.

Read poetry.

Volume and Dynamics

Achieving greater volume requires pitching your voice higher and projecting it more forcefully.

Don't allow yourself lazy reliance on a mike. We've mentioned: Sound systems go dead or scratch and crackle with feedback. They also tend to rob the voice of personality. You may not be able to fill the Hollywood Bowl with your unaided lungs, yet try.

One of the functions of Greek masks was acoustic enhancement: they were fashioned in such way as to concentrate the carrying power of the actor's voice: they formed a kind of tube or trumpet through which the speaker funneled his words. We do some of this naturally when calling from hilltop to hilltop. We lift our chins, aim at the clouds scudding across the sky, and with our lips form a round (though shallow) tube as we extend the last vowels: "Hel-*low-ow-ow*, there! Do you hea*rrrr* me!?" How do you blow out the candles of a birthday cake?

There's a polemic going on: whether volume truly issues from the diaphragm or whether that's an illusion. What I know for a fact is that it makes sense to propel the voice on pneumatic power. This requires tightening of the stomach muscles and thrusting them out, which people conscious of their fitness, or lack of it, and of their 'aving too plenteous a *poids*,[6] resist as unsightly. Singers and actors in the legitimate theater synchronize the filling of their lungs and the expelling of their words with the breath naturally, after long training. Maybe this is why lecterns were invented, to conceal distended stomachs.

Should you have problems projecting your voice without (men) shouting or (women) going shrill, consult that speech instructor recommended at the beginning of this chapter. Meantime . . .

. . .Try this. For the effect of dynamics, do what clavichordists do, whose instrument uniformly plucks sound from the wires, not, as in the piano, hammers on them with felt pads: *increase the velocity with*

---

[6]As in, *J'ai beaucoup trop de poids.*

which you deliver a sentence. This gives the impression of raising your voice. Stepping up the pace of your delivery won't help you reach the far corners of the lecture hall, if your projection is truly weak, but saying what you say more rapidly (and always distinctly) can save you from straining your vocal cords. Remember that *the greater the distinctness of the rapidly delivered passage, the louder will it seem,* because the more clearly will the syllables tinkle into the eardrums.[7]

Pace and Tempo

Begin briskly and conversationally, then vary your pace. Suit tempo to the passage. Do not rush.

Pace is the rate of speed with which you deliver your text. *Tempo* is associated with music, the rate of movement at which a piece or passage is played. To keep tempo is to keep rhythm and to respect the correct mood expressed not only by the notes but by the rate of speed with which they strike the ear . . . The difference in a sonata between the *andante* of a second movement, for example, and the *scherzo* of the third movement being a difference of mood—between the melancholy or poignant or introverted and the joyful dance.

Sweat, Blood, Toil, and Tears: Surpassing Yourself

March, quick time, dance, dirge: All the different tempos must be at the command of the speaker. *More often than speaking too slowly, speakers rush.* They set a breakneck pace that audiences cannot keep up with and so tune out. This occasionally suggests the speaker who is unsure of what he is saying, dubious about what he is saying, and whose nerves at the idea of performing on a stage are threatening to engulf him (see more on stage fright under Chapter 20). Too fast a pace is a bane.

Too deliberate a pace may also be a bane. I've known the most intelligent and intellectually fascinating scholars to place their audiences in anguish (and thus undo the purpose of their appearance on the stage), because it seems that between the iteration of the first syllable of a word and the last syllable of the word, whole eons pass. Galaxies are born out of gaseous clouds, gleam their fierce four billion years or so,

---

[7]This is why we Anglophones are under the impression that Spaniards and Italians are always shouting: it's because they are enunciating every single syllable in their speech, producing a rapidity of percussions. They also shout.

and then implode into a black hole that permits not even light to escape. It takes these speakers a cosmological age to get done with a single paragraph, by which time the sense of what they are imparting has condensed into an impenetrable nucleus and is lost utterly, while the impatience of the audience is hostilely aroused.

Yet it is better to speak deliberately than to race. Permit the audience time to absorb the sense of what you are saying. Keep in mind always how dumb and lacking in understanding and refractory audiences are. Their obtuseness can scarcely be exaggerated.

Your Native Accent[8]

Wherever you come from, *assuming your accent is literate*, do not—no, not ever—succumb to the snobbery of changing it.

There's a nefarious outfit in Atlanta (and I hear that it has spread to Birmingham and Charlotte) which seeks to deracinate Southerners, to teach Southerners how not to sound where they came from, to eliminate their long vowels and their regional locutions. I become indignant. Those people ought to be tarred and feathered, ridden out of town on a rail, and dumped into ploughmud. (Which is pronounced *pluff*mud, and which will set on them like cement.)

Occasionally, we get piteous telephone calls at the school asking whether we can do something about the caller's Southern or German or Spanish or New Yawk accent. I leap up from my desk in fury. I'm sure I shock them, shouting into the receiver, NEVER TRY TO BE A CHAMELEON, EVER. DO NOT TRY TO DENY OR OCCULT YOUR ANTECEDENTS.

There can be no greater mistake. Can there be an accent anywhere in the English-speaking world more euphonic than what philologists call Upper Mississippi Valley? Doesn't your ear delight in the *educated* Texan drawl, or in the funky, smoky tonalities of New Orleans? What about the Vermonter, the Down Easter, the haughtily insouciant flat *Aaas* of the Bostonian, or the streetwise nasal bray of the Bronx? If you were born to any of these dialects, thank your stars! Our country is blessed with the variety of its speech, which is distinctive and filled with such character.

---

[8]Much of this is cribbed from *Speaking in Public*.

There *are* some ugly accents. The uninflected nasal Minnesotan elongations of the late Lawrence Welk, for example, which afflicts the speech of people all across the northwestern tier of states from Illinois to Montana, and renders what they have to say boring, no matter the content. This is a literate idiom, but not enviable. The singsong Oriental intonations of Indians speaking English are literate, nevertheless unpleasing. On the whole, however, once again *assuming that the idiom one speaks is literate*, regional inflections impart great charm to anyone's speech. What would John Wayne have been without his *not hardly* elocutions, or Jimmy Stewart without his Indiana (Pa.) adenoids?

Foreigners speaking English need not fear either. I never heard anyone object to the accent of Greta Garbo, Sophia Loren, Charles Boyer, or Ricardo Montalbán (unless it's the Ford Motor Company, which never heard of *Corrrrinthian leatherrrr*). Even some of the minor grammatical errors that creep into the English of someone not born to the language can be full of charm.

POETRY . . . AGAIN

Read these kinds of poetry for help in what ails you:

1. *Ballad poetry* for cadence and a sense of fun.

2. *Lyric poetry* for attention to the vowels, pathos, strong yet disciplined emotion, requiring exquisite enunciation.

3. *Tragic poetry* for projection of strong emotion also, sometimes contained, but sometimes unbridled, exercising the hard and plosive consonants (<u>Men</u>: Try soliloquies from *King Lear*, the funeral oration of Anthony in *Julius Caesar*, and take your pick from *Hamlet* or *Othello*; <u>Women</u>: The soliloquies of Lady MacBeth test the female temperament through her voice as nothing else).

4. *The love sonnets* of Shakespeare and Petrarch, the short religious odes of Hopkins, almost anything by Yeats, and the odes of Keats for the projection of complex emotion, ranging from disciplined through tremulous; poignant, tender, high, penetrating to the most profound levels.

5. For projection of the intellect in a playful yet mordant
   manner, exercise yourself on *the "metaphysical" poets*:
   Herrick, Herbert, Donne, Marvel, and toss in William Blake.

These suggestions are limited, sufficient for the purposes of this book.[9]
The reading of just a little poetry *out loud* will discover for many
readers a new world, one that can develop into a source of permanent
joy. In common with training the ear to great music and the eye to high
art, reading poetry (*out loud*) can turn the phlegmatic temperament
into a vital force. It can sublimate the dangerous passions and reveal
kingdoms of the spirit that some people live and die without ever
having tapped, without ever having attained or been given the least
awareness of. That's tragic. It's to weep over—such a terrible waste! For
these deprived and emotionally starved fellow human beings, it's as
though they had never existed, not on any level higher than minimal
human consciousness. Their carcasses fill the graves. Their flesh rots
and their bones pile up, and their memories yellow in snapshots of
Niagara Falls. Like everybody, in life they suffer a lot and glut on a little
happiness, but existence for them is Hobbesian, *drab*, nasty, brutish,
and short. *Read poetry, out loud.*

---

[9]You'll find more detailed and demanding advice in *Sex, Power, and Pericles*, Part 1, Chapter 6 and Part 2, Chapters 2
and 3. Refer to those chapters should you care to scale the Himalayas.

CHAPTER 13

LITERACY, GRAMMAR, STYLE, AND PROPRIETY

As well as mastering the voice, a speaker must be literate, grammatical, stylish, and decorous. Erring badly in any of these departments can be ruinous.

LITERACY

Just as one should never try to affect some flavorless mid-Atlantic accent—the kind of English spoken by Katie Couric or Deborah Norville (never mind the godawful Beltway, oh-so-superior intonations of Barbara Walters and Nina Totenberg, to which Jane Pauley has been gravitating)—*do not*, out of a desire to ingratiate, make the mistake of affecting a down-homey style of language when you are giving a formal address. Save it for *Hee-Haw*.

The rule is: *Avoid regional locutions that are idiosyncratic of the uneducated classes, unless for ironical effect*. For example, *the Yankee* "gonna," or *the Yankee* "doin'." These can grate as badly as the ungracious low-class regional idiom of *the Pennsylvania "Dutch"* ("it's *all*," for "it's [the train, bus, taxi, pumpkin pie] gone") or the low-class churlishness of *Connecticut and Massachusetts* natives, to whom it seems that any utterance beyond the level of a grunt is heroic. Avoid *the Southern* "like ought to," or "I feel like we should," or "more better," or "had oughter." If you hail from *the West Coast*, be less than totally awesome—grow out of Californiaspeak. And for the love of Heaven, eschew *jockstrap locutions*, such as, "He's got good quickness," or "He did good," or "We hope to do as best we can," and even worse, "We feel like we can do as good as we can . . . hopefully."

William Safire be damned:[1] Abolish *hopefully* improperly used as an adverb from your vocabulary. *Hopefully* means full of hope, and only that, *not* it is to be hoped, or one hopes. The Arabs have the word *inshallah* for the sense in which *hopefully* is incorrectly used, and the Spanish derived their *ojalá* from the Arab word. Use *ojalá* when you feel coming on you an urge beyond human power to resist uttering you-know-what. (When Iran quits calling us The Great Satan and quits financing half-mad terrorists to blow up our Marines, use also *inshallah*, but not before.)

BASIC GRAMMAR

You had better take care not to commit grammatical blunders from the stage, bringing shame and ridicule on yourself. But look, this is not a treatise on the correct use of the English language; there are places you can go for that. Here, I just want to point out the three blunders that, at all costs, must be avoided.

Dropping Participles

Nothing proclaims the uneducated and unsophisticated background from which a speaker hails than his dropping the participle. Almost nothing strikes the ear as uglier than this. The audience develop an itch in the recesses of the eardrum; at the root of the tongue and at the back of the jaw, muscles clench, tendons grow rigid, as the hearer awaits the very next comin' or watchin' or sayin', his whole soul silently enunciating *ing . . . eeng . . . eeen-yung*.

Raconteurs of southern or western origin, notwithstanding, may drop as many participles as they please when they are spinning a good backwoods yarn.

---

[1]He has notoriously given in on this solecism.

Personal Pronouns

Mixing up the subject and the object: *For you and I. She spoke to him and I. She and me* went to the ballpark, where a high fly hit her and then I. (It should have hit you first.) You are speaking to *whom*, not to *who*. To *whom* do you wish to address your remarks. The Lord chastiseth those *whom* He loves, *who*ever they may be. THERE IS NO EXCUSE FOR THIS DISSONANCE OF CASES.

Repeat to yourself, *he* is the subject, *him* is the object, *she* is the subject, *her* is the object. "It is *I*," not *him* (though "It's me" is acceptable). Him and me did not go to the ball game; him and me went straight to Hell, where he and I deserved richly to go for committing a mortal grammatical sin like that.

Oh, and don't try to fudge by using *himself* or *herself* or *myself*, as in "He and myself went bananas," which is the future, I promise, for anyone guilty of that solecism.

Mixing Up the Plural and the Singular

None *is* . . . unless you absolutely intend to imply that *not any are.* Which, if this be your intention, say so: Not any are. Otherwise, when you use *none*, it is natural for the hearer to assume that you mean *not one is*, not *any are*, and be left twisting in the wind, waiting for the singular case to follow. *The crowd gathered in the forum, and they shouted, Caesar, Caesar, Caesar, and when he at last appeared to it . . .* Please.

I know, *like* for *as*, *good* for *well*, *that* for *which*, and one for all: there are many other grammatical faults that plague this analphabetic age, but the three mentioned above are the very worst and among the most common. It's not too much to ask that you memorize the rules on these three grammatical niceties and rehearse yourself in them.

Sweat, Blood, Toil and Tears: Surpassing Yose'f

Read Gower or Strunk or James Jackson Kilpatrick's *The Writer's Art* for grammatical polishing (refer back to point 20 of the list in Chapter 10), which will do you immeasurable good to study at your leisure, assuming you have any. Meanwhile, strike the errors from the list of sins that you must repeatedly confess. Remember, like all grammatical faults, *they are an affectation*, they are an *acquired vice*, they are *learned*.

STYLE: JETTISONING USELESS BAGGAGE

Be simple. Be straightforward. Be yourself.

Don't try to be fancy! If the intellectual content of your talk leaves you with no recourse but to use unusual terms or complex syntax, *do your level best to reduce those terms to the vernacular and to straighten out the syntax.*

Among the most difficult concepts in this world is the ancient one of the Trinity. One can chew on this for hour after hour, yet the simple phrase, one God, three Persons, says it in a nutshell.

Meanwhile, there are syntactical addictions to avoid.

Sweat, Blood, Toil, and Tears: Surpassing Yourself

These empty expressions are the junk bonds of the English language:

Never say *the question as to whether*, say plain *whether*. Never say *there is no doubt but that*, say plain *no doubt* or *doubtless*. Never say *used for fuel purposes*, say plain *used for fuel*. Never say *he is a man who*, say plain *he*. Never say *in a hasty manner*, say plain *hastily*. Never say *this is a subject that*, say plain *this subject*. Never say *his story is a strange one*, say plain *his story is strange*.

The same goes for redundant syllables. It is not to *disássociate*; it is to *dissociate*. It's not to *disénfranchise* (as some illiterate contemporary dictionaries allow): it's to *disfranchise*. And it's, of course, *regardless*, never *irregardless*, irregardless of the low temptation you may feel to tack on a rhetorical superfluity. You do not want to get into the habit of metastasizing from simple *establishmentarianism* to *disestablishmentarianism*, and thence to *antidisestablishmentarianism*, which leads you ineluctably into *antianti*disestablishmentarianism. Were you an antianticommunist? Are you pro-choice or simply antiantipro-choice?

What this boils down to is: Don't be rhetorically pompous, be simple. And—pray, please—also—pull the plug on sententious fillers, like *the fact that*.

Just don't use that awful verbaltic. Instead of *owing to the fact that*, say *since* or *because*. Instead of *I'd like to call your attention to the fact that*, say *I'd like to remind you*. These matters may all be elementary. It nevertheless behooves every one of us to develop good quickness when we come out of the pocket . . . hopefully.

Never end a pulling of the leg with *just kidding*.

Which brings us to a subject that boils my blood: grossness from the stage, which is an act of capital discourtesy.

PROPRIETY

Gutter language belongs you guess where. It is not *macho*. It is no calibration of true toughness.

I go into this because big-time corporate executives here and there seem to have become prone to the delusion that four-letter obscenities in boardrooms and—inter alia sometimes, too—in an exhortation are big time. But though riches and industrial preeminence do not make the man, his speech can betray him. We don't need barbarians at the gates.

What shocked the nation when the Watergate tapes were first played in living rooms across the land was not so much the deed in itself, which, in the beginning at least, was in the nature of a political prank, but the coarseness and vulgarity of the highest echelons of the Nixon Administration, including the late President himself; and it earned the disdain of all America. It insulted the Oval Office; it was an indignity to the Oval Room. In short, it was a difference in class: between the gentleman and the rabble.

The Book of Sirach Chapter 27 verses 4–7 tell us:

> When a sieve is shaken, the husks appear;
>> so do a man's faults when he speaks,
> As the test of what the potter molds is in the furnace,
>> so in his conversation is the test of a man.
> The fruit of a tree shows the care it has had;
>> so too does a man's speech disclose the bent of his mind.
> Praise no man before he speaks,
>> for it is then that men are tested.[2]

---

[2]Curiously, Demosthenes (384–322) echoed these sentiments: "As a vessel is known by the sound, whether it is cracked or not, so men are proven by their speeches, whether they may be wise or foolish."

CHAPTER 14

THE DELIVERY:
PACING, TIMING AND ENERGY

PACING

Pacing is the speed at which an address is delivered.

That speed is correct which (a) is sufficiently deliberate to permit the audience to keep up with the speaker, (b) is sufficiently brisk to keep the audience alert, (c) is varied, (d) best suits the personality of the speaker.

1. Speak at a rate that you can comfortably handle.

2. It's better to be deliberate than to rush.

3. A deliberate pace (on the whole, good) is not the same as a plodding pace (bad).

4. Pause between thoughts, clauses, sentences, paragraphs, segments.

5. Vary the pace according to the content.

6. Develop your idiosyncratic cadence.

Sweat, Blood, Toil, and Tears: Surpassing Yourself

1. Speak at a rate that you can comfortably handle.

Some people suffer from a speech impediment. Others are not used to verbalizing.

Do not try to rush your speech beyond your capability of keeping it clear and crisp. Do not attempt a speed of delivery that will cause you to (a) stumble over words, (b) elide syllables, (c) swallow syllables whole (jumping from consonant to consonant with scarcely the valley of a vowel between, as in *Metnik, the German chansler*), (d) drop participles (very nearly as wicked as dropping principles), (e) slur, and (f) glottally suck in word endings, especially *verb* endings of the past tenses (as in *he was stop't* instead of *he was stó/pe/túh*, or *she abdicat't* instead of *she ab/di/catéd*).

To rev up your speed, read poetry out loud. (Do what you should have been doing since reading Chapter 12.) When you can utter *the Thessalonians* without a moment's panic between the two *the* sounds, you are doing all right.

2. It's better to be deliberate than to rush.

Heaps better. The speaker who rushes his delivery not only risks poor diction, that speaker tires his audiences out.

Audiences can become mentally breathless listening. Some people shoottheirmouthssofast, in suchunrelentingflow, that audiences quickly give up trying to keep up.

3. A deliberate pace (on the whole, good) is not the same as a plodding pace (bad).

Taking one's time is preferable always to rushing madly, but do not permit the pace to plod, the best safeguard against which is maintaining a high infusion of energy (see below).

Boring people speak boringly, which is almost always ploddingly, even when they have interesting things to say. "Did   you   know   that I   discovered   that   toe   tal   en   ergy   equals   the   squareof   the speed   of   light   times   the   mass   which   of   course   means   that mass   and   en   ergy   are   e   qui   valent   now   is   n't   that   ex   citing?"

Anyone speaking in this manner could slow light. Generally speaking, if a typewritten, double-spaced page, containing about 250 words, takes one more than a minute and a quarter to speak, one's pace is too slow.

4. Pause between thoughts, clauses, sentences, paragraphs, segments.

This requires an instinct for timing also.

In the roar of a rushing waterfall, the splat of how many individual drops of water can you hear?

Thoughts must be allowed to sink in. Speakers can be faulted for lack of imagination. They seem sometimes oblivious to how difficult it is—what a task it is, requiring more effort on the part of the audience than they are (at least initially) willing to devote—to absorb anything through the ears; the newer, the harder; the longer and more complex, ditto. That's why listening to a master orator is such a pleasure.[1] Every nuance is clear; every drop of meaning splats on the tympanum with its individual impact.

Unless there's some pathological physical reason for it, rushing in ordinary conversation is a rude expression of the ego: the speaker will be hanged if he won't have his full and complete say this minute, and don'tyoudareinterrupt. In the formal speaker, rushing defeats the whole purpose of getting up there. Resist leaping breathlessly from crag to crag, from thought to thought, from sentence to sentence. *Pause*; permit listeners to catch up. *Always keep present in your mind that though you may be addressing Nobel Laureates in Washington's Cosmos Club, they are in the aggregate obtuse.* You had might as well be speaking to a congregation of Teamsters Union goons, or to New York taxi drivers from Kurdistan, or to your teenage children. From the speaker's point of view, it is well-nigh impossible to overestimate how dumb audiences are. Speakers, on the other hand, show how dumb they can be when they fail to take into account, and allow for, the extreme difficulty we all have absorbing sense from the spoken word.

When you come to a major turn in your argument, therefore, announce it, flag your intentions to the audience. Not only alter the pitch and tone of your voice, cease vocalizing altogether—permitting a lengthy cessation of sound—prior to launching into the new course. (This is the moment for a piece of planned choreography. See Chapter 16.)

---

[1] My sister Priscilla, then managing editor of *National Review*, went to West Point to hear General Douglas MacArthur pronounce his farewell address, which was brilliantly written in MacArthur's high baroque style and delivered with his usual instinct for high drama. She said admiringly of it to me, "You could hear every comma, every semicolon, every full colon, every full stop." The punctuation dropped in like metal slugs into slots.

5. Vary the pace according to the content.

The story goes that when a startled novice discovered St. Teresa of Avila in her cell consuming a rich *perdiz podrido* on Holy Thursday, she exclaimed, "Oh, Mother Teresa, how could you!" To which (my newly favorite saint) replied, "Young lady, there's a time for penance, and there's a time for partridge. And this is a time for partridge."

There's a time for deliberation, and a time for high velocity.

When explaining a difficult intellectual concept, slow down; when speaking about a grave or sorrowful subject, slow down; when delivering statistics, slow way down (or drop them altogether).

When telling a narrative, become conversational, brisk: speed up. When delivering a whimsical aside, speed up. When generating excitement, gather velocity as you gather your energies.

When driving to the crescendo of your talk, in the gripping stillness of your passionate peroration, pull out the stops: slow to a crawl, permitting each syllable of each word to take its effect; explode, expelling the words like a toboggan whooshing and thundering down a chute; slow suddenly again, hammering on the brainpans and consciences of the audience with your most deliberate intonations; then speed pell-mell into your climax . . .

Let it all out, put it all together.[2] There's a time for penance, and a time for partridge; for fasting, and feasting. The main course of the speech should display as many variations in tone, volume, attitude, and velocity as the peroration contains in its compact statement. Keep in mind that *salsa* is the spice of life. (And if you won't take that from me, take it from a saint.)

6. Develop your idiosyncratic cadence.

Just as the gait of your walk and the sound of your voice are indisputably you, just as a writer or a painter develops a style, so, as you gain in the practice of giving talks, should you develop a cadence that defines you. (Even if only to be able to surprise your audiences occasionally by changing it.)

---

[2]Read novelist Max Byrd's description, in his novel *Jefferson*, of Patrick Henry winding into the conclusion of his famous oration before the Continental Congress—the "give me liberty, or give me death" speech. Or see pages 176–177 of *Sex, Power, and Pericles* for a summary.

Your text will partly determine the cadence; but your personality will choose the text, sieve it through your consciousness, and tinge the manner in which you deliver it. I can still hear, in my mind's memory, the cadences and mannerisms of John L. Lewis, Franklin Roosevelt, Winston Churchill, Douglas MacArthur, Walter Judd, Jack Benny, Robert Kennedy, Martin Luther King Jr., Pablo Merry del Val. They are indelible. Some are (or were) orators in the grand style, some not. I'm not referring to each their idiosyncratic accents—which, of course, impinge on the memory—but on the rhythms deriving from their speech patterns, the lilt and style of their syntax, the peculiar way in which they addressed whatever they were talking about.

There's no quick acquiring such personality: it evolves. You'll become aware of it. Never make the mistake of imitating yourself, as, say, in their prose, Hemingway and even Faulkner did upon the decline of their powers. But seek your true voice. Your peculiar cadence may one day identify you, so that your beat on the tympanum may also lodge in the mind's rich larder.

TIMING

Timing is knowing *when* to bring up a subject (or suppress it), *how* to elicit the response you desire.

The first depends on seasoning and sensitivity, the second on instinct and control. The speaker blessed with a sense of timing will almost always succeed, if for no other reason. The poor sad fella without it falls flat.

1. Check your impulsive desires, the importunate demands of your wit.

2. Exercise sensitive political judgment; never risk being too far in advance of the times. Unless you are a professional polemicist.

3. Always subordinate wit and even your notion of truth to (a) humility, (b) compassion; out of love of your neighbor, learn to respect what you cannot hold.

4. Create the anticipation of the response you want; flag your intentions.

5. Take your time, relish the moment, feed the expectation.

The first three rules address themselves to the *when*, the last two to the *how*.

Sweat, Blood, Toil, and Tears: Surpassing Yourself

1. Check your impulsive desires, the importunate demands of your wit.

Don't bring up the plumbing as the family sits down to a meal.

Don't impose your American superiority to every other race, nation, ethnic origin, power, or dominion on guests from the Third World—though it's demonstrably so. Don't bring up paedophilia in the company of Roman Catholic priests, the theory of evolution to Creationists, God Creator to astrophysicists, growth of government to New Democrats, the utter folly of the 1996–1997 GOP congressional agenda to Newt Gingrich, Don Juan Huang to Bill Clinton, Gennifer Flowers to Bill Clinton, Monica Lewinsky to Bill Clinton, or, for that matter, Hillary to Bill Clinton.

And contain the malicious eruption of wit, as evidenced in the preceding sentence, as insuppressible as it may seem.

This is difficult for the compulsively honest or (and) compulsively irreverent personality. All it requires is that I contemplate Al Gore half a second for funny, cutting, and *true* jabs to rise up in my breast, begging their expression and that brief fling of existence to which their delicious malice gives them the right. All it requires is one more pious reference to Native Americans on TV nightly news for me to desire to talk about Native Whiners, or Native Sanctimoniousness, not to mention Native American Stone Age savagery. But as a speaker, I may not, should not, do not indulge in any of these temptations.[3]

When I was a young man, I liked letting blood. I was satisfied with having gained and held the intellectual high ground. I made enemies wholesale, converts none. Now that I am an old man, I have buried the tomahawk. (Sometimes, I still gleefully, fondly imagine, in the skulls of

---

[3]Even as a writer. I have cut other jabs at political correctness in this book at the entreaty of my editor, who is too darling to disoblige.

my opponents . . . for which reversions I scold myself.) The speaker's
mission is to win the crowd: not basely, not through demagoguery and
falsehood, but through charity, tolerance, fairmindedness, goodwill,
and patient argument. Sure: The fatuousness of certain (false) accepted
attitudes needs to be pierced with a red-hot needle, allowing the pus
of deception to drain: in the interest of truth, of public sanity, of clear
thinking. But that time may not be now, this minute.

Restrain your own self-righteousness.

2. Exercise sensitive political judgment; never risk being too far in advance of the times. Unless you are a professional polemicist.

Well, I covered much of this above.

There's a time for penance, and a time for partridge; and good judgment dictates the timing.

That judgment is egregiously lacking in American society. We are
a nation of hortatory zealots and fanatics to whom common sense is as
strange as a lunar landscape. As witness the jihad against those poor
people who are addicted to nicotine or the sex education dispensed to
tots in the schools. I'm not speaking of egregiously *wrong* or hysterical
*mis*judgment, such as ACLU extremism on the rule of the First
Amendment; I'm talking about having the sense not to discourse on
graphic sex to a classroom of 6- and 7-year-olds.

The time *is* coming when blunt talk will be appropriate in
discussing a whole lot of taboo issues, but the general speaker is well
advised to claw off such reefs. Why risk alienating that sweet old lady
in the seventh row by (a) calling her a lady, (b) calling her old, (c) calling
her sweet? You are not a political polemicist, nor are you a professional
controversialist. Whatever you may believe privately, don't make fun
of religion, don't openly despise traditional sexual morality, don't bash
gays, don't ridicule Mother Teresa, don't begin to snore before Al Gore
has opened his mouth (wait a little), don't talk dirty, or be profane, or
crack blasphemous jokes, or tell about the witch doctor in Zaire who
went about lighting the faggots under the pot in which a bound Belgian
missionary was to be boiled, saying, as he smacked his lips, *"Plus ça
change, plus c'est la même chose."*

3. Always subordinate wit and even your notion of truth to (a) humility, (b) compassion; out of love of your neighbor, learn to respect what you cannot hold.

No matter how outraged you may yourself be by the wrongheadedness or ignorance of others . . . hold your tongue. Is your topic tonight the politically motivated exaggeration of the peril to straight American society of the AIDS virus? No? Then don't mention it.

Don't respond candidly to a question on the subject: say pleasantly and courteously that you understood that you were invited to talk about the morphology of the Japanese beetle. (There is the most awful tendency in the United States to assume, on the part of the audience, that anyone situated on stage or in front of a microphone is *ipso facto*, automatically, an authority on TOE.[4])

Did your boss instruct you to include a disquisition on corporate morality in your financial report? Then don't get dragged into the subject. Were you asked for your opinion of the seven CEOs of major tobacco companies who, one by one, swore before a congressional investigating committee that no way did they believe nicotine is addictive?

My opinion—who cares?—is that they should be stripped of their corporate rank, docked ten years' pay, placed in the stocks, spat upon, and pelted by rotten eggs and tomatoes. (As a prelude, of course, to being hanged, racked, drawn, and quartered by Mel Gibson, the whites of whose cornflower-blue eyes never even got bloodshot.)

But even if this is my (private) opinion, (a) I have no business vociferating it unless it is germane and necessary to the topic of my talk, and (b) my opinion itself is wicked.

Not just self-righteous. Bad. Because uncompassionate and unforgiving.

Take a harder case: the inerrancy of the Bible— in which so many good people believe—down to the exact date when the Holy Spirit breathed on the void.

In my opinion (for what it's worth: probably nothing), modern scholarship and science render such claims . . . preposterous? foolish? innocent? uneducated? stupid? Wrong and false, certainly. But is it my mission as a speaker to shake that poor old woman up, embarrass her in public, cause her grief and anxiety?

---

[4]The theory of everything, an astrophysicist dream, not to be confused with GUT, standing for grand unified theories.

Make it tougher yet. I'm a Roman Catholic. I believe in my faith wholly. It is the *true* faith. It came from Jesus in uninterrupted apostolic succession down to me and my children. Jesus is God, the second person of the Trinity, and there is no salvation without Him. I was never horrified by religious wars, as all good secularists are; I can't imagine any other justification for war. All other wars are either frivolous or venal. If the wars against Hitler and the Evil Empire hadn't been religious in nature, my allegiance could be questioned.

Consequently, I believe that orthodox Jews possess an incomplete knowledge of God and the drama of human salvation; that Protestants are heretical, Muslims infidel, nonbelievers pagan.

According to my beliefs, these people profess incomplete truths, blasphemies, idolatries, and in the case of pagans, perpetual enslavement to the Hobbesian view of life.

Untruth is evil; error is evil. In the hard sciences, error and superstition are ruthlessly stamped out. Do I call for a holy war or pogroms or dusting off the Inquisition?

No.

Am I, then, a hypocrite?

No.

Have I, then, no proper ardor for my expressed beliefs?

No.

Am I, then, one of those "cultural" Catholics, or one of those convenient Catholics—like John Kennedy, who in 1960 called a press conference solely to reassure America that his Catholic faith would in no way influence his decisions as President?

Neither: I personally despised John Kennedy from the day he made that statement, which in my book was tantamount to denying Christ.

Well, what the hell am I?

A pilgrim, a sinner, a poor wretch. Neither more nor less. We are *each* of us absolutely essential to the Lord's program for salvation, and as such, of an inestimable value. We are otherwise, and at the same time, nothing. Sanctimoniousness ill suits us, who are called upon to love and respect our fellow man because they are our brethren, because of their sacred rôle in the drama of salvation.[5]

---

[5]One of the few times her children were indignant with my mother was when she was discovered in church upon the announcement over the radio of Stalin's death, praying for his soul.

Sure, I believe it is my express duty to help knock the scales off the eyes of people who, sadly, don't believe as I believe: to explain to them the terrible error of their thinking and convert them. Implicitly, by the way I try (failing too often) to conduct my life. Expressly—if they ask me. My primary obligation is to love them and pray for them, just as I fervently pray for the salvation of my own soul and beg that they too, out of their goodness, pray for that.

Again, though my faith saturates all my thinking, *as a speaker*—unless these questions have been specifically imposed upon me—*it is not my business to proselytize*.

We have waded into deep waters with this example, but I think it has been necessary. The speaker must exercise judgment; there's a time for penance and a time for partridge.

4. Create the anticipation of the response you want; flag your intentions.

5. Take your time, relish the moment, feed the expectation.

These two tips, relating to timing as crowbar (of timing as a device for extracting, principally, mirth—as the slipping of the blade between the valves of the oyster), can be addressed together.[6]

Humor depends absolutely on timing, which means that the same instinct, sensitivity, and judgment must play their part as when making the rapid decision whether to broach delicate questions or permit oneself certain quips.

The blunder is to smile or laugh before the folk out there smile or laugh. Few sensations can be so excruciating (or so lonely) as to slap one's sides gasping at one's inspired sally, only to find the audience staring at one in stony silence. That's like being seated between a Minnesotan and a South Dakotan at a reading of Mark Twain.

How to provoke an audience into responsive smiles or foot-stomping guffaws is a matter not so much reflecting the intrinsic humor of the remark as the sly timing with which it has been uttered. The

---

[6] I crib here from *Sex, Power, and Pericles*.

stock exemplar is Jack Benny in his most famous routine. A masked mugger thrusts a revolver into Benny's ribs, demanding, "Your money or your life!" Benny considers this, permitting his chin to bob on an invisible cushion of air as he revolves his head to face the audience, lips clamped prissily, a faint humming sound issuing from his chest.

Seconds pass. The mugger jambs the muzzle once more into Benny's side and shouts, "Didn't you hear me? Your money or your life!" To which Benny responds in his high, whiny voice, "I'm *thinking*, I'm *thinking!*"

Bringing down the house time after time, dozens and dozens of times. It wasn't the lines, which audiences spanning two generations had heard since the days of a crackling RCA radio set in the kitchen, it was the total composure and deliberation of Jack Benny's delivery.

His timing. He was a master of it. All his acts were primarily a matter of timing. Groucho Marx's cracks were mostly awful puns. It was his timing that made them hilarious: the tapping of the ashes off his cigar, the wild rolling of his eyes.

Have fun watching reruns of *I Love Lucy*, Bob Newhart's early shows,[7] Sid Caesar and Imogene Coca, episodes of *Gilligan's Island* and *Three's Company* . . . and, of course, the incomparable *Seinfeld*. All these master comedians rely on exquisite timing for the hilarity of their effects. The secret is to "flag" the imminence of a shaft of wit or a one-liner. By the foxy look, the shimmer of amusement (or dumbfoundment) on the lips, the pause whose every second of delayed response brings gales of laughter from the audience (who know what that response inevitably has got to be), or the drawled word kept in suspended animation—before completing the unexpected statement, delivering the punch line. The audience must be let into what is coming. *As in the art of persuasion, the speaker permits the audience to identify themselves with his act and participate in it*. The audience must begin to savor the humor before a syllable of it is pronounced. The speaker's pacing of his words should slow down, the voice go dry. A cunning, malicious, *reluctant* grin should be displayed at that critical instant when the audience are just beginning to apprehend the witti-

---

[7]Newhart's unsurpassable television interview, for example, when he plays the rôle of a psychiatrist being sizzled by a venom-filled blonde interviewer on a Chicago morning show: I have watched this skit now 56 times over the past 56 months, and I still howl with laughter. Newhart's eyeballs alone are a lesson.

cism but have not yet surrendered themselves to it. Or the expression of the face should go deadpan at the moment of delivery, and then feign surprise that the audience are laughing, conveying bewilderment ("Did I say something funny? Will someone let me in on it?"). This can intensify the laughter.

Some speakers are able to widen their eyes in exaggerated innocence, or waggle their eyebrows or their ears, thus coaxing the appropriate response out of that dumb beast facing them. A Bob Hopian leer will do. The witticism itself must be delivered distinctly—with an absurd, precise distinctness. Each separate syllable. And if the witticism is world-class, it can be repeated after the first roar of laughter rolls through the audience and subsides, in a wry manner, or with candid relish: which will elicit a second round of laughter. (Master raconteurs never fail to repeat their punch lines, extracting ever more juice from them.)

Study these comedians. The audience are a fish on the line; the speaker must be an expert angler. The essential thing in humor is to develop patience, the faculty for exhibiting total composure while keeping the audience in suspense. Timing is the key ingredient.

ENERGY

Nothing happens without it.

The speaker must expend energy. He must inject every word, every gesticulation, every movement of his body with energy. He must fill his moments of seeming calm, or withdrawal, or even ostensible rest with suppressed energy, energy that sizzles, energy that creates that tumbling current of ergs[8] flowing from the speaker to the audience and back. They must become two naked hot wires put in contact.

The catalyst must be the speaker. The audience are under no obligation to listen to him, much less heed him. It is *his* task to rouse them from their lethargy. For this reason, one must first rouse oneself, intellectually and emotionally. This requires that one has discovered something interesting and maybe even important to say. *If you can't ignite your own interest in your talk, it's bound to fail.* If you can't give that

---

[8] —like microscopic high-speed 9-mm copper-sheathed bullets—

same talk ten, twenty, even a hundred times and *still* be intellectually and emotionally excited about it,[9] then you cannot hope to succeed.

1. Before the performance, the speaker must psyche himself into giving it all he's got.

2. The speaker must never permit himself truly to relax, not for an instant.

3. The speaker must guard fiercely against any distraction conducive to a leak in his reserves of energy, a slackening in his resolve.

4. The speaker must sweat from the effort of his performance; he must end elated, moody, bone-tired.

I don't feel that any of these four prescriptions requires individual comment.

The speaker is the seeker, the yearner, the supplicator. He is also the predator. He must seize his prey by the throat. He must approach his task with all the patience and all the fierce tingling concentration of a leopard beginning its stalk. If he has not sweated, if he is not thoroughly wrung out at the conclusion of his performance, he has failed . . .

To grapple. To contend. To expend energy.

Anyone who doubts a word of the above will give dull talks, leaving audiences cold.

---

[9]—because it is intellectually wanting—

C H A P T E R   1 5

FACIAL EXPRESSIONS, GESTICULATIONS, BODY LANGUAGE

INTRODUCTION[1]

We tell our students at the School that audiences do not so much listen to speakers as read them, which is why facial expressions, gesticulations, and body language (or eurythmics) are so crucially important.

Even in the age of heavy metal rock and boomboxes, literate societies are more accustomed to absorbing information through the eyes than through the ears or other senses. Vision is the primary sense. Vision is what alerts all living creatures to danger, food, drink. The human eye is biologically incredibly elaborated and informs the neocortex of a vast array of information.

A recent study showed that only 7 percent of any message about our feelings and attitudes comes from the words we use, 38 percent from our voice, and a startling 55 percent from facial expressions and body language. (How they determine these matters is beyond me, but there it is.) *U.S. News & World Report*[2] tells us that "Though we think of sensory abilities as independent, researchers are finding that each

---

[1]Much of what follows is stolen from both *Speaking in Public* and *Sex, Power, and Pericles*.
[2]January 13 , 1997.

sense receives help from the others in apprehending the world. Unconsciously, the eyes of listeners flick everywhere, searching out visual clues. Given the chance, the article reported, "the brain integrates visual clues while processing language."

Acoustics are muffled by human bodies, clothing, draperies, the upholstery of seats. They are distorted by feedback and competing sounds—traffic outside, buzzing murmurs and coughs in the audience. Beyond the fifth or sixth row, individual words can become indistinct. Beyond the fifteenth or twentieth row, they may be virtually indecipherable. Watch people as they listen; see how active their eyes are, constantly flicking from one part of the speaker's physiognomy to another. They are lip-reading, virtually. They are absorbing the sense of what he is saying by construing from his attitude of body, his gestures, and the clues that stream across his face. Deny audiences these aids and you deny them comprehension of what you are saying.

FACIAL EXPRESSIONS

If your descent is Irish, Welsh, Spanish, Italian, French, Austrian, Hungarian, Polish, Rumanian, Jewish, or African, you are blessed. Your problem will be to tone down the vivacity of your mug.

But if your descent is English, German, Slav, American Indian, or Protestant, you must be concerned. You may be emoting, but that's probably not apparent, and if the audience cannot see plainly on your face what you are feeling, whatever your emotional state may be privately won't show, wherefore won't communicate. The ridiculous lurks in the deadpan expression, which is fine if you are Jack Benny saying something droll, but not good if you are petitioning, describing the horrors of a famine. *You must liven up your physiognomy, else you will deaden down your audience.*

Practice what you are going to preach into a mirror. Professor Paul L. Soper puts it well in his *Basic Public Speaking*:

> [This] is indispensable to your knowing what your face does as you speak. Study it. What do the eyebrows and forehead do? If frowning wrinkles appear, iron them out [not always, see below]; if your brows are pulled down into a scowl, relax them

[ditto]. Perhaps most important, does your face do nothing at all as you speak? If you are a "deadpan" speaker, practice to relax and lift the muscles about the mouth and cheeks. Experiment in delivering sentences expressing various emotions: sorrow, joy, anger, curiosity, and so on.

Sweat, Blood, Toil, and Tears: Surpassing Yourself

Discover what is your natural, most relaxed expression. Should it be too cloying, or coy, or offensive, or too gloomy, or too stupidly cheerful, or vacuous, modulate it. If you *wish* to frown, because a frown is appropriate (expressing your concern, or your disapprobation), do, by all means, wrinkle up the eyebrows. If you wish to *scowl*, do so also, when a scowl is expressive of the sense. *Never assume an expression that is out of character for you.* A smirk accompanying Alan Greenspan's latest admonition about speculative fever on the stock market would quite undo his professional affinity for gloom and doom; a totally serious mien on Seinfeld shocks. Use body language appropriate to each expression. For instance, if you have a happy thought to communicate, smile, rise up on your toes, lift your arms and shoulders.

Some people need to be physically reacquainted with their faces. It's as though they suffered terrible burns in childhood and scar tissue has accumulated on their foreheads, cheeks, and the corners of their eyes and mouths; it's as though they are like bears, which are expressionless (and therefore doubly dangerous) because they are deprived of the underlying muscles permitting expression. And sometimes people deprive their faces of feeling for social and professional reasons: the imperturbable field marshal in the Pomeranian Junker tradition, who squeezes down on the naked glass rim of his monocle to avoid betraying the slightest emotion when he is told that his only son was killed in the attack he has just ordered; the Englishman who was taught at Eton that a display of emotions is unmanly; the CEO who believes it compromises his authority to permit human feelings (especially the kinder ones, such as benevolence or humor) to surface.

There is a place for the iron visage . . . but it is not on the podium. One should gaze at oneself in the mirror not only to rediscover one's natural expression but also to diversify it. Put your hands to your face.

Pinch the cheeks; knead them until they show red. Hook index fingers to the corners of your mouth and pull them wide. Squinch and winch into the mirror. *Feel* the muscles there. Wiggle your ears, if you're able. Practice lifting both eyebrows, then a single eyebrow (not easy). Practice quivering the upper lip (to foreshadow pleasure, approbation, or humor), or one half of the upper lip (to express disdain, disgust). Try drawing the whole scalp back (for astonishment). When arching the eyebrows and consequently corrugating the forehead, first smile . . . then slowly pull the corners of your mouth down; see how totally and astonishingly your expression changes from surprise or delight to disapproval. By widening or narrowing your eyes, intensify these expressions.

An impassive countenance knells death to attention. Attempt smiles that convey amusement, bemusement (there's a tough one), genuine frivolity, a touch of wickedness. Harden your heart next, allowing your lower face to portray anger, frustration, indignation, and so forth. Jut your jaw forth doggedly; shake your head like a mastiff. You'll notice something by this time: *Your facial expression, to be successful, will depend upon your actual feelings.* You must summon inside your breast the appropriate feeling in order facially to express it.

The speaker must keep this foremost in mind: The intensity of his interest in what he is saying must be reflected in his whole attitude and mien, but intensity as sole expression is neither sufficient nor always a good thing. Just as a silk-skinned thoroughbred shivers all over with pleasure at a touch, so the face of the speaker must reflect every nuance of meaning and feeling in his text. His face should be so sensitive that these nuances are in perpetual permutation across his countenance, and so faithfully defined that they can be read by the audience. Richard Burton had a magnificent voice before drink and debauchery destroyed it, but never would he have rivaled Lawrence Olivier on the boards. Burton's face was stolid and suety, the face of a butcher; over the face of Olivier a vagrant thought or emotion traced its passage as subtly and as evanescently as a subatomic particle on a spectrograph. Yet the fleeting ghost of expression alerts the audience that Hamlet is in a mood to jest with his friends, or to take regicidal revenge on his uncle, or to skewer Polonius—or cruelly to drive Ophelia insane. That's the mastery of facial expression that speakers should strive for.

<u>A note on smiles</u>: The dour or forbidding or severe personality must smile on occasion. The friendly person must make sure that her or his smile neither prolongs itself into a simper, nor degenerates into a smirk, nor transmogrifies, for hanging around too long, into something vapid and silly. The single major technical fault in President Clinton's delivery is the persistence and, on occasion, radical inappropriateness of his half-smile.[3] Rapport needs to be established, sure, but too naked a desire to ingratiate oneself is unworthy of an orator. It is contemptible in an orator; it is proper to hucksters of the lowest rank, slugs, skinks, and other slimy creatures found under rocks. Give a good, broad, heartfelt smile; let it flash brilliantly to warm your audience; then turn it off!

GESTICULATIONS

Communication between earliest hominids probably relied as much on the intelligence conveyed by hands and arms as on grunts.

The speaker who neglects to get these appendages into the act denies the audience the most vivid aid to understanding at his disposal. Incessant and meaningless agitations, on the other hand, irritate.

This subject divides into five parts: (1) what one must do, (2) what one must avoid doing, (3) what not to do with the hands when one is doing nothing with them, (4) differences between the sexes, and (5) sophistication. Before getting into any of that, however, here's a simple recommendation that will do wonders for your *ability* to gesticulate and your *willingness* to do so: *play charades*.

Or The Game, as charades are sometimes called. With your family, friends. No pastime is so useful in this matter. Using hands, arms, body, and facial expressions, you must mime the sense of the quotation (or whatever is assigned to you), transmitting it to your teammates without uttering an intelligible sound. Inasmuch as you are racing against the clock, there's an intensity to the game that compels a person to hurl body and soul into the purpose, producing sometimes inspired acting out of the meaning. And it's fun. Play charades . . . meanwhile keeping in mind the following:

---

[3]Mr. Clinton's isn't a glazed blue-eyed exophthalmic rictus—the dazzling idiot's grin made famous by Jimmy Carter, which caricaturists derived so much (cruel) pleasure from. No, his comes across as a kind of winsome, juvenile appeal for tolerance and affection that undermines his authority and can be offensive when he is commenting on a disastrous flooding of the Red River or the loss of life and havoc caused by a tornado.

What One Must Do

There are five constituents to the telling use of one's hands on which most everybody agrees:

1. Gestures must arise from the emotions.

2. Gestures must conform to the person's individuality.

3. Gestures must be timed to synchronize with the sense of what one is saying.

4. Gestures must be broad and readily interpreted by the audience (graphic) yet disciplined.

5. Gestures must be appropriate to the time, the place, and the message.

Sweat, Blood, Toil, and Tears: Surpassing Yourself

1. Gestures must arise from the emotions.

Genesis occurred, physicists speculate, because a kind of primeval urge *to be* moved in the insensate heart of nothingness.[4]

Speculations during the early 1920s by the Russian physicist Alexander Friedmann, following on Albert Einstein's special (1905) and general (1916) theories of relativity, implied (Friedmann did not seem to be aware of it) that matter began from a state of infinite compression. Call it a Zeus-sized headache, from which sprang all that is; because from it was inferred what Fred Hoyle dubbed the "big bang."

In analogous fashion should gestures be generated: from a gut-ache to carve meaning out of the void.

Gestures must therefore arise out of the emotions, out of the intellectual tension that throbs at the temples of the speaker when he is himself immersed in his topic. They must be generated, and come fully to flower, simultaneously with the emphasis or rise in pitch of the voice, reflecting that intensity. The entire body (read *will*) must be put behind a gesture, following through just as it must follow through with a swing

---

[4]They agree with Christians on this point: *ex nihilo*, something. Christians explain this mystery as that of the Holy Spirit breathing upon the void. That majority of physicists who are nonbelievers wiggle and squirm, but no matter how brilliant and inspired their stupefying delving into origins, wondrously explicating for us the mechanisms of the universe back billions of years *to within one second of the "big bang*," the essential will that operated on the void—that fluctuation in the vacuum, as it has been called—resists their reductions.

or a punch. When the voice rises, the tendency will be for the heels to lift slightly and the torso to thrust forward. When voice (and the concomitant emotion or intensity) drops in energy, the body will tend to slump, the heels to descend to the floor, and a step backward to be taken.

In your mind, sound out the word *eu*-ryth-*mics*.[5] That's the completed gesture, from initiation to end.

Remember, don't be static on stage. Don't lightly (or lazily) ignore opportunities to render what you say visually palpable to the audience. But unless the urge develops from the depths, refrain, because you won't do the opportunity justice.

2. Gestures must conform to the person's individuality.

Gestures will vary depending on personality type.

The restrained temperament may employ few gestures (too few gestures), and these will be precise (too precise). It is incongruous for a person of this type to thrash around from the lectern like Kramer bursting through Seinfeld's apartment door.

On the other hand, in a disciplined speaker, as in a disciplined actor, the extravagant gesture at a suitably climactic moment can have extraordinary effect. Recall Sir Lawrence Olivier's black-and-white film version of *Hamlet* (1948), when, utterly alone in a chamber off the cloister of the castle, he suddenly thrusts both arms above his head and shrieks, "The *play's* the thing / Wherein I'll catch the conscience of the *king*"—spinning like a dervish the while, hooting the last word so that it sounded like the wail of a locomotive. It startled. It shocked. But it worked.

This is a daring prescription. One may have to boast the histrionic talents of an Olivier so to do violence to the temperament to which one belongs. On the whole, people best execute gestures natural to them, developing a repertoire from which to draw.

3. Gestures must be timed to synchronize with the sense of what one is saying.

One doesn't shout at a friend across the street, "Hi, Fred!"—and only then wave one's hand at him. It looks as foolish and awkward on the

---

[5]*Eurythmics*: expressing bodily movements usually coordinated with improvised music. Merriam-Webster.

platform for the complementing gesture to lag behind or by too great an interval to anticipate the sense of what one is saying.

Incongruity results also if the gesture isn't consonant with the emotional pitch of the message. That is, one doesn't pound the lectern when suggesting that maybe a compromise is in order, nor shrug one's shoulders when petitioning Congress for a declaration of war.

4. Gestures must be broad and readily interpreted by the audience (graphic) yet disciplined.

Are you able to *describe* a circle, *square* a box, *swim* like a fish, or *beard* a lion in its den? (To do the latter, you raise one hand, *grasp* the lion by the tussock of whiskers sprouting from its lower chin, give a good *yank down*, then *yank it hard toward you* as you *lean forward* into its muzzle, all the while *glaring* into its ferocious eyes.)

Gestures must illustrate, they must be graphic. They should, ideally, tell the tale almost independently of your utterances, which is why they should be practiced before a mirror until one has become accomplished in their execution.

Yet . . . practice restraint (for more on which, see below). Suit use of the hands to the words; use them purposefully, and unless one is in the business of tripping the consciences of kings, *sans* exaggeration. Speakers who windmill nonstop from the lectern tire audiences. Let the digital extremities be when there's no need to emphasize a point; let them fall as naturally as possible to the sides, or grasp them behind you, or cock them on either side of the waist, or hook one thumb in the belt (never both, and *never* a thumb in the armpit of a waistcoat), or even place them on the lectern a little while.

Do not, however anent this last position, succumb to the habit of leaning into the lectern thus held, every so often flicking the spread fingers of left or right hand out to the sides, like a bird stretching its wings. This can drive an audience nuts.

5. Gestures must be appropriate to the time, the place, and the message.

A gesture may fit one occasion, not another.

Older people prefer parsimony in gestures: they don't like to be lectured to, and too much hand-flinging about in their faces irritates them. (Think of Robert Young.) Children, on the other hand, respond to enthusiasm, the more exaggerated the better. (Think of Danny Kaye.)

Full-blown gestures are out of proportion in a small room, and before an intimate audience. But caution: The subtle gesture—that slight lifting of a single eyebrow, or that fastidious, disapproving twitch of the upper lip—won't do in an auditorium. It passes unobserved; it is as though lapped up by space. The energy of one's gestures, moreover, should be determined by the power of the voice. A weak voice accompanying a strong gesture is like a high voice piping out of a big man.

Keep always in mind that incessant chatter by the hands is a bane. Watch José Ferrer's *Cyrano de Bergerac*, particularly in the scene where he is baiting the fellow who made rude remarks about his nose (they cost him dear). The gestures are both sculptural and exquisite. Sufficiency and eloquence are equally demanded of the speaker. Recall Burt Lancaster in the film version of *The Leopard*. Playing the prince, Lancaster receives a letter from a butler, who holds to his master a silver platter. In an explosion of unexampled arrogance, Lancaster lifts the envelope from the platter and, giving a forceful downward thrust of dismissal with that one hand, manages somehow to tear the missive inside the envelope out, coming up with it open as the envelope slips to the floor. The entire character of the prince was contained in that awesome dismissal.

What One Must Avoid Doing

There are bad habits of which speakers are often unconscious that undermine the purpose of gestures while irritating the audience.

1. Wagging or jabbing the index finger at the audience.
2. Pumping one or both hands at the audience, often repetitively.
3. Keeping the elbows clamped to the ribs, gesturing solely with the forearms.
4. Keeping the hands at the top of the tummy, or second-shirt-button level.
5. Keeping the hands at belt-buckle level, or lower.

6. Gesturing sideways from these positions—permitting the hands to, as it were, fly apart and then snap back toward each other, as though attached by an elastic band.

7. Gesturing at or slightly beneath the level of the shelf of the lectern.

8. Gesturing at the level of the thighs.

9. Gesticulating with one hand and arm only, or alternately— first with the right hand and arm, then with the left.

10. Falling into the habit of the Dread Tick-Off Gesture.

Most of these faults require little comment. One common denominator characterizes them all: The hands are neither truly at rest nor doing anything. They're simply discharging nerves.

Sweat, Blood, Toil, and Tears: Surpassing Yourself

1. Wagging or jabbing the index finger at the audience.

The pedagogical index finger is hortatory, arrogant, and condescending. Nobody likes it.

It *may*—rarely—be used as a grave admonition or as a threat.

2. Pumping one or both hands at the audience, often repetitively.

Women fall into this infuriating habit more often than men. The hands are usually paired, fingers extended, clamped together, and whacking at the audience.

Duh-duh, duh-duh, duh-duh, duh-duh, the hands emphasize each word issuing out of the speaker's mouth, successive percussions. (When resorted to with extreme moderation, at exactly the right moment, this can be effective.)

3. Keeping the elbows clamped to the ribs, gesturing solely with the forearms.

It looks as though the upper arms are glued to the speaker's sides. All gestures thus made are perfunctory, nondescriptive, and ineffectual.

Liberate your elbows. (Free yourself of inhibitions.) Lift the full length of your arms from the sides. Reach with them well above your head, elbows sprung wide at ear level—to get the hang of how properly to talk with your hands. (Playing charades liberates the arms in no time flat.)

4. Keeping the hands at the top of the tummy, or second-shirt-button level.

5. Keeping the hands at belt-buckle level, or lower.

6. Gesturing sideways from these positions—permitting the hands to, as it were, fly apart and then snap back toward each other, as though attached by an elastic band.

The hands are generally paired in these positions, to which they return after brief and meaningless forays to the sides, the forearms becoming doors, flapping or swinging on the hinges of the elbows—opening and closing, opening and closing. Or the hands clasp each other with fingers interlaced, as though holding the belly in; or clap together in the fashion of Oriental petitioners; or worry each other, as though the speaker is seeking to dry them under one of those hot air blowers in public restrooms; or one hand obscenely milks the extended index finger of the other.

All these habits distract and annoy.

7. Gesturing at or slightly beneath the level of the shelf of the lectern.

Whatever the hands may be doing (which is little) is obscured. The movements pop or whisk out at the audience and then whisk back out of view. This exasperates.

8. Gesturing at the level of the thighs.

Again, audiences get glimpses only of whatever the hands may be doing. If the lectern is one of those monstrosities resembling upright coffins, the gestures can't be seen at all. The hands are doing little in any case. They are mostly twitching, discharging ergs. Audiences become disgusted.

9. Gesticulating with one hand and arm only, or alternately—first with the right hand and arm, then with the left.

In the first instance, audiences wonder whether the unused arm, which often dangles down the side, as though loosely attached to the shoulder, has been disabled. In the second instance, a metronomic effect is produced; the speaker resembles a windup toy soldier.

10. Falling into the habit of the Dread Tick-Off Gesture.[6]

This is typical of TV hucksters: ". . . and you get thermostatic temp control, remote door locks, dual airbags, ABS brakes, 4-wheel independent suspension, a full set of rubber tires, a steering wheel, a roof, a dashboard, a rearview mirror, and windshield wipers, all for the amazing low price of a second mortgage on your house . . ."

It's endemic. It's awful. It is one of the worst sins of the apprentice speaker. Sportscasters, for some reason, are peculiarly tempted.

What Not to Do with the Hands When One Is Doing Nothing with Them

To be avoided are several default carriages:

1. *The Buck-Toothed Bunny Rabbit*, or *Chipmunk Position* (Hands clasped at sternum level.)

2. *The Parade Rest*, or *House of Windsor Position* (Hands clasped behind the back. Watch out! Elbows may tend to dig into the ribcage, inducing hyperventilation.)

3. *The Fig Leaf Position* (Hands clasped as though protecting the crotch—adopted by Adam and Eve when they discovered the concupiscence that lies coiled like a serpent in the heart of existence . . . *The Flapping Fig Leaf Variation* can be obscene.)

---

[6] There are several variations. One is tapping the pinky of one hand with the index finger of the other . . . proceeding to tap the other fingers as one verbally ticks off points. Or grabbing and tugging on the fingers of one hand, starting with the index finger. And so forth.

4. *The Praying (Mantis) Position* (Fingertips touching in sublime satisfaction at having consumed one's mate or having established exclusive communication with one's Creator.)

5. *The Nixon/Bush/Clinton* Faux *Macho Fist* (Fingers curled in and tightly clenched, thumb protruding at the top, which can seem threatening or hostile to the audience when men do it, but which more often makes the speaker look foolish.)

Differences between the Sexes

The sexes do differ in the matter of gesticulations.

Men, when they gesture, should always, always present their palms toward the audience, fingers spread wide. If they happen to possess handsome, broad, sinewy, virile hands, so much the better. Men should *never* thrust one or both hands into trouser pockets (the audience may wonder whether they are seeking to reassure themselves about something), but . . .

Women, particularly if they are dressed in a pleated skirt, may do so: it can give them a wonderful air.

More about Women

1. Some women permit their hands to dangle close to the tops of the legs, touching their upper thighs. Don't.

2. Women with beautiful hands and elegant arms should display these attributes generously when they first take to the stage as speakers, but frugally as they gain in maturity on the stage (see below).

3. Women innately have the ability to do magical things with their hands and arms, and they should take advantage of that . . . while always observing the rules of grace, discipline, and *mésure*.

Back in the 1960s, I had the good fortune to get to know well Pastora Imperio, maybe the most sensational female dancer in the history of Flamenco. She was the intimate friend of Arturo Rubenstein, mistress (it was bruited) of King Alfonso XIII of Spain, and married to one of the great matadors of his time, El Gallo.[7]

In her time, Pastora scandalized all Madrid. As uninhibited as she was flamboyant, she was the first female dancer to dare to lift her arms above the head, exposing the seductive, gleaming, scented, convex mounds of the pits. Yet she was herself scandalized by a crop of young women dancers who, she said, flouted Flamenco traditions, wagging their behinds outrageously, flaunting their satin-sheathed pelvises . . . wicked enough, but what incensed her most was their lascivious use of the hands, which she denounced as vulgar and improper. At lunch one day in my flat, she became vehement, saying of "La Chunga" and other '60s, liberated-generation stars, "The *sinvergüenzas* [shameless ones] know nothing, nothing! They possess not a shred of elegance or art. It is not the *sex* that one sells from the *tabla'o*; it is the *illusion* of love, of dalliance, of amorous abandon. They lift their arms without an idea what to do with them except to twist them this way and that, *permitting the hands to fall forward and hang from the wrists*! That's not how it's done!"

She was then in her late seventies, and corpulent. But unable to contain herself, she hissed under her breath, "*Verás!*"—and plucking up a long-stemmed crystal tumbler of ice water by its round base, she shoved her chair back from the table, rising majestically to her feet— snapping the third finger and thumb of her free hand in the cadence of a Fandango de Huelva that her granddaughters (also dancers) picked up with sharp, high rappings of the four fingers of their right hands flat against the palms of their left hands, producing that staccato gypsy accompaniment that snaps against the eardrums like bullets ripping through the sonic barrier—she, meantime, humming the melody to herself, toes and heels rapping the floor in a brick-breaking descant, black eyes flashing, wide hips and buttocks suddenly voluptuous as, reaching down to twitch the hem of her black skirt above fat knees, she went shuffling along the table toward her son-in-law at the other end, those famous arms with their marbled flesh now lifting to the insistent rhythm, higher, higher, elbows bent forward and out from her head,

---

[7]Her two grandsons—Curro especially—bore a striking resemblance to the late Don Alfonso de Borbón, elder son of Don Jaime, eldest of the sons of King Alfonso XIII. (A sad, gentle soul, Don Alfonso was brutally decapitated in an accident at Vail, fourteen years ago.)

hands drawn close above tightly bunned black hair—languidly inter-
twining them in patterns as intricate as the coiling of a wisteria vine—
turning sharply and shuffling back toward the head of the table, where
I sat, rotating those pudgy little hands as though they rested on gimbals,
one hand continuing to support the goblet *by its base*, finishing right up
close to my chair, gazing down at me with the lewd, amused, knowing
smile of a practiced *grisette*. As suddenly as she had begun, she ceased,
presenting me with that crystal goblet, not a drop of its water spilled.

The old lady slumped back down into her chair, wheezing at me,
"*That's* the way it should be done, without sacrificing dignity or decency
or respect for the public!"

Women's hands on stage should be kept palm up always, as though
cupping rose petals speckled by the fresh dew of dawn.

Sophistication

What follows is difficult stuff. It applies equally to men and women.

As the speaker advances in skill, she learns how to communicate
essential information by hands and arms alone. If one speaks of the *ebb
and flow* of an ocean swell, using the flat plane of one hand to mimic
this perpetual, rhythmic motion, the vocalization should accompany the
hand: "*ebb*" (gesture) "*and flow*" (continued gesture). And any gesticulation of this kind, describing motion, size (big beach ball), shape
(triangle), vector (soaring budget deficit), or direction (plummeting
economy), should be gazed at by the advanced speaker *while* she
is executing the gesture. The speaker's eyes should study the beach ball
in her hands, her eyebrows should lift at the zooming deficit, she should
stare disapprovingly—frowning—at the declining economy. (This
concentrates the audience's attention on the graphic simulation,
implanting the idea—the text—in their minds.)

Another example: When saying, "He went that-a-way," the left
forearm and hand might flick back from the elbow, over the left
shoulder; the speaker's eyes should (briefly) follow that indicated direction, face turning (slightly) in the direction the fellow went. Such
miming shouldn't be tried too often.

The master—the orator—need not speak at all when executing a
particularly graphic and well-conceived gesture, vocalizing only when it
is done or nearly done. The minds of the audience anticipate what the

eyes see and what the ears, following the visual intelligence, hear. In cognitive effect, this is tantamount to repeating something three times. *The inexperienced speaker* must practice his graphics and remember to use them. *The advanced speaker* must draw attention to them occasionally by himself gazing at them, thus encouraging the audience to gaze at them and absorb their message. *The mature orator*, however, confident of the precision and sufficiency of his gestures, and having established total dominion over the audience through the intensity of his eye contact, *normally* should maintain visual contact with the audience while gesturing, *rarely* averting his eyes from them, permitting his hands and arms to be eloquent on his behalf.

This is mastery—Burt Lancaster as the prince in *The Leopard*. The merely competent apprentice speaker dare not relinquish eye contact with the audience, not for an instant. The advanced speaker and the orator may: to render all the more graphic the conceptualization of an important point or image. This is not the prescription for every gesture, nor for every man jack or woman who mounts the podium. Passion and art can transform an old lady, briefly, into the smoldering gypsy beauty of her youth; dominance and restraint are at the core of that art. The excess that one does not permit oneself is suggested by the discipline that one imposes on oneself. That tension defines the art.

BODY LANGUAGE

One must throw oneself heart and soul and *body* into the performance.
. . . As in charades . . . whether one likes to or not.

Hey, you protest, I'm no actor, and I don't intend to become one. Hey, retort I, *tant pis*, you bloody well will acquire attributes of the thespian art, assuming—I'm assuming—you are serious about expounding and winning acceptance for your ideas. If you are merely a dilettante, I—we, the audience—have no further use for you.

It's no good to be diffident or reserved. (One aspires to the *art* of being spiritually detached from what one is doing, in the sense of maintaining one's spiritual independence, but one does not get there until one has subjugated all the kinetic energy of the body to service— expressing the ideas of the mind and soul.) The stiff (and remote) speaker at the supper table or on stage will chill, alienate, and even offend audiences. Nobody warms to a wooden performer. Certainly that speaker will bore audiences, because the undemonstrative body, unwilling to play the game, almost certainly will end up chilling and stiffening hands and facial expression, voice too.

1. Practice loosening up the torso.

2. Limber up the waist.

3. Master the art of shrugging.

4. Learn how to draw the shoulders close together from the intensity of one's feelings.

5. Learn how to crouch from that intensity.

6. Practice shrugging, drawing the shoulders together, and crouching, simultaneously or in quick succession.

7. Practice stalking the audience's attention.

8. Expand the lungs with hope, gladness, joy, triumph.

Sweat, Blood, Toil, and Tears: Surpassing Yourself

1. Practice loosening up the torso.

Become reacquainted with your body.

It's not a bad idea to stretch mightily a few minutes before stepping on stage, if given the opportunity. Grasp the right wrist in the left hand, pull and stretch hard; relax; then grasp the left wrist in the right hand, pull and stretch hard. Breathe deeply several times, expelling the breath the way bulls do, with a *huff!* Swing your arms from the socket, as though you hold a tennis racket or a baseball bat. *Lift and revolve the shoulders.* Get the *feel* of them. Swivel the head on its neck—right, left. A few isothermic exercises aren't a bad idea, either: the fist pushing into the opposing force of the receiving palm, stiffening the bicep. Moderately. A few deep kneebends.

2. Limber up the waist.

Most of the energy associated with body language comes from the waist up.

Clasp your waist and rotate the upper body, to the right and then to the left, leaning well forward as you do so, leaning way out to the sides, less so to the rear. The older and more out of shape you are, the more advisable this exercise becomes. You are not limbering up for a footrace or a pole vault; don't overexert yourself. But gently do remind yourself of the physical body you inhabit—with the intention of making use of it to help project your ideas.

3. Master the art of shrugging.

Just as a surprising number of actors don't know how to sneeze on stage, so a surprising number of people don't know the first thing about shrugging.

Lift those shoulders up and down, first one, then the other, then both. Raise and expand the diaphragm with each shrug. It's a pleasurable sensation. There are barely discernable, subtle shrugs; there are enormous, exaggerated shrugs—in which the whole body participates, a sigh of contentment escaping.

The point is: Shrugs, in conjunction with facial expressions— eyebrows lifted, forehead rolling up—convey attitudes and emotions. Practice, shrugging, these feelings: disdain, dismissal, faintest approbation, resignation, heaving consent, enthusiastic acceptance. Watch yourself in a looking glass until you convey the intended sentiment.

4. Learn how to draw the shoulders close together from the intensity of one's feelings.

Both shoulders should push forward from the axis of the chest and toward each other.

The body bends forward from the waist. The upper spine stretches in this movement, and cords of muscle on the sides of the neck tighten, as do the triceps. (The arms are usually bent at the elbow, hands outstretched.) A frown generally deepens ruts on the forehead. The eyes widen and pain at the inside corners as the brows screw together, and the skin of the facial mask from the bridge of the nose upward rises tightly. The arms may begin to tremble. All depends on the depth and urgency of one's feelings.

Practice this before a mirror. One is drawing one's feelings up from the gut. I place their physical origin in the region just above my pelvis; the lateral muscles there swell and grow taut. Others may locate the welling of intensity elsewhere.

5. Learn how to crouch from that intensity.

I mentioned that the upper body bends forward. The knees must also bend, the weight of the body favoring the balls and toes of the feet.

This is histrionic, but when high emotion needs to be conveyed, the speaker must respond. The crouch is almost predatory. It is feral. It must be anguished. Use that mirror!

6. Practice shrugging, drawing the shoulders together, and crouching, simultaneously or in quick succession.

This combination of body attitudes can inject spellbinding dynamism into the performance.

Body thus getting into the act, the speaker is playing the audience as an angler plays the fish. The better one gets at doing this, the more closely does one get to reeling in the catch.

7. Practice stalking the audience's attention.

One accomplishes this by a combination of intensity of eye contact, severity or intensity of facial expression, modulation of the voice, and body language.

The purpose is to capture fullest attention to a particular point or line of reasoning, to build toward a crescendo of emotion that corresponds to the intellectual content, or in peroration.

Exploit the vertical space behind the lectern, meager that it may be; taking a step, two steps, three steps—a half step—back; lowering the tone of the voice. Then—employing the combination of attitudes described above, depending on your attitude and sentiments—move back forward, the pitch and projection of the voice rising the while. Toward the lectern, leaning over it into the audience; alternately, if circumstances permit, striding out to the wings of the stage, in the direction of the footlights, until one is virtually looming above the audience—utterly dominating it.

You will have achieved their maximum attention. You had better have something on your mind worthy of it.

8. Expand the lungs with hope, gladness, joy, triumph.

Some speakers are extraordinarily inhibited when it comes to expressing the lighter and happier emotions.

Their bodies aren't being put to use. Fill your lungs with oxygen! Raise your arms joyously, tilting the chin up, straightening your head—rising up on your toes as though you are lifting the whole burden of the human condition with you, triumphing over it.

You will have triumphed over the dread of surrendering yourself to the moment.

*   *   *

The orator must cultivate a kind of thoroughbred *frisson* about the business he is engaged in up on the speaker's stand that translates to the body. He must physically respond to his ideas as the mount trained in dressage responds to the subtle pressure of heels, legs, and knees. This means that to develop appropriate body language, the orator must have crafted a talk that is intellectually so challenging and so entertaining that he himself is continually entranced by what he has to say, though never to the fatal degree that he forgets his audience and his purpose, which is to persuade people to his convictions; but, yes, to the degree that no matter how often he has delivered this particular address, his whole body shivers with anticipation in the excitement of his message. The Sermon on the Mount produces this *frisson*, as does the Gettysburg Address. It isn't a bad idea at all for the orator to begin as a genius.

CHAPTER 16

CHOREOGRAPHY

INTRODUCTION

No matter how small it may be, the stage is elevated and set back from the public for two reasons: (1) in order visually to sequester the performer, and thus help concentrate audience attention on him, (2) *in order to give the performer space in which to build meaning.*

As a speaker, you are a performer. Never forget that. You must excel yourself, be better and bigger than your natural self.[1] Lectern and stage magnify. They endow one's least word and most vagrant expression with a significance that these would not ordinarily be meted, which is why a speaker or an actor must exercise such perfect control over himself, such fidelity to the purpose of his performance.

Sometimes a speaker is given precious little liberty and next to no space to work with. He is penned in—at the center of, behind—a banquet table or dais; he is restricted to the lectern by the sound system or by a bristling festoon of media mikes; or his talk is being filmed for company purposes, his movements confined. Worst case: He is jammed into the wooden chair of a TV station's "news room" (this is a medieval experience), instructed to stare rigidly into a designated square on a wall three feet in front, receiver plugged into an ear, lavaliere mike clipped to his tie or lapel. (Ankles, legs, arms, and hands may not be strapped down by high-voltage conductors, but he feels anyhow as

---

[1]Cornelia Otis Skinner once told me, "You can always tell an actor. They have more face."

though he is about to be electrocuted.) Under such conditions, the speaker must be both agile and inventive to dress out his remarks.

Assume, however, plenty of space: a stage in an old-fashioned movie house, or in a college assembly hall. Why does one wish to move about it?

Well, in order to release some pent energy and inject dynamics into the performance. These mustn't be the primary motivations, however. The stage must be used to: (a) create immediacy, urgency, and close personal—*intimate*—rapport with the audience; (b) hammer down this or that essential point; (c) help paragraph the case, so that its careful construction transpires; (d) give visual form to the meaning; (e) partition and choreograph the text—that is, to associate in the visual memory of the audience a given physical space with a specific point, example, or judgment, so that when one returns to that particular space on stage, making reference to the point, example, or judgment, these leap readily into the minds of the audience.

1. Plan out all your movements about the stage beforehand; if necessary, scribble them into the margins of your text as a reminder.

2. Remain 60 to 80 percent of the time behind the lectern, sallying forth infrequently.

3. Exploit vertical space behind the lectern.

4. Allow yourself impulsive, impromptu desertions of the lectern when these are inspired by passion or opportunity, but be frugal about this!

5. Do not wander ceaselessly and aimlessly back and forth across the stage.

6. As a rule, do not talk while you are in movement from or back toward the lectern, or from one location on the stage to another.

7. Be careful during your movements never to turn your shoulders or rear end toward the audience.

8. When you get wherever you are going on stage, take a firm stand; do not fall into a box step.

Sweat, Blood, Toil, and Tears: Surpassing Yourself

1. Plan out all your movements about the stage beforehand; if necessary, scribble them into the margins of your text as a reminder.

Think hard about how you intend to give shape and form to your talk
. . . though the fact of the matter is, prior to delivering the talk at least once, your choreography won't gel.

It tends to define itself in the heat of the actual performance. Notwithstanding, set yourself to the task beforehand. Where do you want to be when declaiming this or that point? Where would it be most useful and effective for you to be?—remembering always that the lectern must be the spine and gravitational center of your performance.

There are what can be called "grand sallying forths" from the lectern and "minor sorties."

Belonging to the first category might be *a narrative* that exemplifies or helps materially to advance the text: it should almost always be spoken to one or the other side, stage front. *A major development* in the argument deserves major choreography. So does the pronouncing of moral or intellectual judgments: all the good things supporting one's case or point of view should be expounded either at home base or to stage right (in debate, depending on which side of the stage one's teammates are sitting, the preferred location may be to stage left); all the bad things about the opposing case or view should be expounded on the opposite wing. One wants to associate in the audience's minds the good with *a physical location*, the bad with a location as far as possible removed from the good.

Occasions for *minor sorties* to one or the other side of the lectern include recital of a *spiel of statistics*, the reading of *a quotation*, posing *rhetorical questions*, or *parenthetical remarks*. Do not come out quite so far from behind the lectern, or so much stage front. Occasions for minor sorties are best sparingly taken advantage of.

2. Remain 60 to 80 percent of the time behind the lectern, sallying forth infrequently.

The lectern anchors the speaker and anchors the sense of his talk. It shouldn't be abandoned except for deliberate, useful, advantageous reason—and it should then be promptly returned to.

Like anecdote, the stage should never be treated ornamentally—as mere rhetorical embellishment. Pound its boards maybe twice in ten minutes, three times in twenty minutes, four times in thirty minutes. The grand sallying forth must be the exception that cleaves like a hatchet into the brainpans of the audience.

3. Exploit vertical space behind the lectern.

. . . Especially if you are confined to the lectern, for the reasons mentioned above.

Taking three steps, two steps, even a half step to the rear, then coming briskly forward, can be amazingly effective; not simply as emphasis, but in rendering points intellectually vivid and memorable for the audience's receptors.

4. Allow yourself impulsive, impromptu desertions of the lectern when these are inspired by passion or opportunity, but be frugal about this!

Often during the delivery of a text, instinct will decree departure from the lectern.

Something occurs that makes one wish to leave it and come stage front, to the very rim of the footlights: a collective sigh from the audience, restlessness. The senses signal: *I need to get this across to them better; I need to take stronger command of their attention.*

Don't repel these psychosomatic messages. Embrace them. Always be responsive to your audience, but never promiscuous in your movements.

5. Do not wander ceaselessly and aimlessly back and forth across the stage.

Few faults are so distracting, irritating, and dizzying as the speaker who abandons the lectern almost at once, crisscrossing the stage, prowling it left-right, right-left, never stopping an instant.

This utterly negates the theatrical advantage of erupting from one's base. It's a foolish wasting of resources. Moreover, the thread of the restless, undisciplined speaker's argument is rendered confusing to the audience. He generally babbles in his meanderings, displaying hopeless disorganization—breaking eye contact and carelessly flinging his words into the wings of the stage, where, like moths in an open flame, they are consumed.

People prone to this major error are those—often salesmen—who pride themselves on their ability to "wing" a talk. They are better off flying a kite.

6. As a rule, do not talk while you are in movement from or back toward the lectern, or from one location on the stage to another.

In the school, we've dubbed this sin "walk-talk."

Rarely, it's okay Much more often, it isn't. The tendency is almost always to talk into the sides of the stage, as mentioned above. And speaking before one arrives at one's destination forfeits the drama and the editorial signals that are the purpose of deserting the lectern.

This isn't to say that one must always come to the full stop of a sentence completing a segment of the talk, permit silence to reign, stride out to a location in the wings, take a stand, and only then begin speaking again. That can be awkward, or seem artificial and programmatic. (A lot depends on how graceful one is about one's bodily movements.) One may instead flag one's departure from the lectern while still standing there, in this manner: *"Look . . ."*—pronounced while the speaker is yet behind the lectern, the sentence suspended in midair. He strides briskly out to the right, the hall still reverberating to that single word. This isn't a planned departure. He has noticed someone in the fourth row, left of center, registering doubt or skepticism at his remarks. He arrives where he intends to go—stage front and directly facing that person. Planting his feet firmly, he continues: ". . . I found this tough to credit myself, when I first heard about it. One can't take any projection from the Congressional Budget Office on its face value, first, because the Office has been politicized, second, because projections with reference to single mothers on welfare commonly fail to take into account . . ."

The speaker should continue explaining and justifying his point where he is standing, and only when he has cleared that countenance in the fourth row of its disaffection, *shutting his mouth*, return to the lectern, there resuming his discourse.

Major departures from the lectern must stand out. This is what you wish for: After the talk, a member of the audience says, "I just don't believe the CBO issues false data," to which another answers, "But don't you remember what he said when he came out from the lectern—explaining how politics influences statistics and how they never include . . . ?"

The unpremeditated sally has been successful, lodging at least this single point in the mind of at least one person in the audience. That's a triumph.

7. Be careful during your movements never to turn your shoulders or rear end toward the audience.

Which occurs most often when the speaker continues babbling while he is striding across the stage or back to the lectern, so engrossed in his thoughts that he becomes oblivious to the audience.

Look out. Turning a shoulder to the crowd can project contempt. Turning one's back . . .

In Copenhagen, where, at parties to which Embassy Row may have been invited, falling-down drunkenness goes unremarked (is even encouraged by the host), and where fornication and adultery and other extra-Biblical sexual concourse are considered *divertissements*, turning one's back to a crowd may educe gasps of horror. Which means that if one is seated center row, center, in a theater, and be summoned by Nature, one must turn one's buttocks to the backs of the heads of people sitting in front of one, one's face and front to those sitting along the same row and to the rear of one; which in turn means that edging out to the aisle demands that one's knees bend in a direction that Nature (though every second the more urgently summoning one) did not intend, so that instead of feeling the knees of other spectators push softly against and slide discreetly by the soft yielding inner hinges of one's own knees, their knees and one's knees rap hard, knobbily, sometimes painfully, as one awkwardly sidesteps out to the aisle, thump-thumping with one's fanny the backs of the heads of those sitting in the row in front of one's own, obliging one to gaze into the faces of those whose kneebones have bruised one's own, or whose kneebones one has bruised with one's own. You should have stayed at the Tivoli.

8. When you get wherever you are going on stage, take a firm stand; do not go into a box step.

. . . Or a shuffle.

Get where you are going, then plant your feet like Juan Belmonte.[2] Say what you have to say with those feet nailed to the floorboards, expressing energy and body language from the knees up, keeping the feet still.

When you are through, cease speaking, turn, and stride back to the lectern.

❖   ❖   ❖

The open posture, the candid, happy face, the smile, the lift of the shoulders, the rising to one's toes, the wide-flung, outthrust, audience-embracing arms and hands, and the vulnerable stance taken as far stage front as the stage permits: All these motions and attitudes signal good news, truth, sincerity, faith, conviction. Don't neglect cultivating such silent persuaders.

---

[2]One of Spain's greatest matadors; founder of the modern style. He was famous for planting his feet like posts before the bull, never budging them, though he risked almost certain collision with the charging bull's prow and impalement by the horns. He was a close friend of Ernest Hemingway, whose suicide he anticipated by his own.

PART 6

CHARACTER

CHAPTER 17

WIT AND HUMOR/
DISCIPLINED EMOTION

INTRODUCTION

Can anything be more fearful for an audience than to be visited by
the awful foreboding that they have become prey of an undisciplined
speaker?

That he may talk on and on is prospect horrible enough; but that
he may drench the hall in sentimentality, or scald it in shrill outbursts
of ranting ire, or seek to amuse the crowd through clumsy excursions
into third-rate humor, the point of which escapes everybody, chills the
imagination, casts down the spirit, and fills the breast with foreboding.

Please don't get me wrong. I'm all for the heat of conviction, and
I'm all for fun. If one could spike the breakfast coffee of Washington
with laugh gas, our country would benefit enormously; and if one
could instill in Congress and the White House true moral fervor (right
or wrong), Mr. Smith might come to town again, and, gee, shucks, you
know?—we just might be able to read the papers or watch the news
of a morning without feeling embarrassed. Nevertheless, *purpose*,
relevance, and *timing* (see Chapter 14) are the essential virtues of wit
or humor, without which either is superfluous. *Self-control* must gird
the spirit, ruling the emotions, or they become rampant, ugly, and
self-indulgent.

WIT AND HUMOR

There are major differences between them; where one won't do, the other may.

Wit is more intellectual and usually more topical. It is associated with "lively intelligence, perspicacity, understanding,"[1] the latter two qualities signifying that wit can penetrate to deeper levels than the almost immediately consumed surface sparkle of a wisecrack or one-liner. Webster pins wit not only to "lively fancy and aptness of talent for clever expression" but also to "expressing brilliantly and amusingly ideas which are startlingly incongruous in association . . . Wit"—Webster continues—"consists typically in a neat turn of speech by which disconnected ideas are unexpectedly associated," like fun guy and Al Gore.[2]

Humor "commonly implies broader human sympathies [Webster's again]," whereas wit is not only "more purely intellectual [and again]," it is (in my opinion) inherently cruel. Wit is a rapier, inflicting wounds; humor is a salve, healing wounds. When one is said to be the "butt of humor," more often is one the pierced hide of wit.[3]

Wit

Sans wit, anyone at the lectern is mortally handicapped. In the scale of value, wit wins over humor. Decisions may more often be gained by the fortuitous turn of phrase than by the logic recommending them. Ronald Reagan quite clearly lost his debate against Jimmy Carter on domestic issues, judged by the soundness and coherence of the individual points raised; but he won the night, and the Presidency, by his since-famous summation, beginning, "There you go again!"

1. The witty shaft should rarely be reused.

2. Bear in mind that wit tends to wound and invites retaliation.

3. Wit is handy for penetrating to the heart of an issue.

4. Don't confuse wit for a gag.

---

[1]Webster's Dictionary

[2]Over whose grave countenance steals an expression of faintly costive distress whenever he encounters something that he suspects may be funny.

[3]For more on wit, see pages 183–184, *Speaking in Public.*

5. If you entertain any doubt about the appropriateness or deftness of a witty jab, discard it.

Sweat, Blood, Toil, and Tears: Surpassing Yourself

1. The witty shaft should rarely be reused.

Ronald Reagan did that crack to death, as, in his second run for the Presidency, he did to death, "You ain't seen nothin' yet!" (For more, see Chapter 2, Commandment 4.)

The temptation to recycle wit is a product of sloth and a naive assumption that owes its existence to bucolic Currier & Ives prints of nineteenth-century America, when news traveled about as fast as the horse and buggy. The Internet may be the best metaphor (to date) for the speed and pervasiveness of modern communications. Or a computer virus. I get the feeling as I type that somehow, somewhere, these words are being engraved on a universal hard disk, or are inspissating on thousands of screens world over with a kind of ghostly resonance. You may not buy this book because somewhere, somehow, you've already read it.

Literary "conceits" like the one just told have a half-life only slightly longer than that of a witticism.

2. Bear in mind that wit tends to wound and invites retaliation.

Wit seizes on human foibles, which are funny to everyone who doesn't happen to be the target or harbor that particular weakness.

Why am I beating up so on poor Al Gore? I just don't know. Such a decent sort—solid, besides. There's the story of Jebediah Snodgrass, of course, who throws himself to his knees on the lawn of his burning house, which is being consumed in flames to the last rafter, wailing, "Lord, Lord—what have I done to offend thee? My poor father has been vegetalized by a stroke, my dear mother is suffering from terminal cancer, my beloved wife just told me she's lesbian, my son and heir shoots heroin and steals from the church poor box, my precious daughter walks the streets, my business is bankrupt, and now my house is burning down. Lord, Lord, what have I done to offend thee?" At which piteous cry, a dark cloud gathers overhead, bolts of lightning rip down, and a voice in a peal of thunder intones, "I don't know what to tell you, Snodgrass; there's something about you that just pisses me off."

It's nevertheless easy to invite a hostile reaction from the audience unless the wit is sufficiently funny and free of malice (wit is *never* wholly free of malice). Make certain the target fully deserves the venom in the shaft and that the shaft is as narrowly focused as possible on that target's idiosyncrasies, to the end that few people in the audience will be alienated, the majority amused.

You are, notwithstanding, playing with fire.

3. Wit is handy for penetrating to the heart of an issue.

Wit tends almost always to be aphoristic. It is compelling. On his deathbed in a shabby Dublin rooming house, Oscar Wilde cocked an eye at the horrible wallpaper and said, "One of us has got to go." (These are purportedly his last words.) The witty shaft may, alas, be the only thing the audience remember from your performance.

When my brother Bill ran (facetiously) for mayor of New York back in 1968, he was asked one evening on television what his first act would be upon getting elected. "Demand a recount," he shot out. (From the heart.)

It was wonderfully funny, expressing his puckish humor, while adroitly leveling a riposte at critics who harped on his lack of political experience. And though his campaign made its point—that a conservative running even in the most liberal of Northeastern cities could attract votes (brother James two years later was elected to the Senate in a three-way race)—my guess is Bill has got awfully tired of being reminded of his quip over and over again these past thirty years, when so many of the gut issues of the campaign have been fudged by political expediency.

Wit is a compression of argument, a shorthand; it pierces to the core of complicated issues, reducing them to something concrete—to a paraliptic metaphor. That was the strength of "There you go again!"— and in an earlier campaign, of Walter Mondale's wonderful jab at Richard Nixon, "Where's the beef?" (Which, of course, he borrowed from a Hardee's TV ad.)

When—as you contemplate them—boiling arguments down to their essence, try composing the witty turn of phrase that exemplifies what you mean. ("In a nutshell" was a clever reduction from the mouth of its first utterer.) Ask yourself: "How can I put that better, more compactly, more suggestively? What will make it clear—and stick?" Some reductions spring spontaneously to mind. Others resist. But the habit of turning phrases over in the mind for possible witty extrapolations or extrusions bears fruit. Ponder the extraordinary mathematical wizardry, the elegance, and *the wit* of $E = mc^2$. True, just as Albert Einstein thought in parallel lines that eventually crossed, some people are more verbal than others. In all cases, practice and application help.

4. Don't confuse wit for a gag.

A gag palls even faster because it is loaded with little intelligence. To be first rate, the witticism must succeed in an intelligent fusing of disparate references that, when joined, throw a spotlight on what was not comprehended, or was no better than implied, by each on its own. "He brays like a jackass," uttered of anyone, is devoid of wit and tells us little about the person other than that his words are windy (and maybe also colicky) and stupid. But, "If he could bray, a jackass could speak," engages the mind more and tells us . . . I'm not sure what, but I'll work on it. (Now, "If wishes were horses, then donkeys could neigh"? No . . . no . . .)

To such false starts, some of the best witticisms owe their genesis . . . ("If his proposals could fly, so could a dodo." Closer?) Some, of course, like the dodo, never get off the ground.

5. If you entertain any doubt about the appropriateness or deftness of a witty jab, discard it.

". . . Witticisms can be even more dangerous than humor when they misfire. A heavy remark that just misses the point is gravely embarrassing. If one flubs a joke, the audience may shrug sympathetically, even laugh, with a modicum of sympathy. But the witticism that bombs is painful, intellectually uncouth, making listeners deeply uncomfortable, at once putting in question the smarts of the perpetrator. When what may sound like a witticism ignites in the mind, hesitate just an instant before delivering it."[4] In short, if it's a dodo, it won't fly. (If it's a dumbbell, it won't clap?)

---

[4]Lifted from *Speaking in Public*, p. 185.

Humor

Humor can be black, can be bitter, but that's not its true nature.

Humor appeals to our sense of the ridiculous. Humor is often witty, but its proper tendency is to tell a story that reveals human beings in their sometimes endearing innocence. The buffoon is our natural state. The happy bonobo, for example, cousin of the fratricidal and savage chimpanzee, is our caricature in the primate world. We share 98 percent of the bonobo's DNA, but unfortunately, only a smidgin of their carefree lust. The bonobo's is *Playboy*'s ideal lifestyle; to observe them in their natural environment, doing their thing (which they do almost all the time, unself-consciously, without a notion of how gross or ridiculous they are), fills us with peals of merriment over the tendentiousness and simplicity of Hugh Hefner. Our recognition of the universal human condition, which bonobodom comically illuminates, binds us together. Laughter is the common denominator of the human primate, disarming the naked ape.

Cause an audience to laugh and you have gone a long way to winning its sympathies for your point of view.

1. Humor is utterly inappropriate on some occasions.

2. Ill-begotten or poorly delivered humor is a curse.

3. The best humor is personal narrative.

4. If you must tell a canned joke, choose one at least a generation old.

5. Humor must serve a purpose unrelated to itself.

Sweat, Blood, Toil, and Tears: Surpassing Yourself

1. Humor is utterly inappropriate on some occasions.

. . . When a casket is being lowered into the ground; when a death sentence is being pronounced; when survivors of a commercial jet crash are testifying before a congressional subcommittee; when a corporation announces it is applying for Chapter 11 bankruptcy, or dismissing 10,000 employees.

Or, I suppose, when Oprah is announcing her new diet, Liz Taylor introducing her umptieth husband, Bill Clinton expressing his shock at O. J. Simpson's lack of candor, the GOP its devotion to bipartisan rule, or when Little Nel expires, at long, long last.

That's the trouble, you see. The exuberant and irreverent temperament finds humor too joyous to resist on almost all occasions, saving the assassination of a President (and then it might depend upon whom); as, for example, by way of relief at funerals, or solemn state occasions, or watching horse shows ("Horse shows are where horses' asses go to watch horses' asses"[5]), or retriever field trials ("Field trials are where the men look like women, the women like men, and they all look like their dogs"[6]). That person must restrain himself or herself. Not only can humor be in poor taste—for being ill-considered—it can plunge one into the bad graces of an audience.

The joke that bombs blows up the speaker.

2. Ill-begotten or poorly delivered humor is a curse.

Some people have little talent for humor and tend always to muff the punch line.

If you don't possess the knack, don't fret, but don't take risks either. (You may be gifted with wit, which can compensate for humor, though never make up for it.)

3. The best humor is personal narrative.

It's original to the speaker; he can't easily muddle or bumble it; it will have intimate appeal and firsthand authority. (See Chapter 1, Cardinal Sin 2.)

---

[5]Attributed to famed thoroughbred race-horse trainer, the late Burly Cocks, when asked his opinion at Madison Square Garden (at that time still a social event high on the New York calendar, men in tuxedos and women in evening gowns). His comments were mistakenly broadcast throughout the Garden on the loudspeaker system. He was not invited to officiate again.

[6]Acid dropped by the late William Huntting Howell when he had been dragooned into serving as a judge at an event held by the Long Island Retriever Field Trial Association; after which never again was his judgment invited.

Both the above epithets are, of course, characterized by wit more than by humor: which is why they reaped the retaliation that both men hoped for.

4. If you must tell a canned joke, choose one at least a generation old.

A chestnut like Snodgrass, above. (See pages 235–236.)

5. Humor must serve a purpose unrelated to itself.

Only an expert raconteur can get away with a funny story that is its own justification, and that's because the purpose of his presence on the stage is to spin yarns—like a Justin Wilson, the Cajun gourmet cook, who tells tall tales about bayou shooting and is (or used to be, he's getting along in years) invited often to address meetings of major Ducks, Unlimited chapters.

❀   ❀   ❀

Timing is the essential ingredient of humor: the ability to cause the audience to anticipate it; the talent for coaxing yet more laughter out of the audience.

The essential control is of a different order when it comes to passion and sentiment:

> Would you recognize a Spanish Cartagenian stallion? It's the short, chunky war-horse of the Crusades, which bore the weight of knights in full armor. Few sights are more awesome than one of those animals in action, powerful quarters hunching, muzzle tucked in at the throttle, pink nostrils flared, neck bowed like a spinnaker in a 30-knot gale. Veins bulge. Sweat has blackened neck, withers, and loins, which are slimy with it; foam drips from retracted lips in long yellow-white skeins. Eyeballs roll wildly in their sockets. The animal is about to explode . . . yet it is being contained by silken reins and maybe a rubber bit, nothing more.
>
> It is the delicately maintained tension between passion and discipline that enhances emotion; that can awe an audience or whip it into a frenzy."[7]

---

[7]From *Sex, Power, and Pericles*, Part 2, Chapter 3, "The Greek Mask: Disciplined Emotion."

DISCIPLINED EMOTION

If you care to live up to Plato's definition of the art of public speaking, whose purpose, you'll remember, is to exercise dominion over the souls of men, exercise that dominion over your own soul.

It was character that defined the greatness of the orations of Pericles. It was his control over himself translating to his rhetoric. There are times when it is appropriate to "let it all out," to thunder, to fulminate . . . but these are rare, rare occasions. Times occur when high emotion may be, must be, expressed: but oh, so carefully, so skillfully, with such reserve and intellectual austerity that it is all the more heartrending or tender.

Mastering this restraint is the difference between the amateur and the pro.

1. Never rant from the lectern.
2. Spare us as well those tender, intimate concerns that cause one to weep at the thought.
3. Never lose your temper from the lectern, or at a press conference or other pig stickings.
4. Rinse your emotions in stoic fortitude, in the Book of Wisdom, in Christian resignation and forbearance.
5. Acquire philosophical detachment about yourself, your opinions, your self-importance.
6. Learn how to love Adolf Hitler.

Sweat, Blood, Toil, and Tears: Surpassing Yourself

1. Never rant from the lectern.

Erect a wall between your private beliefs and emotions and your professional obligations.

What a hard prescription this is!

Go out and starve fifty pounds of fat off you. Go run three miles a day. Study two hours every night when you drag home from the office. Read the manual . . . *then* try to put the damn thing together.

So let's begin with the understanding that what's demanded of us is too hard; that we will fail; that it is inhuman to ask anyone to persist in trying.

I could entertain you with stories about my staggering list of passionate biases, my heartfelt unalterable opinions: why I go up the wall when I hear some solemn fellow talk about "social justice," or why I want to scream when I'm put on hold to the music of André Kostelanitz, or . . .

But then you would insist on telling me about the crotchets in your own intellectual closet, and I would be neither entertained nor improved.

As the testosterone weakens, so do other passions. That may be little consolation to men. Yet it is their salvation, the bulwark that professional discipline can become against our naked selves. Discipline imposed from on high can work or not. *Self*-discipline is of a different order, because it is our response to the demands of survival. In pursuing our daily lives, we don't lash out at small provocations; even when that provocation is major, we bite our lips and bear it. (See below for more on this subject.) Maybe from fear of the boss do we hold our tongues, or because professional reasons dictate that we maintain cordial—at least neutral—relations with the fellow worker who offended us. We steam . . . but in the privacy of our offices.

Fear of retaliation may have been the balance persuading us to swallow our pride, but it was an act of self-discipline just the same. That same professionalism we must take to the lecture stand.

Here, understand, I am not speaking about being goaded by a reporter or someone in the audience into an intemperate response. I speak of resisting within oneself the temptation uninhibitedly to loose from the lectern one's sentiments and passions, wallowing in them. We have the audience at our mercy! Wow, maybe two hundred people are out there whom we can harangue to our hearts' content. So if I'm a feminist, I'll rant about incorrigible male chauvinist piggery in the workplace; if I'm a pro-lifer, I'll fry in the burning spittle of my rhetoric anyone who dares frame abortion in any terms other than that of infanticide; if I'm a charter member of the Sierra Club, I'll, by gum, show how all loggers seek to chop down the very last giant sequoia in

California, and how all cattlemen and sheep farmers despise the gray wolf for totally selfish anthropomorphic reasons, even though there is no recorded instance of a wolf on the North American continent ever having attacked and bitten a human being, perhaps because there was nothing left of his bones to bear witness, inasmuch as it is difficult for some of us to understand that Canis lupus americanus is different from his first cousins, Canis lupus siberianus or Canis lupus scandinavianus . . .

Now, one can be these things—a deeply offended and embittered woman; a person to whom, in fact, abortion cannot be discussed other than as murder of a human child in the earliest stages of its life; or a lover of wildlife furious about the self-serving hypocrisies of commercial lobbies in our country—but at the podium, it is nevertheless *inadmissible* to exploit one's power by lashing out at one's enemies, *unless one has been specifically requested to hold forth on these subjects* (in which case, the audience should know what to expect). Even then, having been asked to talk on controversies of high emotional octane, *assuming one hopes to persuade*, instead of indulging one's bitter passions in a tirade, *one should shun ad hominem remarks, cheap shots, low blows, exerting the professional self-discipline to state one's views with due respect for the contentions of one's enemies—rationally, fair-mindedly, and with restraint.* One may burn with passion top to toe, be consumed inside by love or hatred, but in neither case may one allow oneself to be extreme, acrimonious, mean-spirited, and fanatical. It's a breach of manners.

Throw up that wall between your emotions and the professional detachment that any seasoned campaigner must learn.

2. Spare us as well those tender, intimate concerns that cause one to weep at the thought.

Neither should we take advantage of our position as a speaker to sauté the audience in a sticky sauce of sentimentality.

One must impose strict discipline over the tender feelings also. We must learn: People are *not* interested in the dreams of other people, in the bellyaches of other people, in the pets of other people, or in the children of other people; nor should it be assumed by the speaker that, like it or not, they must be, as some kind of obligation proclaiming our human solidarity. One has no right to make such a claim or exercise such an imposition on the privacy of one's listeners.

If I'm a Christian, I will not gush about my love for our Lord, Jesus Christ, with such saccharine sweetness that I'm likely to alienate a plaster saint. Though I may cherish cats, I'll not emote thirty tear-bedewed minutes on how cute and cuddly and *darling* kittens can be.

One must *earn* the desired reaction: by wit, metaphor, sprightly anecdotes . . . One fine September sabbath a year or so ago, a curmud-geonly Irish priest at a convent school in Madrid that grandchildren of mine attend began his homily with the announcement that the schedule was hereby changed, there would no longer be a 10:30 Mass, there would be instead an 11:00 o'clock Mass, and he would brook no objections on the part of the congregation about this—most people were arriving for the 10:30 Mass at 11:00 o'clock anyhow. (Without permitting himself a twinkle in the eye.) He then expressed his discom-fort with the gospel for that Sunday, in which we are instructed by the Lord first to talk to our friend about his evil ways; and if he fails to reform, to talk to him again privately about them; and only if he remains obdurate, bring him before the elders for reprobation. The old priest said he preferred getting across the good news in a different manner. For example, he went on, three of the nuns of the parish set off on their regular round of bringing victuals to the poor in the Guadarrama Sierra north of Madrid, when their little Citroën of a sudden stopped. Lo, it was out of gas. The nearest gas station, a sign advised, was several kilo-meters up the mountain. Thence the sisters trudged, carrying emptied milk cartons with them. A hot and sweaty hour later, they were back by the Citroën, carefully tipping the gas from the milk cartons into the tank's port . . . when an open truck filled with day laborers trundled by them, the men waving and *huzzah*ing and shouting at the nuns, "The power of prayer, sisters, the power of prayer!"[8]

That's the way to preach the good news.

3. Never lose your temper from the lectern, or at a press conference or other pig stickings.

I could regale you with stories about my red-hot temper also, against which I have waged war sixty-eight years, with little noticeable improvement.

---

[8]See Part 2, Chapter 3, "The Greek Mask: Disciplined Emotion," pages 130–132, in *Sex, Power, and Pericles* for more on how to handle subjects involving the deepest human emotions.

One must never permit oneself to be provoked into a flash of temper by some nasty remark from the floor. Keep your cool always. Tips on how to do this come below. But always be prepared: some people attend lectures with the sole purpose of hurling darts at the speaker, which they hope are so venom-tipped that he'll fall in a heap. They despise him personally, or ideologically, or even professionally.

Which brings up the media. To be a journalist is to be part crank, part misanthrope, part cynic, part ideologue, part snob, and a whole lot invested with a sense of unparalleled moral superiority over all other creatures. If you are a person of affairs, do not hesitate getting help from pros on how to deal with the media. (In-house training is not likely to do you as much good, for reasons mentioned previously.) The training you get will help you maintain your composure under all conditions, including when you are wheedled into giving a speech to the Kiwanis Club, free of charge, as a personal favor, your topic announced as "Putting the Icing on the Cake," and to your astonishment, someone in the audience rises up at the end of the talk violently to charge you with committing a crime against humanity by coddling to the sweet tooth of desire, which will rot the gums of civilization down to its root canals.

The totally unexpected attack from some amazing far-out quarter is what most often undoes speakers—or chairmen of press conferences. A national insurance company (hereinafter X) headquartered in a southern city (hereinafter Y) of the state of Z (no reason not to be candid) asked us to coach a team that was scheduled that next week to fly to San Francisco and there, at a press conference, unveil to the world an array of new products. It was important for the company, whose sales were lagging.

We held our clinic at the premises of X. The founder of the company quietly took a seat in the rear of the room (we were unaware of this) just as his senior vice president in charge of marketing was coming to the end of his remarks, telling how the new spectrum of insurance policies would bring bounty to all concerned, subscriber and shareholder of X alike.

He concluded. My friend Glenn Tucker, a veteran journalist, built no taller than a keg of carpet tacks, but sharper, opened the attack. "Mr. B., how many people are there on X Life & Casualty Insurance Company's board?"

A. Well, twenty-four, I believe . . . but what does that have to do with . . . ?

Q. How many are women?

A. Well, I'm not sure, one, I think, maybe two . . . we didn't call this press conference to . . ."

I jumped in:

Q. We can read the handout, Mr. B. Do you have one woman or is it two on your board?

A. I . . . I don't understand. What's the number of women on the board got to do with . . . ?

Glenn Tucker:

Q. We've had a complaint filed with my newspaper by NOW that your company is notorious for excluding women from significant executive positions, including the board.

A. But that's not so, that's . . .

I jumped back in:

Q. Mr. B., will you please answer the question: How many women do you have on your board; is it one or is it two, and how come there are so few women in other top positions?

At this point, the founder stood up and walked down the aisle, climbing on stage to succor his beleaguered vice president. A mild, kindly looking individual, he introduced himself.

A. I'm Jerry A., chairman of X Life and Casualty. I believe I can answer that question. We have two women on the board. We've been actively searching for others . . .

Glenn Tucker (not a whit taken aback):

Q. Yeah? How long have you been searching?

A. Oh, I suppose it must be ten years . . . maybe twelve . . .

Q. How old is your company, Mr. A.?

A. I founded it in 1946. It was called The Workers' Life and Property Insurance Company back then, we . . .

Q. So your company is forty-eight years old, you've been searching ten, twelve years for a qualified woman in the city of Y and the state of Z, and you tell us that you can't find one!

A. Well, I mean, insurance is a complex business, not many women . . .

I:

Q. Mr. A., are you asking us to believe that in the city of Y, with a population of 1.3 million, of whom some 800,000 are female, and in the state of Z, with a population of I don't know how many millions of females, you and your board have been able to discover just two women—two women!—capable of exercising the professional judgment to grace the board . . . ?

Tucker:

Q. Yeah, do you really mean to insult all those women with that statement, Mr. A.? Is that your answer?

A. Well, I . . . no! No! That's not . . .

I:

Q. But that's nevertheless the answer we've heard! You and Mr. B. have told us that after twelve years, you haven't been able to come up with more than two qualified women out of millions, which goes to prove either that your company, and your industry for that matter, have been holding back on executive appointments for women or that your search for a qualified female to sit on the board is pretty hypocritical.

Tucker:

Q. Hypocritical? Good ole boy-critical! And what about blacks, Mr. A.? Do I dare ask you about them? What about you, Mr. B. How many blacks are there on the board of X Life & Casualty Insurance Company?

A. Are you asking me?

Q. Yes, you, Mr. B. Who do you think we're asking? You called this press conference.

A. Well, I . . .

"None," said the founder and chairman of the company.

Now, several high officers of the panel were made furious by the questions we hurled at them (which were more virulent and extensive in the original transcript) and wanted to dismiss us on the spot. They went into private conclave with the chairman. But he apparently overruled; he wished us to continue to drill them any way we thought best. So we worked these poor gentlemen over for the balance of the afternoon, several hours: of which there were two happy results.

The first was a call from San Francisco some eight or nine days later, Mr. B. on the line, who said, "Thank-you, oh, thank-you. I'd no sooner got through with my opening remarks when a woman reporter jumped up to ask how these policies were going to help single mothers in the ghetto, and another, a Hispanic, wanted to know whether we even cared about poor people . . . They came at us from all sides, just as you warned us they might, with irrelevant and infuriating questions, but we were prepared. We handled them! We kept cool and bridged right back to our agenda, refusing to be trapped in theirs. It worked. The reports this morning in the newspapers and on TV are great!" [Read: factual and unremarkable.]

That was the first happy result. The second is that this company has become one of our most generous and loyal clients.

The point: Professionals can assist you in acquiring the composure and the wit to deal with hostility generally, whether at press conferences, in the office, or on stage speaking. Take advantage of that.

4. Rinse your emotions in stoic fortitude, in the Book of Wisdom, in Christian resignation and forbearance.

One can be schooled by top, tough pros in composure, wit, and agility. It nevertheless requires a personal act of will to bear up under fire.

Adopt the traits mentioned above. Train yourself in them. Begin with minor irritations, such as those so common in business: a rude switchboard operator or a snotty secretary; being kept on hold forever (while being subjected to recorded puffs for the company's wares); being told, "I'll see whether he can speak with you," subsequently, "I'm afraid he can't," or—coldly, distantly, laconically—♪"She's not a♪♪♪vail♩♩♩able."♪ Practice steeling yourself against these common rebuffs, perhaps with a mild, unmuttered, "May you fry in your phlegm, my dear," or "May he [or she] be 'unavailable' on Judgment Day."

My patience, which is . . . thin, is tried in such fashion on a daily basis, and many times a day. Lawyers are never available. And if they are, it's because they have lost a suit or have no clients, in either which case they are unlikely to attend my school. But doctors are worse. They are the high priests of our society. Their administrative RNs were begot by Chimera, brought to term by Medusa. "What is it you wish to speak with Doctor about? Doctor is a very busy man. Doctor is in surgery at the moment. Doctor will be teaching a class at the university this afternoon. Doctor is in conference. Doctor is seeing patients . . ." And Doctor never calls back.[9] I am perforce constrained to remind myself that my business requires trade, whose quest counsels patience and forbearance. I liken the soliciting that I am doing (which I loathe) to fishing for a steelhead of monstrous size in a wild western river or stalking ruffed grouse on a New England hillside. The checks and frustrations will be many, but the catch, the prize, is worth them many times over.

Some such strategy, make your own to thicken the skin and develop an unruffable inner tranquility. *Don't* let the dirty you-know-whats get you down.

5. Acquire philosophical detachment about yourself, your opinions, your self-importance.

This is even tougher, but it helps enormously in acquiring the sanguine temperament recommended above.

People react volatilely under provocation or commit the sin of abusing the privileges of the lectern to rant or proselytize, in direct proportion to their vanity, to their inflated estimation of the importance of themselves. Take this from an expert.

I possess a justified high esteem for my intelligence, sagacity, discrimination, judgment, wit, and talent. They are obvious to everyone I meet, including myself every morning when I shave.

. . . Though I don't understand math. Though I've made crooks my partners in business and several times confided in people who have betrayed me. Though I have not set the world on fire. (Nor, at this late date, am I likely to.)

---

[9]When terminally exasperated, I permit myself this retort: "Ms., kindly tell Dr. Jencks that in this case, he is the patient, I am the doctor; he is the solicitor, I am the dispenser; he needs the help, I can give him that help; and if he wants to attend my school, he had better call, because I don't accept patients I haven't first spoken with."

There is our humbling ontological destiny, now made even more potentially bleak by the new cosmology of the collapsing universe. There is also an honest scanning of our personal faults. Either of these serves to collapse the ego, which, when deflated, makes it less easy to pontificate, easier to bear the rebuff.

Try candor and philosophy on for size; the swelled head shrinks marvelously.

6. Learn how to love Adolf Hitler.

I'm not a good hater.[10]

Worse, I am a bumbling and an ineffectual hater. Some people, moreover, are utterly without shame or pride.

A student acquaintance at Yale, now dead, was a blackguard. He was Gollum. He was a toady, a sycophant, an inveterate stabber-in-the-back.

One morning I stopped him on the busy concourse of York Street, right outside the entrance to Davenport College, and yelled at him in front of mutual acquaintances, "Tony, you're a snake. I've just found out what you told Sid Hellman[11] that I said about him, which I never said about him. I despise you. Don't ever call me or speak to me again. I'll insult you. I don't want to associate with you in any way. Got that?" And I strode off, trembling with my indignation, but proud of myself for having spoken my mind.

Next day I was walking the same street, returning from class, when someone across the way shouted at me, "Hi, Reid!"—waving his arm exuberantly. "Oh, *hi*," I yelled back, peering through my weak eyes, at last—to my inexpressible disgust—to see inspissate out of the gray winter afternoon the face and features of that odious Tony A . . .

Whom I now remember with a certain scurvy affection!—the *faiblesse* of old age, I guess—further fueling my self-disgust, because this is rankest sentimentalism.[12] I have not forgiven Tony, nor have I applied

---

[10]That business about permitting the sun to go down on one's anger.

[11]Son of "Clear it with Sid" Sidney Hellman, of FDR fame; who was himself brilliant, whom I respected, whom I grew greatly fond of; who died young.

[12]One can take satisfaction in outliving one's enemies (though it would be a shame to outlive them all, and possibly a poor reflection on one's character), but whether one should wish to outlive one's *enmities* is dubious. Alzheimer's disease for an Irishman is forgetting everything except a grudge.

to his memory a whit of compassion, nor the Christian (and Jewish) injunction to love even those for whom we can summon no justification for loving.

... Though we must, Christians and observant Orthodox Jews for their reasons (they are commanded to), others for whatever reason they choose. Which may be capricious, unreliable, flimsy, and grossly sentimental, but which has to do. The idiot, the mean, the poisonous; monsters like Hitler, or Stalin, or Pol Pot. For the sake of civility, if none other. For Heaven's sake.

CHAPTER 18

THE VICES

INTRODUCTION: VIRTUES AND VICES

As has become plain to you, we've been shifting grounds these past several chapters from craft to character.

Character is the primary element that a speaker brings to the stage. Everything else can be learned.

Craft is demanded of the performer—how to make the most of one's voice, one's face, one's hands, one's body—which, when perfected, can be lifted to the level of art. But these are useless artifices unless the speaker projects certain virtues, suppresses certain vices.

In this and the following chapter I've selected the good and the bad that, in my forty-five years as a performer and fifteen years as a teacher, strike me as paramount. Keep this in mind: *You must extrapolate.* We shock clients at our school when I say that we haven't the slightest interest in them as human beings. "We couldn't care less," I tell them, looking them each in the eye, permitting this to sink in. Then: "All we care about is what you project from the stage."

Which is almost the whole truth. Because there's a distinction to be drawn between the social personality and the stage personality. They do differ; they can even be antipodal. The convivial person at the cocktail party, on stage, can be struck stiff and dumb; the social boor, whose face your fist squeezes tight shut resisting the desire to smash, can, from the stage, ooze charm. The highly intelligent person may sound like an idiot, the idiot like . . . no no no. I must stop this . . . like an Alan Guth in physics, a Joseph Epstein in literature, an Irving Kristol in social criticism, a Bill Gates in cyberspace.

Our concern is *what one projects from the stage*, not what one happens to be. Of the vices and virtues discussed in this and the following chapter, therefore, you may be afflicted by none personally, graced by none; but their projection may either undermine or fortify your performance. We're talking about virtual reality.

The vices covered are arrogance, pomposity, belligerence, over-seriousness, excessive solemnity, fanaticism, truculence, sarcasm, too cool for words, uptown blues, the ego.

Virtues covered are honesty, candor, decency, sincerity, passion, personal magnetism, humility of spirit.

I cannot tell you, the reader, which of these, if any, mark you. You must come to me, or go to another professional, for a CAT scan of the impression you radiate from behind a lectern. But maybe you suspect that in your public performances you exhibit this virtue or that vice. Skip to what you think pertains.

We depart from the format in these two chapters: there are no quick fixes for next week's performance. The best you can do is run down the list, underlining what you conjecture may weaken or strengthen the job you have been given to do. Then, when the chore is done, come back to these pages, browse on them, and ruminate.

THE VICES

Principal among which is . . .

Arrogance

Traits

Characterized by conveying aloofness and condescension to the audience, who bristle with a silent snarl.

The arrogant stage personality projects that he cares little for the reactions of his audience to what he says—for their opinions—and less for gaining their support. (Their opinion is that he is a snotty SOB whom they will resist supporting even though happiness and prosperity may hang in the balance.) He comes across as an intellectual snob, set and bigoted in his thinking, unyielding, bereft of compassion. The arrogant speaker invites hatred.

Treatment

Smile, even though the stretching of the lips may be physically painful to you, from being so unaccustomed. Pay special attention to eye contact. Try to remember that you are *soliciting* the good opinion of your audience and *entreating* them for their support. (They are not obliged.) Toss in self-effacing and self-deprecating remarks every chance you get. Tell a story on yourself: how your expectations were deceived; something that makes you the butt of your own (as the audience view it) obtuseness and insensitivity. If you succeed in giving them a good laugh at yourself, they'll warm to you, and you'll feel warmer about them, which will become apparent in your stage personality.

Pomposity

There are people who possess the face (blond hair cut short; small, regular, handsome though unexciting features) and build (not too tall, verging on stoutness) to *be* pompous, and that's what their stage personality *ought* to suggest. An air of pomposity on stage *in which they do not take excessive stock* becomes them, though with generous lacings of self-effacement to render the act tolerable and to let the audience understand that it *is* an act, a pose.

Traits

A liking for orotund (sonorous), grand-sounding phrases. They are unctuous, given to rhetorical furbelows (flounces, ruffles, showy trimmings). "My distinguished colleague . . ." "The gentleman in the seventh row . . ." "I submit to you . . ." "All things being—which, of course [*har-har*], they are not—equal . . ." They relish in, they are infatuated by, the sound of their voices. The carriage of their bodies is stiff. They may beam on the audience with (excessive) avuncular goodwill, because it is their immense satisfaction with themselves that they are expressing.

It's easier for me to envisage the pompous man than a pompous woman. In my experience, pomposity tends to be gender-specific, though that's not absolutely so. I have known few pompous women. (Vanity, on the other hand, is more a female trait. I have known a few, though not as many, vain men.)

The pompous fellow takes shape (in my imagination) in blue blazer and wonderfully creased gray flannel trousers. He loves waistcoats, sometimes showy ones. He was born with a foulard around his neck. His sandy hair is thinning, his cheeks are full, his complexion florid, his eyes pallid, and he stands with his weight back on the heels, inasmuch as he is, as I mention above, stout. He may be a bachelor. His chin bobs in the air as he winches lower jaw this way and that in the effort to liberate folds of skin at the neck from a too-tight collar. It's as though he is constantly seeking to lift his chin above the masses, upon whom, down at, with an abundance of benevolence, he gazes. His mouth may be habitually pursed in an unidentified though ineffable distaste, or it may lift at the corners with palpably false bonhomie. He's not comfortable in a men's locker room. He may belong to the Union Club, and the Racquet Club, and he may have walked Harvard Yard, but from a vintage prior to when that sacred turf was trod by women, blacks, Hispanics, and other minorities or representatives of, to him, the inferior sex and lower classes. He is, notwithstanding, in his mid-thirties or early forties, an anachronism. He is distinctly unenamored of modern air travel, because though he travels first-class when possible, he must still queue up with other people, and no distinctions of person are observed in customs or police lines. He broods on his fate in not being able to afford a private jet. He prefers circumlocutions in his sentence structuring, the grandiloquent phrase, the thickly syllabled Latinate synonym with wallows of long vowels, lush sibilances, and mounds of extended diphthongs, as though his tongue is coated in crême brulé. He listens to himself with evident approval as he speaks. Oh, how he begs for the ice pick to punch holes in the full sail of his vanity.

Treatment

This is a creeping disease, to which anyone is prone whose ego is periodically palpated by public attention. One must keep a regular check on oneself, appealing to one's spouse, one's colleagues at the office, and close friends for candid assessments: "Was I okay tonight? Did I please the audience? How did I come off?"

Absent which candid reaction by intimate acquaintances, a healthy lacing of self-effacement and self-deprecation on stage is salutary, along with, of course, anecdotes in which one figures but does not star. Evident devotion to what one is saying is a good antidote to pomposity also, inasmuch as the degree to which one is dedicated to the message is the degree to which preoccupation with the (fine) figure one is cutting will be lessened.

The cure for extreme cases of pomposity is to snap (and keep in the locked front drawer of one's desk) a photo of oneself while one is suffering from loose bowels on the toilet, or vomiting, or engaging in any other bodily function that is (a) repulsive (coughing up the night's collection of phlegm) or (b) ridiculous (such as slurping down baby eels). You will learn whether you are truly infected with pomposity to a terminal degree should you enjoy these pictures.

Belligerence

The overly aggressive stage personality can intimidate and anger audiences. A touch of insouciance (lighthearted unconcern) and even pugnacity are desirable, putting the audience on guard, provoking their interest; but spilling over from these desirable attitudes into disdain or outright aggressiveness prejudices opinion.

Traits

An unrelenting and badgering manner, projecting the notion that one is speaking for the good of the audience, who had better damn well listen, but who won't (the damn fools). The tacit assumption conveyed by the speaker is that he is dead right, everybody else dead wrong, which causes him to be gruff, rasping, scornful, sarcastic, irritable, and in an unrelieved state of wrath.

He has been his own boss always; he has never been mistaken. That fellow hiding his face behind a newspaper is planning to cut into the line ahead of him. If he doesn't watch her closely, that woman at the check-out counter will shortchange him. In attitude, he is pessimistic, because he is talking to idiots, and idiots will not agree with him, let alone listen to him. He does not intend to brook opposition from fools, never fear. He wonders why he was such a fool himself as to agree to talk to them, little good that it will do. His voice grates, his expression is bilious with contempt, he pushes his mug up front the better to growl and dare anyone to disagree, and his hands are commonly clenched into fists, with which he hammers on the blockheads below him . . . who, as they sit, are planning to spike the tires of his car or disconnect the brakes or place a plastic explosive in the engine—those, that is, who are not so cowered by him that they have ceased listening altogether (as he expected) and just wish he would go away.

Belligerence is an affliction of both sexes. The belligerent female is more to be feared and avoided than the belligerent male.

Treatment

Smile. Smile. Smile. Lighten up the tone. Alter the voice: stop it from booming or growling or rasping. (In the case of a woman, from shrilling.) Soften it, honey it. (In the case of a woman, make it dulcet.) *Entreat* agreement from the audience . . . with open hands, as though inviting them all to a wedding. Stand well back from the lectern, don't crowd it. Neither risk striding stage front, looming over the audience. Look up three words in the dictionary: the noun *humor*; the verb *to ingratiate*; the act of *persuasion*. Read James Thurber. (Read Florence King.) Post a sign on your office door: I FART, THEREFORE I AM ONE. Repeat three times a day: *To err is human; and I, too, am human.* Repeat twice a day, morning and evening: *Nobody has ever been absolutely right about anything, not ever; not even me.* (Tsk, you should have said *I.*) Go to bed reminding yourself: *One can lead a horse to water, but one catches more flies with honey* (as any savant will tell you).

Overseriousness

This platform manner is tedious beyond enduring, defeating the purpose of the serious person.

The overserious speaker reminds one of the recent convert, or the one-note obsessive. The attitude slips easily into hortatory hectoring.

Traits

This speaker deems every word he (or she) utters is of utmost importance. Though he/she preaches salvation, he/she does so in the knowledge that the state of man/woman is the state of a fallen nature. Not only, therefore, is he/she excessively earnest about everything, he/she is glum. And if he or she ever encountered humor, she or he resolved never again to strike up its acquaintance, for fear of frivolous infection and subversive effects.

He/she was never popular at birthday parties. She/he read *Dead Souls* with never a laugh, and *Catch 22* in a major/majorette state of confusion. He/she enjoys the organ music of Bach, toccata and fugue, but is impatient with Bach's cantatas and cannot believe the *Concerto in G Major for Two Mandolins* by Vivaldi. (Why two, and why a mandolin at all?) He/she shines in a crisis, which is what she/he lives for. But he/she will put the audience to sheep/sleep before one can say Jack/Jackie Robinson/daughter. Who when they do wake up, thank their lucky stars that they do not think or believe like him/her.

Treatment

Acquire the grace of regarding existence with an indulgent (if never quite happy) smile. Seek out humor and embrace it/it. Cultivate the aristocratic attitude that makes sport of the worst hand that destiny may deal from its dark deck, loaded always with misfortune, shrugging the blows off with elegant shoulders. Recall always the wit of Mercutio, who, upon receiving the mortal thrust of the foil into his bowels, quipped of the wound, ". . . 'tis not so deep as a well, nor so wide as a church door, but tis enough, twill serve . . ." And even punned: ". . . ask for me tomorrow and you shall find me a grave man."

To maintain my own composure in contemplation of the dread worm, I think up last words. For the adolescent, on his tombstone: *At last, a space of my own.* For Indira Gandhi, as she falls to the fusillade of her assassins: *Sikh transit gloria mundi.* The Ayatollah Khomeni, gargling up his last breath: *Oh, Shi'-ite!* William Clinton, when his time comes: *Hillary, is that you?*[1] Such pastimes put perspective in place, which keeps overseriousness at bay.

---

[1] The staff at my school threaten to carve on my tombstone, *Shut up at last.*

In a word, the speaker who is by nature (or from the platform) too earnest must acquire grace. One's opinions and beliefs may never be cavalier, should not be, but one's attitude in expounding them may be bettered by a touch of detachment. Leaven the message. It won't hurt; it may earn the attention and patience of the audience.

Excessive Solemnity

This condition is related to overseriousness; it is a more radical, even glummer state of being. Night is never relieved by daybreak; winds never abate, nor rains relent. The eye of the hurricane signals the worst to come. The eye of the beholder is dull and glazed and gone to sleep.

Traits

Gaiety is not their bag, these folk. They are sewn into the hairshirt of their bourgeois state of correctness and public duty, with which they rise in the morning and tumble abed at night. Almost all occasions strike them as fit for portentous, even gloomy, reflections. They detect widening ozone holes in circus balloons. They see in a bundle of kindling hundreds of thousands of acres of tropical rain forest razed and irrevocably destroyed. They bite into a tuna fish sandwich and ponder the fate of dolphins. They (like their overserious cousin) fear humor, which they suspect. Is that raillery? Are they being mocked? Don't people realize that an unnecessary trip to the grocery store simultaneously exhausts the finite supply of fossil fuels while incrementally polluting the atmosphere?

Treatment

Lighten up! Oh, please. Solemnity has its uses, more often its abuses. Again, as above, get a handle on the absurdity of existence and your prominent place in it; be ribald. You were screwed by your government before you were born. You will be merrily screwed, if you are lucky, all your life. The fates conspire. Your certain end is long and dreary, filled with suffering, phlegm in the lungs. Your passage to that end is fraught with fraughtness. Even worse. Your certain fate is oblivion, existential and cosmic.

What do you intend to do about it? Defy the gods? *Rage, winds, crack your cheeks!* Beat your breast forever? Weep? (Spare me in the audience.) A Christian is, of course, exempt. He escapes human destiny, has been liberated of the human condition, is made by the Second Coming indifferent to, and sanguine about, the mortal sentence in the stretched gases of the expanding universe. He likens doom to a yo-yo, or to a rubber ball attached by an elastic to a paddle, which he will swat with gusto and good cheer.

There is no excuse for him to be overly solemn. (That's an affront against the Savior, in Whom he professes.) The non-Christian and the nonbeliever have more of a case for the gloom and doom of their attitude. Pity. But come on! Suffering and death and comedos on the chin are the grown-up bumps of life, and cosmological catastrophe is some sixty billion years in the offing. Eat, drink, and be wary of casting such a pall over your audience that thick night descends upon their senses as though of hemlock they had drunk.

For your audiences' sake, make yours Dom Perignon. And when next you catch a cold, analyze your condition for what is hilarious in it, treating your audiences to a newfound composure and sophistication.

Fanaticism

This is a vice for which there is no cure except shooting. Almost everyone is susceptible. Even people with delightful senses of humor can succumb to fanaticism. I have a delightful sense of humor. It keeps me company all day long and lifts my spirits in glummest weather, though it plays a lousy hand of pinochle. But just scratch me! I find nothing funny about; I find in wretched taste; I abhor and shrink from and become angry upon hearing; jokes to do with the Virgin Mary or Jesus Christ, Our Lord, unless they are lily-clean, free of malice and derogation, and reverent. The subject is sacred to me. I would happily throttle that blasphemous scumbag Andrés Serrano until his eyes bulged and his bladder turned purple—and I mean that. I look at Madonna and lust for the return of the Inquisition. To the agnostic or atheist, I am a fanatic.

Traits

Characterized by projecting a sense of moral superiority and self-righteousness, in which there may also be an admixture of intellectual superiority. The eyes may be dark and brooding, or pale blue and exoph-thalmic. There's a tightness at the temples, beneath the skin of which a swollen vein may throb. When the sacred subject is broached, the whole upper torso flushes from chest to crown, the angry crimson or a high pink reaching high up into the scalp and visible between furrows of thinning hair. The jaw is stiffly set. The voice can be steely hard, brittle, but as the turbidity of the emotions intensifies—at the slightest hint of opposition—the voice may quaver. Tears or a tantrum equally may ensue. The audience listen in an ague of discomfort, ranging from pity through embarrassment, disapproval, rejection, anger, and horror. The cause is of course lost.

Fanaticism is no respecter of sex, but women seem to be infected by the fault more often than men. One of our senior coaches wrote in her critique of a female client,

> Women in particular must be careful about seeming too serious, overly committed. They sometimes give the impression from the speaker's stand of being perfervid, which causes audiences deep unease. The relaxed (though deeply committed) woman speaker who is able to poke fun at her subject—get off a wry crack about it; show her own emotional detachment (as distinct from her intellectual conviction)—endears her at once . . . and enhances respect for her opinions.

The difference between male and female fanatics is that the men shout louder and sometimes lose control so utterly from the floor that they threaten, or seem to threaten, to do the audience violence. Brought to this emotional pitch, the female fanatic is sometimes seized by help-less (and pathetic) weeping. Both are terrible sights. Fanatics deserve pity, though in virulent form—when their emotions translate into action—they themselves are merciless.

Treatment

If you exhibit any of these symptoms, if on certain subjects you tend to be possessed by indignation, rage, burning passion, you are emotionally and, I dare say, psychologically in trouble. You may have to seek profes-sional help.

Meanwhile, one can help oneself by practicing self-conscious *exercises in humility*.

The first is historical: to chastise your emotions by recalling the universal failure and ultimate ludicrousness of causes that have been deeply tinged with fanaticism: the futility of so many "holy" wars down through the centuries; the grotesque, bloody, monstrous failures of fascism and communism in this century; the charnel house that Cambodia was turned into under the Khmer Rouge; the horror and brutality of fundamentalist Muslim fanatics in Algeria, who just the other day slit the throats of four young boys for having been caught in the terrible sin of playing dominoes. All fanatical faiths are characterized by the same furious emotions, which are diabolical in origin and diabolical in their manifestation. Contemplating the torture, murder, rape, and pillage of which fanaticism has been guilty since the world began should produce a healthy disgust.

The second exercise in humility is moral in nature: contemplation of the hideous extirpation of compassion toward which self-righteousness inexorably conduces. *The third exercise is intellectual*: the resignation with which we must all acknowledge that no one, not any one, is capable of possessing the whole truth about anything. Astrophysicists can (awesomely, amazingly) theorize to within one second of Creation, of the Big Bang. They employ hindsight in the literal sense, with the aid of the Hubble telescope peering into the eons billions of light years gone by, with their sensitive instruments recording the magnetic afterglow of the eruption of matter from nothing at all, of genesis, temperatures that begin in excess of one trillion degrees cooled now by what Alan Guth calls the giant refrigerator of the universe to 2.7 degrees Kelvin, which is 2.7 degrees centigrade above absolute zero, which is defined as an unimaginable 273 degrees below zero centigrade, or 460 degrees below zero Fahrenheit. Yup, all these extraordinary deductions can be made, but of the future one nanosecond after the nanosecond being this instant consumed, not even science can do better than conjecture. We are all trapped in the ontological paradox that so irritated—while humbling—Eric Voegelin: We are a drop in the mighty stream of existence, paradoxically the only creature in existence capable of coming to a self-conscious understanding of the mystery of being, yet prevented from doing so by virtue of our own containment within

Time. No telescope is capable of penetrating the future; imagination may. One may project from past performance and physical laws. It is unlikely that the sun will not rise in the morning, but we can never be certain that it will. Though moral fervor can be justified, the self-righteousness of intellectual superiority flies in the face of knowledge and experience—of what can be dubbed the Human (not Hubble) Constant: the doomed imperfection of our knowledge at any given time in history.

The cure for fanaticism is to get real.

Oh, and to my fellow Christians: Fanaticism in the cause of Christ puts us at once at loggerheads with the humility and goodwill that is the essence of the Savior we profess. We are called to pray for Andrés Serrano and to love him, though this goes against (our fallen) nature.

Truculence

Defined as feeling or showing ferocity; as being savage and scathingly harsh. It don't win friends.

Traits

The speaker exhibits some of the impatience of a fanatic; perhaps more of an intellectual than moral superiority. Truculence can be expressed by excessive pugnacity. The truculent speaker seems to be in a bad humor and delivers his text as though expecting to be contradicted or disbelieved (probably both); which (almost certain) prospect is exceedingly annoying to him, because he is right, the audience ignorant; which attitude is evident in his frown, severe set of mouth and jaw, reluctance to smile, neglect of the slightest touch of humor or wit, and an air of general pessimism. A touch of truculence, of limited duration, can be okay, because it can convey the spirited conviction of the speaker, but it must be at once resolved in a smile of great sweetness and charity.

Treatment

This speaker may be truculent—a grouch—in person, in which case he should cease instanter; or his attitude may be rooted in self-doubt and insecurity. The message that the audience can get is that *he may*

NOT *be entirely convinced of what he says*, nor satisfied with it.[2] He may be expecting rebuffs because he himself acknowledges (deep down) that what he proposes hasn't been thought through sufficiently or is in other ways inadequate. Beneath the bearlike, partly querulous attitude, he masks his uncertainties when he should iron them out.

Homework can be a cure. When he has sifted the evidence and rid his thesis of what may be dubious or unsustainable, his frame of mind should improve. What he proposes now makes palpable good sense. He will be able to confide in the discernment and good sense of the audience. He can afford to like them . . . and maybe permit a little sunshine to percolate into his attitude.

Sarcasm

The sarcastic temperament has its uses, principally in enabling the speaker to maintain a detached view of the issue, which can prevent him from being naive or credulous or from going overboard in fanaticism. Sarcasm is the best attitude for pouring scorn on what is truly disreputable, revolting, or wrong. But should sarcasm become habitual in a person or a speaker, which is an almost certain peril when left uncompensated by charity or true humor, it can sour into disposition; amusing, maybe, in the beginning of a talk, but which spills corrosive acid over everything and ultimately alienates the audience because of its negativism. Sarcasm can project its own special breed of arrogance.[3]

Traits

The attitude can often suggest a juvenile sneer. The upper lip is lifted under the nostrils in an incipient snarl or smirk of superiority. The upper lids of the eyes tend to cast down over the eyeballs, gimlet[4] fashion, as though the speaker is examining a laboratory specimen of stupidity preserved in formaldehyde. The speaker is *oh* so blasé, has seen or encountered this or that *oh* so tediously often. There is little

---

[2] I want to emphasize once more that what we're concerned with are the pejorative vibes that the audience may be receiving.

[3] See page 191 of *Sex, Power, and Pericles* for more on this vice.

[4] Dictionary definition: "a small tool with screw point and cross handle for boring." Synonyms: auger, drill, ice pick, marlinespike, tap, reamer, punch. The metaphorical use is a probing look of cold steel digging out the soft insides of whatever is being inspected.

sense of fun in the sarcastic temperament; it does not surrender itself to joyous laughter because it views so little under the sun genuinely to be amused by. There is a rotten core in any apple; there is a worm coiled in the heart of existence. Along with what can be high intelligence, there's meanness in the sarcastic temperament.

Treatment

Charity. Indulgence for the human comedy. The habit of laughter. And the acknowledgement that one is neither superior nor immune to those venalities, foibles, pockets of obtuseness or stupidity, foolish enthusiasms, or ingenuous credences that beset the human race. A particular thing, or belief, or attitude, or policy may be beneath contempt, meriting only scorn, *but not everything*. The sarcastic temperament must be ever so careful to draw the distinction between sin and sinner: to assert the flatness of the earth may be blind denial of reality, but those who harbor this Bronze Age delusion may in most other respects be kind, good, and even reasonably intelligent.[5] The speaker to whom sarcasm is natural must do his best to respect his audience despite all, or he will alienate his audience despite all: his wit, his intelligence, the rightness of his views. He must ask himself: *If there is no hope for the audience, no possibility in their remediation, then in the act of getting up on stage and speaking to them, am I not myself displaying an unregenerable stupidity the equal of theirs?*

If your answer is yes to that question, step down: never again accept an invitation to speak, never more attempt to persuade anyone else to your (superior) views. But should your answer be not quite yes, subject your own soul to examination, admit remorse, aspire to repentance. And next time you speak in public, display in the mildness of your attitude the humility you have acquired, while every now and then spiking error with the same old fervor and malicious delight.

Too Cool for Words

When at the service of whim, a cool perspective is, on the whole, desirable. The uncompromised speaker is marvelously poised to be the witty

---

[5]Curiously, though the earth is round, the observable universe is as good as flat . . . so two cheers for the Flat Universe Society.

and humorous speaker; to engage audiences with his emotional and intellectual nonchalance, which tends to keep him intellectually liberated. His lances may be dreaded; they never miss their mark, toppling cant, unhorsing pomposity and bluster, piercing hypocrisy to the quick.

This speaker is an ornament to society and a bastion of civility. *But he will never do as an orator.* His tendency is to gravitate toward vanity (the vast unwashed become sullied by their passions; he is pristine) and cruelty (his barbs are loosed for their own sake; he takes such pleasure in them that he becomes insensitive to the blood they draw).[6]

Traits

The too-cool-for-words attitude exhibits some of the traits of the sarcastic temperament, but with less bitterness and little underlying anger, humor burbling beneath the surface in refreshing amounts. This speaker can be genuinely funny, inasmuch as the cool perspective exposes human beings at their most ridiculous. But there is an epicurean quality about his presentations from the floor, a certain languor, a weary disinclination to expend energy or passion by identifying himself or herself with any position. Too hot can burn up; too cool will never ignite. The person who has become bound to this temperament is best pouring cold water over enthusiasms; but he is no leader, he will never motivate a crowd.

Treatment

He must acquire passion. He must arrive at the intellectual decision (he is moved more by the intellect than by the heart) that some things matter, even matter supremely. He must decide that if he is to accept an invitation to speak (or be told to speak by a superior), he will—having first placed the topic in perspective, exploiting his talent for wit and humor—put himself in wholehearted support of, or in firm opposition to, whatever the issue may be . . . as inconsequential, perhaps, as whether to hold a barbecue before or after the softball game.

A speaker ideally is at once *dégagé* and *engagé*, in the sense that the French existentialist, Albert Camus (1913–1960), made famous.

---

[6]From pages 191–192, *Sex, Power, And Pericles*. Read more of that section, spilling over into page 193.

He must maintain his intellectual and spiritual independence (wit, humor, sarcasm—wry perspective), while at the same time throwing himself body and soul into his mission (conviction, commitment, passion). Every topic will want its own special mix; the speaker must be flexible. He must be all things to the purpose, though never else than his own man.

Uptown Blues

I refer to those unhappy souls who have been born to and nurtured in privileged enclaves of blood, money, and education . . . and also to those who, thanks to their talent, drive, and unremitting hard work, have entered into the realm of their betters.

They are all to be pitied.

Three weeks before he died, sensing that the end was very near, my father developed an urgency to impart to me, his youngest son, things that none of us had ever heard about his hard upbringing on the southeastern Texas frontier. One afternoon he told me, "There's a gift I have not been able to give to you children. You weren't born poor, as I was." I thought I comprehended what he meant at the time (I was 28), but not until thirty years later did his wisdom fully sink in.

We have had high society at our 'umble institution of learning (I once wrote, recollecting my father's round blue eyes and his wry, sardonic smile whenever the least falsity or fatuousness crossed his ken). They come to us from third-generation corporate boards and fourth-generation country clubs. The uptown corporate bodies . . . are stiffly at ease mingling with the more common folk in the seminar. Should two such book the same passage, they spot each other at once and at the reception at my house that first evening, fly to each other's bosom. They ski in Vail or Gstaad and know where Skunk's Misery Lane is; they pop across the Atlantic on the Concorde; they are charter habitués of the latest New Jimmy's in Paris and Annabelle's in London; they are . . . blasé about Chateau d'Yquem; and they are not awfully amused by the Garth Brooks or Pat Benatar tapes that . . . I . . . put on the sound system. The men are hard enough to take (superior, insolent, refractory about accepting the advice they badly need and get, whether they like it or not); the women are to throttle.

We get some high-flying corporate bitches (no other descriptive term does them justice), but they are in the main poor little rich girls from New York and other major cities or the daughters and wives of European merchant princes from Milano, Biarritz (where they summer), and Bilbao. Pampered all their lives long, they require constant reinforcement; they need to be taken by the hand over the slightest bumps in the road; they just *can't* do this and just *can't* do the other; they wail, they whine; they look piteous; they are as vain as peacocks and sometimes as spiteful as she-cats, and their instinctive last resort is to give up in haughty or forlorn hopelessness.

Top-rank male executives can be no less spoiled and difficult, especially those from humble backgrounds who have been cast up on the foam of LBOs. The last vestiges of royalism in Western civilization reside in the chief executive suites of major corporations. The CEO may have struggled to gain this eminence, and his reign may be brief. Once there, however, he lives as no one else (save his counterparts in other major executive suites), an absolute despot, his every whim tended to by squadrons of fawning subordinates, his coffers filling with riches beyond the avarice of even Spanish monarchs in the age of the conquistadors, when treasure galleons from Peru, Bolivia, and Mexico, fat with the gold and silver of the Indies, dropped anchor in Cádiz. It does not take long for memory of leaner years to dissolve.

The attitudes implanted in both sexes by the environment of inherited or suddenly acquired wealth, rank, and social position can be destructive in the extreme. For a speaker, those attitudes can be ruinous.

Traits

<u>In men</u>, the uptown vice manifests itself in a refusal by the speaker to exert himself for the benefit of the audience and in a personal removal from the common herd that is immediately sensed and resented. Though the uptown speaker invests little effort in the acceptance of his words, credence he expects as divinely ordained right. His sense of exalted station exhibits itself in facial expression (gazing down at the audience along the length of the nose, or side long, or not at all, ennui plastered across his countenance), physical attitude (slumping on the lectern, a pervasive lassitude, or, in some top executives and entrepre-

neurs, a brusque and impatient manner), and voice (either patronizing, "This may be difficult for the lower orders to understand, but believe me, what I say is correct; in fact, I dare say, the *only* thing to be said on the subject," or flat and curt in tone, as though giving orders). The reaction he provokes is that he is insufferable. If there is an alternative to the course he favors, the audience will opt for it.

In women, the insecurities of their high rank and lifelong privilege surface disastrously: tense pallid faces; frozen smiles; catatonic bodies; hands wringing each other wet; faint, whispery, or hoarse uppercrust (sometimes also whisky-ridden) voices. They come in two personality types.

The first and least attractive is overbearing. These daughters of wealth or high corporate position anger easily. They can become strident as well as ill-tempered, turning audiences off.

The second type takes refuge in po' l'il me. They seem often as though on the point of bursting into tears, flushing and then going deathly pale at the first criticism or obstacle, pride of birth coursing close to the surface of the skin, naked and vulnerable. The audience may feel sorry for them; they are also made impatient and a bit contemptuous.

Treatment

A diet of stale bread crusts and water would help.

Women: The society types undervalue themselves. Since all their lives long they have got by on wealth, position, and personal charm or beauty, and since they are the apple of daddy's (or sugar daddy's) eye, they've rarely been left to their own resources and have rarely been called to perform in anything other than a social setting, to dig in, to use the wit, guts, and heart that—happily—many of them possess. They need to believe in themselves more. Both their haughtiness (which can be infuriating) and their attitude of collapse are defenses. In the beginning, they may require the crutch of a fully written-out text on a simple and familiar topic, but since they are natively well-endowed in the brains and heart department, their progress can be rapid.

The woman who has clawed her way to the top or near-top of the corporate pile is a tougher case, though she, too, needs to believe in herself more strongly. Her deep-set fear is that everything she has achieved is an illusion. Of this *cauchemar*, riding her subconscious haggard, she must be relieved. The tough, unbecoming, churlish attitude is unnecessary. It's safe for her to smile, to inject (unexacerbated) wit, to tell a humorous anecdote, to make fun of herself. She won't be demeaning her person or her achievements, inviting loss of esteem or mockery. Actually, she'll be joining the club at last.

<u>Men</u>: In the case of corporate magnates, they need to be reminded of two facts of nature.

The first is that their glory is terminal. They will one day, maybe not so distant on the horizon, retire; or they may be abruptly ousted. The moment the key to the executive suite is twisted out of their fingers, they become ordinary mortals, richer than most—oh, Croesuses—but no longer figures of awe. Their authority must be newly established; it has to be newly earned.

Second is that their glory is transient. The moment they cease to function at the helm, they are through. *Ozymandias*: historically done with, their temporal power in ruins, their memory fading faster than bleached hair under a tropical sun. Meantime, has their family survived the rigors and temptations of their career? *"The Earl of Fife had a wife. Where is she now? Cawdor had a wife? Where is she now?"* Is there a son or daughter to whom they can open their hearts, whose hearts are open to them? Do they retain any true friends? What about honor, decency, and ethical behavior? And what about their conversation? Is there anything other than the stock market and their particular field of production of which they can boast barest knowledge? Have they acquired (or retained) any culture, any learning, any wisdom? What *are* they going to talk about: yesterday's Concorde to Cairo, yesterday's New Jimmy's and yesterday's Annabelle's, yesterday's corporate battles? Are they crashing bores, has-been mechanics of the managerial class, obsolete technocrats? Do they possess any interior resources whatever?

These reflections should be sobering . . . and inject a little humility in their attitude on the podium. If the only people they are truly comfortable with are fellow ex-CEOs, they are in a bad way.

In the case of men born to the manner, they do need to inquire of themselves whether their talents, persons, or accomplishments reflect—justify—their social position. Money talks, but not always well. Blood tells, but the story may be thin and pitiable. Social rank is accorded its privileges, but they may be as hollow as they are little deserved. It has become boring for the son of inherited wealth to go Left in the effort to assuage his guilt.

Such reflections also are conducive to humility. That one teenager in the audience who scribbles poetry at night; that one mother of three who all along has been writing short stories and maybe a couple of unpublished novels; that small-town druggist who screeches awful sounds on the strings of his violin, but spends evenings with wife and children listening to Monteverdi and Schubert; that seedy-looking lawyer who devotes more hours than he can afford to defending the poor; that bland-faced minister who burns inside with love of his fellowman and fights for racial harmony: these and dozens upon dozens Americans like them may be leading fuller, richer, ultimately more remarkable and historically more memorable lives than the speaker, on whom condescension sits ill.

The cure for most of our ills as persons and as speakers is humility . . . about which see the next chapter.

Finally . . .

The Ego

We need it.

As persons and as speakers.

We require that reinforcement, that goad, that source of self-esteem and honor. But oh, my!

Herewith a comment in one of the critiques we write up on our clients:

> The ego is the principal affliction of the speaker. In those who are comfortable on stage, the ego transpires when the audience get the notion that the fellow up there is being too clever by half, unctuous, or pompous: that in fact he is admiring himself as he speaks . . . Such think they are simply marvelous, and the audience turn off. The ego is also paramount in the fumbling, unsure, or panicky speaker. That person is thinking more of himself (or herself) than of the message that must be imparted. The speaker and his ego must be absolutely divorced. To be flustered or panicky on stage *is a moral fault.*

Traits

The ego is the enemy. One otherwise impressive high executive in a major company—basically a speaker of the first rank—demonstrated all the character traits on stage that repel and ultimately alienate an audience. It was pathetic. He was puzzled, baffled. He could not understand why he wasn't successful in winning the sympathies of his audiences. Read what we wrote in his critique. If you suspect that you are guilty of his offenses, reform!

> There is no doubt about it . . . Conferee is a talented speaker. He has a gift for the dramatic in his facial expression, gestures, body language, and voice. He struts about the stage when others are still clinging to the lectern. And there you have it . . . Conferee is strutting, not fretting, his hour on stage. As good as he is, he is *just too much*. He coerces the listener rather than coaxing him. He points his finger in their faces, he moves into their space, and he psychologically vanquishes them by doing it all with such force. Schwarzenegger be still and let the listener get a glimpse of thy soul! Only in this manner can the bond be formed that brings the audience to your side.

The crit continued:

> What's at the bottom of his trouble? He is not throwing himself sufficiently into his message. He is keeping in mind himself-as-performer. It's as though he is admiring Mr. Nibs up there, thinking: what a wonderfully smooth orator I am! That's the impression that he projects, and this is why audiences will react to him as though he were truly arrogant. They sense condescension in him along with self-admiration. The combination of the two destroys him, which is a terrible shame, because he is so immensely talented. He must remind himself over and over of this: Total expulsion of the self is achieved through total immersion of the self in the desire to get across the message.

The ego calls attention only to the self, and in doing so, unbridled, can consume all. Did Henry Kissinger, for one moment, in the innermost recesses of his mind and heart, believe that the North Koreans intended to keep their word in the Paris Peace Accords? Or was Talleyrand-Metternich-Pitt-Canning-Richelieu admiring himself?

Treatment

Humility, humility, humility. He who approaches the lecture platform in the frame of mind other than that he is a humble petitioner—which doesn't at all signify that he can't at the same time be witty, mischievous, funny, acerbic, and passionately convinced of the truth and right of what he is saying—is wasting his time . . . and that of the audience.

Now to the necessary virtues.

CHAPTER 19

THE VIRTUES

THE VIRTUES

First of which, though not principal, is . . .

Honesty

. . . That is, to be more precise and . . . honest, *the appearance of which*.

There are circumstances when it becomes the obligation of the speaker to stretch or embroider the truth, tell not quite the whole truth, equivocate, lie.

He is a defense counsel and has come to the personal belief that his client is guilty as sin; he is a tobacco executive, juggling his personal obligation to truth and to the commonweal against his obligations to his stockholders; he is a diplomat, delegated by his boss, the President of the United States, effusively to praise the United Nations, on the occasion of the fiftieth anniversary of that organization's founding, for its contributions to world peace—and not giggle or throw up in the act.

This isn't a book about ethics; it's about how to speak in public well and effectively. There are occasions, alas, when one's duty may be to lie oneself blue in the face, yet one must project from the platform an air of total candor.

Traits

The impression of honesty is projected when the speaker qualifies what he is saying—the policy or cause he is upholding—in the narrowest terms and with an (seemingly) evident desire not to claim too much for what he favors; by citing the arguments against the cause or policy he deems best, and doing them (seeming) full justice; by being quick to cede minor points in which he is proved mistaken (or has been found out eliding), graciously thanking whoever (may he fry in Hell) brought the errors to his attention, and apologizing for having mistakenly (i.e., innocently) given the wrong impression; by being a trifle diffident in praising his side of the argument, using such phrases as "I don't want to claim too much for what I'm suggesting," "There could well be consequences of which we have no present knowledge, nor can predict," "This is no cure-all," "If a better answer is discovered, please tell me, I want to hear about it," "Only under the weight of evidence was I finally myself brought 'round to the opinion . . ."

From the Stage

The speaker's demeanor should at all times be composed, his expression kind and judicious. When listening to an objection from the floor, he should do so with evident total concentration, frowning, head bent, ear cocked toward the interrogator—nodding as though half in agreement, or as though freshly reconsidering his position while evaluating the strength of the objection; and should hesitate before delivering his answer, never flinging a hasty, sharp, or dismissive retort at the questioner (no matter how dumb his objection may be). Oh, he must be a wily, paltering, slippery, smooth, unmitigated son of perdition, projecting himself as Jimmy Stewart facing down Lionel Barrymore.[1]

The Germans call it *ausnützer*,[2] the French call it *culot*,[3] the Spanish call it *cara* (face),[4] we call it brass. I could draw up a list of master rogues in our public arena who have succeeded brilliantly in never telling the truth with such honest mien that they chalk up stun-

---

[1] Of *It's a Wonderful Life* fame: the jowly, merciless fatcatcapitalist banker who tried to bring Jimmy Stewart to ruin when he was unable to corrupt him.

[2] As in *Est is ein ausnützer*, he is one who takes advantage.

[3] As in *Il a du culot. Culot*: literally, the residue of tobacco tar in a pipe.

[4] As in *Tiene cara* . . .

ning approval ratings in poll after poll, lie after lie, year after year . . . but I will not do this, inasmuch as I decry invidious allusions tending to exacerbate (what else?) public opinion, honestly.

Now don't be foolish. The forensic demands of lying well, or credibly, are identical to the forensic demands on the speaker who is in fact truthful. Be fairminded, don't overstate your case, admit errors gladly and graciously, listen hard to objections, weigh alternative proposals well before rejecting them, avoid hasty or irascible reactions, and never flinch from a tough question that demands you to answer with such a whopper that no decent person in the audience could doubt your veracity.

Do not make this common mistake: Using the phrase, "To be honest with you . . ." Hmmmm. Were you not previously being honest with us? Two minutes from now, will you cease being honest with us? The speaker who calls attention to his virtue places it in doubt.

Candor

. . . As in frankness and outspokenness.

A speaker may be, in fact, a straight arrow, but if he does not exhibit candor, his virtue may be wasted.

Traits

Angels could write on this speaker's forehead. His brow is smooth, his eyes wide and pure, his gaze unflinching, his demeanor frank. He interrupts the interrogator before that fellow has fully completed his question, eager to agree: "But of course, you're perfectly right, how often do we make the mistake of assuming that we have all the answers, or the perfect answer!" He will remark wryly in another connection, "We all make mistakes, and I guess I've made more than my share." He will unhesitatingly admit, "I often wish I understood the ramifications better, but I have to work with what the good Lord gave me." He will confess, "Look, some of you in the audience know me. I have been dead wrong before, no question, and am likely to be wrong again. Yet it nevertheless seems to me that in deciding whether Duchess County can afford a new grade school, we should ask first whether the children of Duchess County can afford *not* having better facilities . . ."

Go ahead, *throw* up. This speaker's candor is expressed not so much by what he says as by how he says it, verbally and with the aid of body language.

From the Stage

To convey candor, a speaker must take pains to stand erect, shoulders flung back, head lifted, his whole bearing squared to the audience. If he comes out from behind the lectern, never, never should he step only partially to the side, maintaining his body half in view, half blocked from view. (*What's the speaker hiding? Why won't he come out from behind that thing and face us?*) To the audience, partial exposure is partial concealment. Always get completely shut of the lectern. And when abandoning it, loads of candor are conveyed by the speaker who strides right out to the front, taking a stand as close to the audience as the stage permits, arms hanging naturally by his sides—exposing himself, breast, stomach, loins, to whatever slings and arrows may be hurled at him, trusting in the truth and merits of his case to be his shield and see him through. The audience like the cut of that man's jib. (*He may be telling us things we don't like to hear, but dadblast it!— the guy is a straight shooter.*)

Any facial antics to which the speaker is susceptible must be controlled, which may require the help of a therapist. Tics tend to surface under stress; they project bad things to the audience. (*Is this fellow telling it the way it is? What's the hidden agenda?*) Similarly does a sudden sweat—the damp at the upper rim of the scalp, the glistening (or glossy) knobs on the brow—suggest the agitation of the speaker who is himself (or herself) doubtful about what he (or she) is saying.[5] The speaker should attempt to gaze at the audience always out of the wide open (china blue) eyes of a Suzanne Somers, blinking as little as possible (the hooded Humphrey Bogart or Robert Mitchum stare may be sexy, but it is also menacing and crafty). A self-deprecating smile should twitch incipiently at the outer corners of his lips, rarely blossoming, and not so persistently that the suggestion decays, as it can, into

---

[5]Some poor souls sweat pathologically, from any nervous tension, or sweat easily in heat, from the desert-dry rays of stage lights. They must struggle against this as best they can, though they should resist constant swabbings of forehead and— especially—the mouth (gross) with a handkerchief, calling attention to their condition and heightening the apprehensions of the audience.

a self-satisfied smirk. Hands, of course, should be kept out of pockets (for reasons mentioned in Chapter 11), and the attitude of arms and hands should be frequently open, raised, and outthrust—toward the audience, embracing the audience, identifying with the audience, trusting in the audience.

Oh, irresistible.

Decency

It's so unfair! Some folk—some physical types, even—suggest, with no conscious effort on their part, an essential decency that is mightily attractive to audiences.

Decency is, I think, the social personality that most naturally and most often translates to the stage. It can be faked, of course, though not easily. It seems to be a God-given grace (see below, under Personal Magnetism) that in some people transpires whenever attention is focused on them, either at a cocktail party or in an interview or when they mount the lecture platform.

Should you happen to be one of the fortunate few, lucky dog. You are the envy of speakers. Should you happen to be one of those rare decency-projecting persons *and also clever*, luckier dog yet. You are a rare platform presence, because most clever people, to their rue, project—unless they are careful—foxy disingenuousness, untrustworthiness, and sometimes malice.

Traits

The decent platform presence comes in two major types, the thin and timid, the stout and amiable.

The second type often perspires, not from fear or guilt, but because of that person's physical build. He may sweat freely, unselfconsciously. His shoulders are confidently squared to the audience; his chin is lifted. His physiognomy is often illuminated with a cheerful smile. Friendliness exudes from him—he grins, he beams, he radiates happiness. No hint of malice transpires, not ever. He has never entertained an evil thought. All his life, he has sought to do good and allied himself with good and decent causes. The audience would trust him with their lives.

There's the quiet, pale, scholarly type. This person verbalizes hesitantly. Shyness is an attribute: swift glances at the audience, the flash of an infinitely sweet smile. The audience fall in love with him (or her).

From the Stage

The speaker projecting decency isn't cut out for polemics, for becoming a partisan in a sharp controversy. It's contrary to character, subversive of his major asset. If he is trapped in a polemic, he should seek always reconciliation between opposing views; he should express goodwill unfailingly and unfailingly attribute goodwill to opponents. The audience will lap it up. They will desire to be on this speaker's side, despite intellectual reservations or, on his part, forensic shortcomings.

By virtue of being decent or conveying decency, half the battle is won, but decent persons on stage cannot rely wholly and alone on the grace with which they have been blessed. The quiet, pale, scholarly type may in the beginning verbalize hesitantly, and flash timid glances at the audience that she quickly averts, but as she enters into her talk, she must discard the protective shell and overcome her shyness. Her articulation must improve, smooth out; her voice must gain in volume and confidence; and she must inject energy in her whole presence. The second type, the stoutly cheerful decent person, must permit himself to become serious, take a firm stand—take pains that he is not mistaken for an amiable fool.

For all their deficiencies as speakers, decent souls will nevertheless win many an argument that the cleverest of partisans lose. The reason: The audience identify with them, being themselves, or thinking of themselves as, at heart, decent also. Ronald Reagan was not a great orator, and often in his later years only a bumbling, befuddling communicator, but the core sweetness of his nature, his essential decency, under the harshest attack, won bout after bout in public forums.

Sincerity

This trait assumes intensity also. Projecting sincerity is essential in winning the attention and approval of the crowd.

Here is where "cool," such a commendable trait, can be in conflict. The cool personality on stage can convey that he is unable to work up warmth for, or conviction in, anything at all. (So why should the audience?) He chops the legs out from under himself.

Sincerity is not shouting or hectoring or lecturing or proselytizing. It can be low-keyed, though no less convinced and intense. The sincere speaker has won this much from the audience: *Okay, this fellow isn't wasting our time; he truly means what he says; let's hear him out.*

Which is to have gained much.

Traits

The sincere speaker projects conviction and passion in his entire attitude: *through facial expressions*, which tend to be strong, dour, stern, the brow furrowed, eyes glittering, gaze penetrating, mouth severe, jaw rigid; *through gestures*, which tend to be abrupt, emphatic, biceps swelled and tensely bulging, forearms taut, the fingers of both hands spread wide, bent—clawed—at the last joint, and rigid; *through body language*, which may be hunched, half crouched, torso thrust from the waist toward the audience, shoulders raised and pressed tightly to the sides of the neck and skull, just under the ears, so that wing muscles from the base of the neck across ache; *and through the voice*, which may become hoarse, descend to the lowest registers, and boom.

Sincerity is the intensity of conviction leaking through the whole being of the speaker, body and spirit.

From the Stage

Attitudes of sincerity at once get it across that something important is at stake. Attention is forced upon the crowd. They fall silent. They harken.

But there are dangers in this virtue. Sincerity expressed too unrelentingly and too forcefully quickly tires people, who rebel against the bombardment of high emotion and begin quickly to wish for a touch of levity, a hint of intellectual perspective, respite, a few moments of remission. One can easily rant an audience to death. The strongest expression of sincerity, for these reasons, should be reserved for perorations.

Give audiences a break. *Speakers who are temperamentally intense in their convictions must take precaution that they do not overbellow their welcome.*

Passion

The speaker who is not passionately interested in what he is talking about is wasting everybody's time, including his own.

Passion is not all *Sturm und Drang*. It can be cool, it can be intellectual, it can be judicious, it can be moderate, and it can be modest.

But it must be generated . . . and the audience must be alerted to its existence.

Traits

Energy is required for passion and is closely associated with passion, but it isn't the same beast as passion. Sincerity is necessary to passion, but is no synonym for passion.

The speaker who is passionately *engagé* unmistakably alerts the crowd about that as soon as he steps up to the stage. It's an air, a *frisson*; the discharge of electricity; the announcement and sensing of a powerful magnetic field, concentrated in the lectern, emanating from it. This is for real, folks.

Passion relates to personal magnetism (below), but is not the same thing.

From the Stage

Passion partakes of ferocity—in belief, desire, determination. The listless, ambivalent stage personality might as well stay home. When the evening's topic is serious, audiences want to know that the speaker is committed. If he isn't persuaded of the consequence of his words, why should they be? The strength of that commitment can be in itself persuasive to them.

Passion imbues the speaker with the concentration of energies that permits him to block out of his mind everything other than his mission, which is to convert the audience to his way of thinking . . . by establishing dominion over the souls of his audience: *domar* and *mandar*. Passion energizes voice, facial expressions, gestures, and body language. Passion—conviction in the truth, rightness, and importance of what one is saying—is the dynamo that can generate a rapt and enthusiastic response in the people one is trying to reach.

When disciplined. When controlled. When *contained*. When

deployed with that indispensable French word *mésure*—in measured manner. *Passion is not to be confused with enthusiasm,* a lesser emotion. Enthusiasm can be the hallmark of the unsophisticated and superficial temperament. It cheapens easily. Unbridled passion, like excessive enthusiasm, is a horror, turning audiences off at once. Mature, subdued, dignified, sagacious passion is the goal. Thus held in check by the speaker, his passion can be expressed in the steely glittering of an eye, in his detached attitude, in his diffident tone, in his single, slashing gesture, in his barbed and acerbic sarcasm, in his mordant wit, in his belly laugh, in his loving-kindness . . . in the residue notwithstanding of his unshakable conviction.

Any fool can rant and rave. Fanatics are passionate. The young? Youthful passion is enthusiastic, callow, sentimental; characteristically exaggerated, shallow, fickle, irrational, and *violent.* Young people are the terrorists; they plant the bombs that maim and butcher fellow human beings; they slash the throats of children for playing dominoes. Desirable, mature passion must be acquired. I hazard a guess: One cannot be passionate in the beneficent sense without having bitten deep into long, bitter, sobering experience. Passion must be proofed in suffering, forged in wisdom.

This is the emotional charge that the accomplished speaker must convey: the dominion of wisdom in his soul, thirsting for justice.

Personal Magnetism

Some people seem to have it, others not. We tell our students not to confuse personal magnetism with charisma, which is incorrectly used. To possess charisma is to be filled with the grace of God. (John F. Kennedy was loosely described as having charisma, but if he was filled with the grace of God, so is Madonna.) Charisma is a gift. One is born with charisma or one is endowed with it. By contrast, personal magnetism—the ability to attract and mesmerize the attention of others—is a quality that can be nurtured and that flows from the intensity of interest that an individual puts into his work, his relations with others, his performances on the speaker's podium, or his attitude in conferences and boardrooms. Leadership, we remind our students, operates according to Newtonian dynamics: action begets reaction; energy (from leader) in, energy (from audience or subordinates) out.

More people than they suspect—you may be one of them—possess
this quality.

Traits

The magnetic speaker unites all the virtues mentioned above—honesty,
candor, decency, sincerity, passion—in a personality that commands
attention anywhere, and from the podium, electrically.

Everything seems to flow toward him; everything of any importance originates in him.

The part that strong eye contact plays in establishing this dominion
cannot be stressed too much. The personally magnetic being, when he
or she looks at anyone, transfixes that person with his gaze and focuses
with laserlike intensity on that person and that person alone, radiating
into the intelligence, plumbing the soul. As a speaker, he treats the
entire audience in this fashion, in the ways mentioned in Chapter 11.

What's crucial to the effect is that he gives each individual the
notion that nothing is so important to him as communicating with that
individual. The Pope himself could be standing in the wings, waiting
to be introduced; he will not lift his head nor interrupt whatever
colloquy he is having with this individual. A fire may break out, police
come charging into the hall, ambulances hoot and clang; he will not
notice. He is totally absorbed. And he is sucking the life's juices out of
the object of his attention, emptying that person's will, gaining a voter,
a convert, a disciple.

Analyzed, it's a snap. Anyone can acquire the one-on-one personal
magnetism of a Dwight Eisenhower, a John Paul, a Billy Graham, a Bill
Clinton. It does require sedulous devotion.

From the Stage

The magnetic speaker permits the powerful effect of his personality to
sink in before commencing his talk. He is silent at the lectern, still,
apparently abstracted. When he breaks silence, he begins perhaps
slowly, in a clear but soft voice, permitting it gradually to gain in volume
and velocity. *He is himself utterly unaware of the effect he is having
upon people.* There can be no streak of self-adulation or self-satisfaction
in him. He must be absolutely engrossed in the message, in the way

that Pope John Paul II and Billy Graham are absolutely absorbed in the love of Christ Jesus and the mission they have been given to spread His Word. This religious devotion is necessary to personal magnetism, though from the stage, it is nevertheless not sufficient to endow the speaker with the magnetic aura. He must learn forensic skills, practice the craft brilliantly, as does Rev. Graham, as does, less well, the Pope.

Way back at the instant of the Big Bang, at the first gasp of Creation, the universe was at a point of infinite density, infinite pressure, and infinite temperature, which awesome and mysterious state is known to empirical cosmologists as $t = 0$. That's an apt metaphor for what we describe as personal magnetism: $t = 0$; a compaction of infinite density, infinite pressure, and infinite temperature, all at the moment of explosion. We tremble in its presence.

We come now to the principal virtue, absent which, nothing is possible:

Humility of Spirit

Demosthenes and Cicero made enemies, and this cost them their lives. *If I have not love, . . .* said St. Paul. The desire, the passion, the felicity of expression and gesture, the wit, the humor, the daring intellect: All amount to not a hill of beans if humility of spirit is absent.

Not even personal magnetism, which cannot exist, at least on the podium, without humility of spirit.

Traits

Sweetness of disposition. Self-effacement. The ability to laugh heartily at oneself. Patience. Magnanimity. The ever-present consciousness of one's fallibility. The believer's ontological and eschatological view; the contemporary secular particle physicist's cosmological view. The Devil may be able to fake humility of spirit; you can't.

From the Stage

The speaker attaches to himself no importance, to his mission, every importance. If that mission is to please and entertain the audience, he goes all out. If it is to advance a point of view, he devotes every skill and talent to the purpose, emptying himself in the mission.

He is no glad-hander. His demeanor is modest (he may blush easily). He takes no credit. He is truly embarrassed by flossy, flattering, elaborated introductions, showing this. He shuns rhetorical excesses and fancy language. He subjects the power of language to its primary functions: to communicate and to persuade. He is aghast at any imputation of vanity. Applause pleases him for the sake of his message . . . and, characteristically, slightly surprises him. He is awkward about compliments at the conclusion of his speech, fearing that he may have betrayed his purpose by calling attention to the rhetorical powers whose sole justification is to support and advance the purpose.

He loathes speaking in public.

❖   ❖   ❖

These virtues are all essential. But just as none of us escapes all the vices entirely, no matter how hard we may try, so none of us, in every department, quite lives up to the ideals set forth here.

Which is their major lesson to us.

CHAPTER 20

FEAR, STAGE FRIGHT, AND *LE TRAC* (PANIC)

I got back from a long absence to find the shooting script for *A Summertime Killer* on my desk.

Leafing through the pages rapidly, anger rose red-hot to the gorge. I had written the script. Outrages had been wreaked on it. If any shred of character or touch of class were possible in the second-grade action flicks of the late 1960s, these resided in the dialogue. Dialogue is just about the only element of a script in which the writer can take pride. The rest is an ordeal by humiliation, as first the director, and then the producers, and then sundry other busybodies with neither a modicum of taste nor respect for dramatic integrity mess it up. But worse had been perpetrated.

I called my friend "Joe" (José) Vicuña, who was involved in the production. "Joe," I yelped, "I've just looked through the shooting script for *Summertime*. Joe, I'm hopping mad. I'm *indignant*. The dialogue is riddled with clichés. The idiom is all wrong for the American rôles; I mean, not even people in California truly speak like that. And my car, my beautiful car!"

"We're paying you for that," he reminded me.

"But the . . ."

"Go see Isasi. He's shooting at the Monumental. I doubt anything can be done about it now, but Chris Mitchum agrees with you about the dialogue."

That was Robert Mitchum's strapping young son, playing the romantic lead opposite Olivia Hussey. The Monumental is the bullring. I sped to it at breakneck speed through Madrid's frenzied traffic in my wife's Mini Austin, getting angrier with each collision that I barely zipped my way out of, thinking all the while of my gleaming 360 hp 1963 Chevelle stationwagon V8, lacquered in a dusty golden brown finish, my "Golden Chariot," which for five years I had squeezed through the narrowest alleys in Toledo and challenged the fattest Mercedes on the highways, leaving them in my dust . . . jumping out of the Mini at the *puerta principal* (the main gate) of the bullring and accosting Antonio Isasi, the director, who is charming.

I found him standing exasperatedly off to the right, during one of those frequent intervals in the shooting of a movie when everything is in a high state of confusion, with nothing seemingly getting done, putting everybody in a sullen frame of mind.

"Oh, hello, Reid. Back from Chile, are you?"

"Antonio," I fairly shrieked, "what have you done with the dialogue?"

"Tell him," said young Mitchum, coming up behind us. "It's been desecrated. The dialogue was the major reason I took this effen part."

"Can't be helped." said Antonio wearily. "All sorts of problems came up; you were away; I did the best I was able; Karl Malden's agent told me that his property can't articulate the lines you gave him to say . . ."

"I don't believe that!" I shouted. "And my car, my car, my beautiful wagon . . . *why* do we have to run it off a cliff at the end!"

"We paid you for it, haven't we? . . . Reid, do something for me, would you?"

Cunning fellow, he knew that my fury is almost always sapped when someone asks me a favor. "What?" I asked.

"Walk to that kiosk in front of the *puerta principal* and buy me a paper."

"What paper, the *ABC, Ya, Alerta,* why?"

"It doesn't matter, any newspaper. We need an *extranjero*, a foreigner, an American like you, to buy a newspaper. The extra has disappeared."

"Oh, okay," said I, still riled, yet obliging. I began striding to the kiosk, which was about fifty feet away. As I went, I became acutely aware that a camera was trained on me from behind. Suddenly I became conscious that I was being filmed, *that the entire universe was going to be watching me.* My back felt clammy. My gait turned catatonic. Each leg weighed a ton, as though filled with lactic acid. I reached the kiosk as though I'd been running a 440 into a high wind, tongue thick in my mouth. "Pppperdiódico," I gasped, clutching at the sill. Fluids were trickling down the insides of my legs to the knees, which threatened to collapse on me. The vendor silently handed me a newspaper. I fumbled in a side pocket of my jacket for a coin. Couldn't get my fist into the pocket. What simpler motion than to thrust a hand into one's jacket pocket? My fingers were thickened, unable to sort and grasp the correct size (denomination) of coin. The sun stood still in the skies for Joshua. For me. This was taking an eternity. I pulled out several coins, helplessly offering them to the vendor in an open palm. My hand was shaking. My whole body was frozen against a fit of shaking. He picked out five *duros,* a quarter. *"That'll do, cut"* Antonio Isasi's voice mercifully bawled out behind me.

The point is *not* that *A Summertime Killer* turned out to be every bit as awful as I gloomily foretold, and may, in fact, have dealt Chris Mitchum's career a mortal blow, or that under the tyranny of the script (which, even though I was eventually paid, for weeping, I would not have written), my gorgeous Golden Chariot was driven off a cliff into the briny deep; no, *not* these twin sad tidings, but that I had succumbed to stage fright, and so wretchedly that the sequence ended up on the cutting room floor. Posterity was denied.

DON'T PERMIT FEAR TO TOPPLE YOU

Fear keeps steady company with the performing arts. You can't abolish it. Perish the thought. Without the *faux bourdon* of fear imminent in your entrails, you are worth nothing on the stage; you will persuade no one to your side of an argument; you will move no one to leap out of his foxhole and drive his bayonet into the enemy. Fear absent, you flop.

But natural apprehensions and the bubbling of adrenaline through your veins are different from stage fright or panic. The first you must cultivate, the second suppress.

1. *Tighten your organization.*

2. *Write your entire speech down, word for word.*

3. *Rehearse and rehearse and rehearse.* Three, four, six times, until you are sick to death of it. *Soak* yourself in your text.

4. *Concentrate totally on your desire to deliver the message.* Freshly psyche yourself into this desire just before you go on stage or open the meeting.

5. *Simultaneously abstract yourself from what you are doing.*

6. *Insist on seclusion before you go on.* Detach yourself from banquet table partners; avoid being cornered by someone at the pre-performance reception who may harangue you on a subject utterly unrelated to your topic.

7. *Resist any feeling of well-being; do not permit yourself to be distracted from the impending task, and do not for an instant permit bonhomie to undermine your concentration.*

8. *Develop an acute consciousness of your personal ridiculousness in the scheme of existence.* (Which should be easy.)

9. *Do battle against your conceit.*

10. *Once on stage, seek out a sympathetic person in the audience for moral support; ignore the hostile face.*

11. *Determine to prevail or to die trying.*

Some of these counsels may seem contradictory. When examined, they're not.

Sweat, Blood, Toil, and Tears: Surpassing Yourself

1. Tighten your organization.

The logical assemblage of an essay or a talk is ideally so natural and so inherently integrated that *one* leads to *two* leads to *three* in a progression that to disrupt must defy the interior logic of the brain.

When asked, "What did you have for breakfast?" one doesn't reply: "Toast, coffee, and juice." Both the gastronomic and chronological sequences impose their order. One replies: "Juice, toast, and coffee," coffee being subsequent to toast because it is sipped as an emulsifying liquid in the act of eating toast. When asked, "How did you dress this morning?" one doesn't reply: "I put on my jacket, shirt, trousers, shorts, shoes, and socks." One replies, "I put on my shorts, my shirt, my socks, my trousers, and my jacket," the logical chronological sequence of the action taking command. Maybe you'll be prompted to add, "Oh, I slipped on my tie before I put on my jacket."

Just so must your argument be reduced to a natural flow of one precedent subject to the next, with the natural chronology in place. If one's topic is the Battle of Gettysburg, it's unnatural to write, "The losses were 51,112 dead and wounded, mostly dead, out of a total of 163,289 men engaged. The advantage seesawed, but on the third day the North won, and this victory is considered as fateful for the young American republic as Thermopylae was for the Greeks and Waterloo for Europe. Nevermore was the South capable of mounting a serious threat to the North. The dates are 1–3 July, 1864."

That's disjointed. Topic one does not lead to topic two does not lead to topic three. Just about anything can be tossed in or omitted. A better put-together construction would ask and answer a number of questions: (a) When did the battle take place? *"The terrible battle of Gettysburg began on 1 July, 1864, ending in the afternoon of 3 July."* (b) How were the fortunes of war apportioned? *"The first day favored Confederate arms, the second day was a stalemate, and the third day brought victory to the Union."* (c) What was the military significance of that victory? *"The South was nevermore able to take the war to the North."* (d) At what cost in human carnage? *"This result was achieved at the cost of 51,112 young men in gray and blue dead, out of 163,289 engaged."* (e) Was the bloodshedding worth it? *"The price was awful; it was one of the most desperate and bloody actions in military history, but as Themopylae proved fateful for the Greeks, Waterloo for Europe, Gettysburg determined the destiny of the United States."*

The organization is clear. (a) When did it take place? *The dates.* (b) What was the progress of the battle? *The summation of the three days.* (c) What was the consequence of the battle? *The South is hurled back forever.* (d) At what cost was this great victory achieved? *The casualties.* (e) In the balance of human destiny, how does this battle rate? *"With the great decisions by arms in history, beginning with the Greek victories over the Persians, Wellington over Napoleon . . ."*

When one's organization is limpid, shapely, tangible, logically euphonious (singing in the mind), lucid, pleasing, and dynamic, *topic (a)* suggesting and impelling one to *topic (b)*, *topic (b)* naturally debouching one on *topic (c)*, it's difficult to go off track. Achieving such organization requires a lot of tough preliminary work. Not only must the sequence of topics be sorted out in their natural order (chronology is the simplest, though not always the correct or most advisable determinant), the syntax of the sentences must also reflect that order. Just as *topic (a)* impels one to *topic (b)*, so the sentences expounding the topic should clearly and harmoniously spill into one another, creating a seamless texture.

The human brain is bombarded every second by millions of messages about reality that it receives through the senses. The brain is engaged in a continuous editing and ordering of these messages, with the design of reducing their vast number to a comprehensible prototype. Is that truly a savage about to strike you with a club, or is what causes you to cringe the shadow of a loose shutter being banged about by the wind? When one's thinking, and when one's reflection of that thinking in language, approach beauty—because they so please the organizational bias of the human brain, in the process acquiring an architectonic majesty—then fear on one major level is defied. You are not going to mess up the presentation of your topic by expounding first things last and last things first, the natural authority of your design preventing it.

2. Write your entire speech down, word for word.

Geniuses prefer to wing it. Let them. I guess I've never met a genius on stage. I *have* met a lot of folk with a natural gift for gab—slick folk, usually superficial folk, and often perniciously arrogant folk—who prefer to improvise their talks as they go along. Do not emulate them.

Generally, these free spirits resist cementing their text in a written version because they are (a) intellectually lazy and do not enjoy the labor, (b) vain and resist exposing the shallowness of their thoughts to scrutiny. So they set down a few cryptic, compact headlines and subheads, from which they "wing it."

They can be brilliant on occasion, oh, yes! When inspired. When everything conspires to go just right. But they won't always be brilliant, nor brilliant when obliged to perform day after day, night after night. More often, they will be erratic and (this follows certainly) verbose, taking too long to utter simple things.

Here's the progression. The first time they articulate a particular point, they may do it commendably; the second time, wonderfully. How pleased they are with themselves. (How truly superior they have shown themselves to be.) By the third go, they've become captives of their conceit. They needlessly elaborate, embroidering; they use too many words and too many subordinate clauses to get across what, in the balance, may not be that important, their syntactical constructions becoming more and more convoluted as they wander further and further from the grain. Their parts wax greater than their whole; the drift is obscured. What they are getting at, if ever they get to it, arrives as an anticlimax, as though yanked in at the last moment. I've witnessed this transmogrification in the speeches of high corporate officers and the highest public officials over and over again. Arrogance is their trademark.

Permit them to disdain your pedestrian talent as you laboriously peck out your text on the word processor. When you have it written down, you'll be economical and say in half the words what it takes them twice the words to say, and you will never flounder, never take a wrong turn along the path of your reasoning, never lose track of where you are or where you must go next. *You will never suffer that terrible anguish of the mind drawing a complete blank,* the very pit of panic, for though you may have so diligently rehearsed your text that you need scarcely glance at it, it is nevertheless there in black and white (and in multi-colored ribbons of fluorescent highlighting) for you to pick up on.

3. Rehearse and rehearse and rehearse.

Rehearse not only with the object of so wearying yourself of it that you cut and compress all the more, for maximum economy (as mentioned Chapter 2, Commandment 5), but with the intention of imprinting in your memory the *sense* of what you want to say and *how* you want to say it. When, you see, you contain the totality of your text in the pitcher of your mind, and when you have practiced pouring out each phrase of it so often that your voice and body respond to the sense in just the way you wish, your confidence upon mounting the stage will be superb, because you will know just what you must do and just how you will do it—that confidence insulating you from the treachery of your nerves (those potential mutineers, servants of your will, catalysts of your triumph).

4. Concentrate totally on your desire to deliver the message.

The adrenaline must flow. In the quarter hour, the ten minutes, the ticking seconds before you are announced and take command of the lectern, you must freshly generate in your gut a fierce desire to tell the audience what you have in mind, what emotionally and intellectually you wish to move the audience to do.

Four factors conspire against this: (1)Your particular rôle on this particular occasion may be merely to entertain, not illumine or charge up, the audience. (2) The subject matter may be of little or no intrinsic interest to you. (3) You may have so sedulously rehearsed your text that it's gone flat for you. (4) Social intercourse may have driven concentration from your mind: you may have lost the sense of what you are there for and must accomplish.

That fourth impediment I take up separately, under items 7 and 8.

Keeping nerves at bay while entertaining an audience.

All you're on the card for is to warm up the crowd or give them a good time. Well, throw yourself into that menial job. The secret is to begin having fun yourself before the audience are invited into the fun. When you put your text down in writing, do your best to imagine what will most amuse, surprise, intrigue, cause to wonder, fascinate, or gently outrage the people you must address. Your quips and sallies, your commentaries on this or that situation, should cause you to chuckle to yourself when you summon them to mind.

Refer to Part 3 for more on how to dig out interesting material, but one can begin by musing on the most commonplace matters. One has to acquire the habit of looking at things with a peeled eye and a dose of realism. Take a common experience. People are troubled when they see so many cars scattered along the streets outside a church, so few people within. They remark on this apparent discrepancy all the time, shaking their heads at the puzzle. The phenomenon has nothing to do with the agues of faith in a secular age, however. It's explained as simply as this: Cars are horizontal, people are vertical. Or (another example of digging paydirt out of the commonplace), people are bothered by the arrangement of words on signs. For example,

PARK DISABLED
CARS ON GRASS

These repeated exhortations along the Merritt and Taconic State Parkways in New York drove me crazy during the 1950s, as I inferred a laconic causal relation between the first and second statements. Once insinuated in my mind, I wasn't able to pluck it out. (Where were all those thoughtless cars, ruining the greensward under their rubbery treads!) Verbal ambiguities can drive one batty also, and can be a rich source of humor. I used to wince in jet flight years ago, when, upon preparing to land, stewardesses routinely instructed passengers over the loudspeaker system to straighten the backs of their seats, put up their trays, and "put out all smoking materials." My head wildly swiveled on its neck as I peered right and left for the cushion that was on fire. Such idiocies dig themselves into the skins of people, itching there beneath the surface. It's like looking at the schematic line drawing of a box, the old illusion: first one flat, dimensionless square assumes prominence, then the one behind it. The alternating inspissation, first this, then the other, sticks to the retinal consciousness at the back of the mind in nauseating fashion.

For sanity's sake, one must resolutely put such ambiguities out of the mind. One must be alert in one's prose and verbal speech patterns from suggesting them to others, causing their minds to burr to the unintended (by you) irrelevancy instead of following where your reason leads (namely, that churches are indeed empty because dolts have lost faith). *But exploit them for use on stage.* The wry perspective of the liberated sensibility gave birth in Braque and Picasso to cubism; that same gift can recast the commonplace into something new and different and amusing. "Ever notice how . . . ?" "Ever hear people say . . . ?" Try to weave such introductions into an anecdote that bears narrative power; all audiences enjoy the impulse of a good story, and telling it well can be wonderfully satisfying. That story, needless to say, must be original; true; wholly yours, or borrowed from somebody whom you have known well; and revealing of human nature.

I've collected a fund of them for my personal use. They tend to revolve around a favorite theme, which is the blessed virtue of civility, of intimate (and classless) human interaction: of human beings standing (figuratively) naked and up front before other human beings, with no loss of dignity or affection, gaining ever in respect.

You will have to search long, maybe far and wide also, to unearth a good story. Talk to the old people. Listen patiently. Buy and read old diaries, or the collected letters of authors, statesmen, and soldiers. Stock the larder of your memory with illuminating vignettes that can make a society, a nation, an age, come alive. Then, if your mission must be primarily to entertain, you'll have the materials at hand. Contrive to make what you have to say delicious. It will be sweet to your tongue, sweet to the ears of your audience, and you need not fear.

Keeping nerves at bay though you have been assigned a topic that bores you to tears simply contemplating it.

How can you summon the excitement and commitment in your soul necessary to keep your nerves under control when your boss turns abruptly to you, saying, "Dick, you tell 'em next week about the new hydropress dynaflow injection system we're gonna install—yeah, you're the one to do that," or when the chairwoman at a banquet all of a sudden beseeches, "Mr. Eisenstat, do tell us about the fascinating rides and things we are going to have at next week's 17th Annual 4-H Society Chickenstrut."

The second is maybe the descent into hell, sprung on you as it is. Any time you are selected to be seated near a dais, at any event, no matter how remote from your interest or experience, prepare in your mind against the cackling bird of destiny that may seize on you for a few words. Remember the adage made famous by Winston Churchill: The best extemporaneous speakers are the best prepared. Drive to the event a trifle abstracted (contriving not to run into the rear of the car stopped in front of you at a light). Wring your memory for matter that somehow relates. Here, your native wit must succor you. You must throw yourself into the duty thrust on you with zeal and good humor. You must think foremost of the good people who have labored long and hard to put on the Chickenstrut, for whom its success means a lot and has consumed maybe six months in the planning. If you are deficient in compassion, there's no help for you, nor is there protection against a rampaging attack of nerves. Go back and read again Chapters 18 and 19.

In the first instance, though hydropress dynaflow injection systems may be as intrinsically thrilling to you as polishing table silver or watching a cork bobber on a still day when you're fishing a pond, militating to inspire you is the latent threat that your boss it is who has commanded. No reason can be more motivating than what logicians style *ad baculum*. You must employ your imagination, as with all tasks requiring that you perform. You must compel yourself to become fascinated with the hydropress dynaflow injection system and wonder what the world would be like without it or how the world will become revolutionized because of it. At the least, you're keeping your job, maybe even mulching a raise—if that bloody system works as advertised and you, meanwhile, please your boss. An iron act of will may be demanded of the speaker, forcing him to summon the protective armor of desire whether he is naturally inclined or not.

Keeping nerves at bay though you have so diligently rehearsed the topic that it has gone flat for you.

There's something called professionalism. Broadway actors in a hit play may be compelled to repeat their performances hundreds of times. Back in the 1960s and early 1970s, I gave one fifty-minute speech so often that I suffered from a kind of despair when I saw the topic come up on my schedule; at $500 the throw, it grossed, by my rough reckoning, over $120,000, the demand continuing year after year.[1]

---

[1]"Can Conservatives Be Progressive?" was the fascinating topic.

A pro must do what he or she must do. A certain stoicism must be acquired by the speaker, a fortitude. But there are techniques that I found helpful in keeping my interest up:

1. Almost every time I went over that talk, I scribbled in a correction here, an emendation there. I crossed out phrases, substituted single words. I kept fooling with the text, so that there was something orthographically fresh in it.

2. I compelled myself to ad lib. By typing this

>-----------------------<

symbol across the page, I flagged for myself that obligation (in music, the bars left for the virtuoso to improvise in the composer's style are called an *obligato*, though these are now completely scored, some great virtuoso of the past having defined the passage). These ad libs were usually reserved for illustrative anecdotes. To keep some of the material fresh, I accepted the risk of telling a story superbly (?) one evening, less well on another.

3. Depending on the audience, I slashed some passages out of that day's or evening's performance and inserted others. In other words, some of my material was free-floating, for use on special occasions. After two or three years on the tour, I developed a pretty good feel for my audiences. (Any competent performer acquires this talent.) I knew what would go over big with a rural crowd; be insufficient before students at a highfalutin' ivy league college; bomb at a woman's club; be entirely incomprehensible by an audience in Michigan, Minnesota, the Dakotas, Iowa, and Missouri; delight Texans and Southerners; invite the hostility of southern Californians; please Mormons; turn Jews surly and suspicious (or make them laugh); outrage Catholics; infuriate academe. There were the rare audiences before whom the most difficult reasoning worked, and these were cherished by me. I had my favorite optional passages, sure, and ones that were popular with audiences; but if the statistics grew outworn, circumstances changing the accepted parameters came to light, new studies superseded old verities, or some better, fresher citation flashed on the scene, I dropped them, faithful friends

that they had been. This practice maintained sufficient optional material to keep me interested. My text was, in parts, forever maturing and becoming tighter. I loved teasing my audiences, delighting in their offended or outraged hoots, from which I was careful quickly to draw the sting with a crack.

5. Simultaneously abstract yourself from what you are doing.

Though you throw yourself mind, body, soul, and will into your exhortation, you must simultaneously abstract yourself from what you are at.

I keep using the example of *Hamlet*. The actor must be at one and the same time Prince of Denmark, son of the foully murdered king, and the cold, skilled, professional playing the rôle of Hamlet. One must step back from oneself at the lectern. One must maintain a detached composure, even when one is in a frenzy of exposition, truly experiencing the emotions that one bids from the audience.

This is a difficult feat. It requires experience and maturity. The detachment must never subvert the passion; the passion must never overwhelm the detachment. But this duality must be acquired. It fortifies the speaker against unexpected circumstances—say (to be dramatic), fire breaking out in the hall—or hostility, or sneaking attacks by *le trac*. Inner composure protects the speaker from becoming such a slave of his emotions that he takes himself too seriously for ontology to bear and suddenly, at the yank of the theater manager's hook, or at the skeptic's yanking of the rug out from under his feet, falls apart. This calls for a stoical disposition and maybe even a philosophical metaphysics, taking the virtue of humility of spirit, discussed in the preceding chapter, a step further: *Though I believe in what I say with all my soul and all my heart, and though I will for something to be done with all the power of my mind, I am nothing, my desire is as the dust of ages, conceived to be scattered, and the cause I champion in the last analysis neither so sublime nor so sacred that it will bend space or move time; because though I am infinitely precious in the scheme of salvation, I am fodder in the folly of this life.*

6. Insist on seclusion before you go on.

. . . If you love yourself . . . If you have pity and compassion for yourself . . . If you wish to excel. This necessity is stressed in Chapter 2, Commandment 9.

You must hole up by yourself before you go on. Because you must concentrate concentrate concentrate wholly and absolutely on what you are going to say. You must rev up the engine. You must psyche yourself into the emotional and intellectual state necessary for the task. Any sponsoring chairman who denies you your plea for these few moments of solitude is a slithy tove, whom you have every right to despise, but win your end with that obtuse person just the same, even if this costs you unctuous flattery and false smiles.

When you are alone, empty the oppressed bladder, even though there may be but a few drops to squeeze or shake out; check your tie or your neckline; slap chill water on your face; moisten your eyeballs with drops; suck with your tongue at your teeth; comb, brush, pat your hair into place; yawn like a behemoth; stretch until the heavens part; loosen you shoulders, swing your arms . . . *and think think think of what you intend to say*. This preparation is essential armor against *le trac*, which awaits always the cavalier, distracted, insufficiently concentrated speaker. Once, when I had sought refuge in the men's lavatories of a boarding school, I did not hear the fire alarm siren go off; its *whoop-whoop-whoop*ing failed to penetrate my skull. I am told that when a teacher rushed in to tell me not to worry, the alarm was false, I gazed sublimely at him, saying, "But, you see, it isn't a figment of the fevered imagination, the 'window of opportunity' is a fact, and if we're not careful, we may all be flung through it to perdition"—or words to that effect. At which point—he *insists*—I sat on a can whose first and second lids had been left up.

7. Resist any feeling of well-being . . .

Oh, resist any treacherous feeling of well-being; do not permit yourself to be distracted from the impending task, and do not *for an instant* permit bonhomie to sap your concentration.

Or the fawning of your hosts, which may happen to you. In *Sex, Power and Pericles* I tell how the great Demosthenes was undone by

Philip of Macedon, his suspicions so beguiled and his hostility so disconcerted by adulation that his resolution was sapped. He blew his chance to avert Macedonian subjection, which failure may have condemned all generations of Western man until 1776 to the rule of despots.

The consequences of blowing it to you and me and for those who come after us are unlikely to be so portentous, but the immediate peril is a sudden onslaught of panic, as you stare out over a few hundred faces and ask yourself in horror, "What am I doing here?" I tell in *Speaking in Public* how the sympathy and affection of a woman's club in Kentucky, which had booked me twice before, so anaesthetized my temperament that as I at last began to speak, a cold dank fog of stage fright settled over my being, blurring the faces of the audience into an indistinguishable mass, blotting out my text, numbing my mind, so that when next I knew—when I came to myself—I was winding into my peroration.

I pray this never happens to you. My forehead was cold and dank; I had sweated through my shirt, deep into my tweed jacket; my armpits were sopping; and my knees so weak I had to hold onto the lectern, which was providentially solid, for fear of falling.

I'd been speaking in public since college. When this awful attack of stage fright occurred, I was five or six years into the professional lecture tour, having given hundreds of talks under almost all conceivable conditions and before every variety of audience, including a few malevolently hostile. Yet this meltdown happened while I was gazing into the fond, serene face of a nonagenarian lady who applauded me energetically as I strode to the lectern and then, with my first words, fell fast asleep. Blissfully asleep, consolidating my fondness for her. I had become distracted from my mission, the warm reception from the audience wrapping me in a false blanket of security. Hostility can have the most beneficial effect of triggering one's temperament into high gear. Overconfidence, the sanguine state, is much the worse to fear.

8. Develop an acute consciousness of your personal ridiculousness in the scheme of existence.

Keep panic at bay by keeping yourself in perspective.

I've covered this. See point 5, above—the passage in italics, concluding.

9. Do battle against your conceit.

Which is implied by the above.

I used to be more sympathetic than I am now to people who suffer from acute nervous distress on stage. It's not uncertainty or temperamental shyness or humility that unstrings them: it is their conceit. It is their exalted good opinion of themselves, which they fear risking in the eyes of the multitude.

To which I am not sympathetic. See the several remarks bearing on this in the preceding two chapters.

10. Once on stage, seek out a sympathetic person in the audience for moral support; ignore the hostile face.

Yes, it can be dangerous to let oneself become lulled by well-being, and as in my case in Kentucky, permit one's temperament to turn too sanguine and complacent through gazing at a sweet old face.

Nevertheless, once on stage, scrutinize the audience in search of the sympathetic countenance, the person who gazes happily at you or even beams at you his or her approval. Beam right back at him or her; by contagion, a good feeling will spread through the auditorium. That moral support can be wonderful. It can be encouraging. As you smile back, you'll find that approval almost surely in other individuals. You'll sense a communion with your audience that prompts you to exert yourself all the more. A virile, exhilarating self-confidence will flood your being, laying *le trac* low.

On the other hand, unless you happen to be, as I am, temperamentally pugnacious and a counterpuncher, ignore what you may perceive as the hostile face. Expressions in the dim reaches of lecture halls can be deceptive. Somebody may be yawning because . . . well, because we all yawn at inappropriate times, for one reason or another. Somebody may be laughing to his companion, not out of boorish disrespect to you, the speaker, but because a thought irresistibly funny occurred to him, having nothing to do with you. Or someone may have gone to sleep . . . well, because you put her to sleep. And that *is* your fault.

Permit yourself to be pleased, gratified, and morally strengthened; don't permit yourself to be upset or morally undermined. In the vast majority of audiences, there are multitudes more nice people than jerks. But if you should espy someone out there who unmistakably exhibits puzzlement—by the wrinkling of the brow and a general worried expression around the eyes, indicating that he or she may not have understood you—come to a full stop.

Turn to that person. For his or her intimate benefit, repeat what you just said. Ask the audience—never single out the person who may have caused you to repeat yourself, you'll embarrass him or her—whether the point is now clear. You will have explained yourself doubtlessly to many others who did not catch your drift the first time round, and your extra effort is sure to be appreciated.

Going back to the grouse: Once at the university in Missoula, a young man stomped down the center aisle, glaring grimly at me as he came closer to the stage. He sat himself in a seat to stage left of the aisle, in the front row, glaring up at me; and then, the moment I opened my mouth, he spread an enormous newspaper wide across his face, making a great show of reading it and loudly turning the pages while I spoke.

I had asked for a question and answer period. I was given five minutes to catch my breath before it commenced. In those days, I smoked. Stepping down from the stage, I walked by the ferociously hostile student, who still kept his face buried in the newspaper, and with a flick of my Bic, dipping my knees as I passed him, lit the paper in two flaming pyres.

Which got his attention. Now, I do not recommend such extreme measures, truly I don't. But what you can do with the hostile hearer is to stop as you did for the person who did not quite understand what you were saying. Remark, "You know, at the beginning I found this as hard to believe as at least one of you in the audience." Pause. Let that take effect. Then go on: "But it was the accumulation of evidence that finally convinced me . . ." Having served up this graceful concession to skepticism, *harden your tone*. You may be polite; you are no wimp. Summon the fire in your belly. Lay out the facts. Convince the skeptic of your sincerity and integrity, and if he is so ideologically congealed that he won't respond, you will have wiped that sneer off his face. Or failing even that, you will have so charged your remarks with intellectual passion that you are sure to sweep along the rest of the audience.

11. Determine to prevail or to die trying.

It's as serious as this. Your determination to sway the audience to your position is so important to you, so deeply a desire of your soul, that the gates of Hell will not prevail against you.

I know of no outstanding speaker who is not motivated so profoundly. The podium or the stage are no place for the weak-willed. Desire to communicate, to justify, to elucidate, to persuade, to convince must rage so burningly at the pit of your being that all else withers. Your tactics may differ. You may argue by allusion, appeal by wit and humor, advance by anecdote, thrust through by moral passion, or noose and draw tight the strings by the sheer power of intellection. But whatever you choose to do on the stage must wrap the audience in your will, which you will permit nothing to circumvent.

For panic, there's no room.

PART 7

PARTING SHOTS

CHAPTER 21

SPECIAL PROBLEMS GENERIC TO WOMEN

A woman's preaching is like a dog's walking on his hinder legs. It is not done well; but you are surprised to find it done at all.

—Samuel Johnson

INTRODUCTION

Sam Johnson must have been as popular with women in his time as St. Paul is with women in our time.[1]

To date, women have not been as successful as men at the lectern. That's plain. In listing the great orators, either historical or contemporary, not one woman leaps to mind. Among evangelists, women have held high place; I don't know whether Aimee Semple McPherson was a first-rate orator. My presentiment, however, is this: By the end of the first decade of the third millennium, several women will pop up on anybody's short list of brilliant speakers.

I am talking about an art, and I hazard this prediction on the basis of what I've seen these past twelve years at the school. We have coached many hundreds fewer females in our seminars than males. The reasons—I'm guessing—are cultural. There's the check of male chauvinist piggery: male bosses may not deem female subordinates worth the substantial cost of sending them to the Buckley School, either

---

[1]Ephesians, 5:21–32. Actually, Paul has got a bum rap; the imposition of contemporary culture on the past.

because they do not rate their executive abilities high or because they labor under the Sam Johnson prejudice. (Several women have told me over the telephone that though they badly want to come to us, their superiors won't foot the bill.) But there's also an element of female timidity, of a reluctance on the part of women to put themselves on the line before a roomful of men, attempting to improve in a department that many men assume women (*women* assume) are temperamentally no good at or by nature not cut out for. That is: The women who decline to subject themselves to the rigors of the Buckley School may be victims of a slight cooked in their imaginations.

That's all conjecture. One thing became clear within months of the School's founding: A seminar with no women in it suffered. It took extra effort to get the men to work as hard as they must, and a certain gusto was lacking. The presence of just one woman in a class of twelve can make a difference. The women who do make their way to Camden, South Carolina (wondering, some of them, as they step tentatively into the parlor of the 200-year-old southern residence in which we are head-quartered, what on earth persuaded them to commit such an awful mistake), work very hard and are intolerant of—clearly show their contempt for—male teammates who slack off. A class in which two of the twelve are female will surpass its native abilities. Why? Chemistry? Because we men are boys at heart, ho-ho? Because even aging males seek to shine before young, competent, attractive females, even when the females may be, in fact, no longer so young, nor so attractive, nor outstandingly competent?

I won't press this further, inasmuch as every cliché in the book on male-female relationships and sexual competitiveness elbows tendentiously to the front. Two other phenomena are established, however. In proportion to their numbers, (1) underperforming women exceed underperforming men, (2) women who excel exceed in proportion the numbers of men who excel.

Facts and figures prove the latter. Women have starred in numbers exceeding their proportionate weight. And among our top star performers, my guess is that there is an astonishing numerical parity: of the nine *orators* who stand out in my memory, I count five women.[2]

---

[2]In the third category of excellence, not a single woman has shined so far: that of the raconteur. Which surprises, given the plethora of brilliant female short story writers in the annals of American letters.

The data. Women graduates of the flagship Executive Seminar in Communication Skills constitute just 16.4 percent of the total.[3] We award outstanding performances with special certificates and silver medals. (Sterling silver, let me add.) The awards must be unanimously approved by faculty; and we are miserly about that, because conferring these awards puts the reputation of the School on the line:

The Buckley School of Public Speaking
Certifies That

. . . So-and-so has shown himself/herself capable of an exceptional performance.

In the category of orators, just forty-two graduates have had the silver medal conferred on them. That's 3.4 percent of the total number of graduates up to that time. In the category of debaters, just thirty-two have been awarded the silver medal, which is 3 percent of the total number of graduates. These distinctions are real and earned.

In the first category, orators, women comprise 36 percent; in the second category, debaters, women comprise 16 percent. (Note and store away the difference: one woman for every two men in the first category, one woman for every four men in the second category.)

Lumping all silver medalists together, women comprise 28 percent of the total. To put these figures in perspective, keep in mind how few women (16.4 percent) by comparison to men (83.6 percent) have attended the Executive Seminar. The ratio of their overall success is notable; in oratory it is stunning.

Oh, and there's the super award: to the performer who excels as orator and debater both. Oration and debate require different talents, different skills, and a different mix in the skills and talents that are common to both forms of public speaking. As an analogy, think of the differences between a sprinter and a miler. Five graduates have won this garland. Just one was a woman. Four males for every female have attended the school. *It is combat—debate—that bothers and besets women, not speaking before a crowd.*[4]

---

[3]The number of women and their proportion to the men have been rapidly rising since these statistics were collected.

[4]Since the data were collected, we have had two more women silver medalists in this double category or orator and debater, and they are brilliant. One—23 years old, a *magna cum laude* Barnard graduate—is superlative and may be the harbinger of a new generation.

Again, store away but leave aside that suggestive difference. What these statistics demonstrate overall is that there is no inherent oratorical incapacity in women—far from it. In proportion to their numbers, women seem to be blessed with superior forensic talent—though there are physical, cultural, and *temperamental* obstacles against which some women must (peculiarly) contend, which is what this chapter is about.[5]

THE DREAD FEMALE TEMPERAMENT

Only women will deny that this exists; and get away with it, because they outnumber men, and for the past thirty years have been progressively intimidating men, under the force of . . . their dread female temperaments.

It is not incontestable that all men are wimps. Gracious. But just as one may not have a true perception of what one sounds or looks like (the snapshot that others deem flattering of us, which we cringe to see; the awful surprise when we first hear a playback of our voices), so, by the nature of one's sex, is one sometimes blinded to faults that may not be exclusive to, but can be characteristic of, one's sex. (It is, of course, typical of a *male* writer even to suggest that women may have difficult temperaments—as any woman knows.)

You may therefore skip this part, if it taps the threshold of your dread female temperament. Or, detesting the writer, read on, just in case something he says may prove useful. Such as that women are more sensitive on the average than men . . . and precisely on account of that attribute are they more likely to take offense than men, particularly if the remark or the contention is insensitive.

Irascibility

On the platform, the female flashpoint can be close to the surface. (I'd rather step accidentally on a scorpion fish, which also lurks close to the surface.)

---

[5]The temperamental impediments surface in the low rate of success by women in debate compared to their success in oratory. See below for reasons.

It's distressing to watch an intelligent, professionally competent woman blow up on the podium. Temper loses arguments. Worse, temper loses the audience.

Control is essential. Not permitting one's temper to show may be even more essential.

1. Days before giving a speech, rehearse in your mind those aspects about your topic that can raise your ire.

2. Subjugate your emotional reactions.

3. Exert dominion over physical reactions.

Sweat, Blood, Toil, and Tears: Gaining Dominion over Yourself

1. Days before giving a speech, rehearse in your mind those aspects about your topic that can raise your ire.

Reflect on what you are going to say. At what juncture, and to what degree, are you emotionally committed?

Ponder those passages. What opposing contention or stupid remark most riles you? Repeat that contention or that remark. Examine it for its stupidity and coarseness. Phrase it more offensively yet: make it more stupid, vulgar, sneering. Imagine you're in a locker room with the sweaty half-naked apes of a professional football team and that no PR person is around to correct their manners. Make it obscene and candidly sexist.

Doing this, you will develop familiarity with, disdain and contempt for, the basest opposition. Your emotions are the less likely to engage on the platform; your replies (which you will have practiced) will be all the more sweetly reasoned, all the more pointed, putting to shame your male (or female) heckler . . . and winning the audience.

2. Subjugate your emotional reactions.

As you rehearse step 1, above, take the pulse of your emotions. Are there any bounds beyond which your tolerance snaps?

Are certain words or phrases most particularly offensive to you? Articulate them, then. Nigger? Catholic prude? Jesus freak? Jewish bitch? Hispanic slut? Dumb-ass broad? Bimbo? Pro-life idiot? Pro-choice radical? (There are worse, of course.) They may never—should never—lose their offensiveness.[6] You aren't likely to encounter such baseness or hostility, but you will have steeled yourself against the worst.

3. Exert dominion over physical reactions.

This is so hard!

Having wrung yourself through the wringers of steps 1 and 2, examine yourself for sudden pallor, blushes of mortification (burning cheeks), flushes of ire, rapid pulse, hyperventilation, a cracked, tight voice . . .

I pick hyperventilation, the constricting throat, and blood rising to or draining from the cheeks as the toughest physical reactions to subdue. Yet steps 1 and 2 will help. Emotion to some degree is leached from the offense. A slight coloring or waxing won't hurt. You're upset by that vicious (and inane) question from the floor? The audience sympathizes . . . so long as you, the speaker, display the composure to handle offense in sophisticated fashion.

I *courted* hostility when I was evangelizing on the college circuit in the 1960s and early 1970s. I'd prime myself, thinking as I strode down the aisle or walked on stage, *All right, you snot-nosed bastards, do your worst.* I schooled myself to take pleasure in student boos and catcalls, as well as the elegant sneers of their leaders in ignorance. Epithets often measured the degree to which I was getting to them. It became a matter of pride to keep my cool, smile, shrug—using wit to turn the malice of hecklers against them and wrest a laugh from the audience. Audiences quickly turn against churls and admire gallantry, their ideological bent regardless.

Practice welcoming the worst before stepping on. This can raise your adrenaline to just the right level, toughen you mentally and

---

[6]Women who habitually use *shit* and *fuck*, as a lot now do, I personally find offensive, and off-putting. This may be a generational thing on my part. But I don't like it in men either, and I wonder whether it proves anything other than a bad upbringing and poor manners.

morally, contain your emotions, and help you to eviscerate the bastards with the twist of a wrist.

Taking Criticism Personally

Oh, it gets harder.

This weakness surfaces too often in our female clients, even in women who are otherwise toughened executives.

It's the principal reason why, though excelling in oratory, women do less well in debate (see the statistics above). Under tough attack (or candid criticism from coaches), either they fold emotionally, receiving it as a thrust to the womb, or they furiously resent it and become rattled.

The topic may be as serious as whether government subsidies to single women with children should be categorically terminated after two years, or as ephemeral as whether Oprah is presently thin or presently fat. No matter, for some women, any contention seems to inflate into a matter of life or death, opposition casting them into emotional disrepair.

Which impedes their learning. Which, from the podium, during the rigors of debate, forfeits audience respect, male and female.

Take this exchange:

> ". . . I'm serious, Frank. I won't have it. My father never did it that way, I've never done it that way. And I'll be dadblasted if I'll permit . . ."
> "Then, Dick—sorry, Dick—you're going to be dadblasted, because this is the way it's going to be."
> "Okay."

This exchange, I submit, could not take place even as a comedy routine between two women.

1. Acquire professional detachment on the podium.

2. Do not permit temperamental commitment to undermine composure.

Sweat, Blood, Toil, and Tears: Gaining Dominion over Yourself

1. Acquire professional detachment on the podium.

One doesn't fear for a Janet Reno, a Madeleine Albright, a Pat Schroeder, or an Anita Blair—a rising star in the polemical circuits (and an outstanding graduate of The Buckley School)—but the majority of women seem unable to separate their persons from their ideas.

Don't ask me why. Women may not be used to the verbal rough-housing that men engage in from a very young age. Oh, women can be scathing—rapier-fast in inflicting wounds that sting and sting and sting. They have little trouble on the attack. But there seems to be a temperamental weakness about being on the receiving end in the rough and tumble.

The three steps discussed above on the control of one's emotional commitment will help, but women must go further; they must effectively separate their persons, their egos, their vulnerabilities from what they are intellectually upholding or denouncing, detaching person, ego, and vulnerability from their performances on stage. Men must do the very same thing, of course; but women are compelled to work harder at it.

The best way of achieving professional detachment is to remind yourself that on stage you're doing a job. You're not jousting with your spouse or lover, scrimmaging with your children, engaging in hot, internecine office warfare for the attention of the boss. You're defending or advancing an intellectual position, and you are required to do this deftly, in good spirit, and with professional aplomb.

2. Do not permit temperamental commitment to undermine composure.

"What a stupid idea!" "Who's calling me stupid!" "I never . . ." "Watch your tongue, buddy, I know when I'm being insulted!"

Now, the inference is permissible, imputing the transference also. But (a) he was *not* calling her stupid, (b) whether or not such an implication was intended in his blurted remonstrance ("What a stupid *idea!*"), the woman should have avoided (1) making the inference, (2) taking umbrage. The man spilled grease on a hot grill, and *she* sizzled.

Women have liberated themselves from most temporal lords, yet it seems they meekly assume the livery of their ideology. Where their minds become made up, or partisan, women's emotions seem to identify, so that a thrust against the construct is transformed into a thrust not *at* the intellectual abstraction but *to* the volatile quick—against them personally.

This higher or more intense and unreserved emotional commitment is wonderful for the purposes of summoning passion to one's aid, but dangerous when compacted (see below) or placed under stress. Women need to practice not only an iron external control over themselves; they must achieve *philosophical detachment*.

That is, they must avoid conflating and confusing the immiscible. I'm a conservative. But my identity doesn't hang on that potpourri of temperamental inclinations, attitudes, personal experience, historical extrapolations, dogmas, and philosophy that more or less define my ideological position. They are them and I am me.[7] I am deeply influenced by them;[8] but should they, in any part or dimension be in error, I am not personally humiliated. And should the error be pointed out, or even reviled, I am not personally insulted. Women must distinguish between the importance of the abstract idea, which may be transcendent, belonging to Truth, and the person advocating it, who is mortal, subject always to error, and no more than the servant of what we (dimly) perceive as Truth.

Nor does one permit oneself to magnify all things to matters of the first order. Sure, every concrete issue—whether it be the incompatibility of drinking and driving (speaking of immiscibles); the right of California vintners to advertise the social and health benefits of wine at supper; or the outrageous prejudice of the Bureau of Alcohol, Tobacco, and Firearms against medical use of marijuana to relieve pain—descends from a higher and ordering truth (respectively, above:

---

[7]Many liberals find me charming.

[8]My liberal friends deeply lament this failing, loving me no less for it.

egocentric behavior vs. the common good; violation by the government of one's First Amendment rights; personal liberty vs. state despotism). But BATF agents confiscating a doctor's cache of cannabis are not the Nazi Gestapo; prohibiting winegrowers from advertising the beneficent effects of moderate drinking is not tyranny; drunk drivers do not criminally intend to kill.[9]

Ideological Fanaticism[10]

The high emotional content that associates with intellectual conviction in women can, in excess, encourage fanaticism. Whereas it is the common experience of women that men are pigheaded, it is the common experience of men that women are fanatically attached to their ideas.

Neither is to be denied his/her prejudice. Both can be true. In men, pigheadedness (and fanaticism) is sometimes expressed in surly demeanor; in women, fanaticism (and pigheadedness) is sometimes expressed in eardrum-shattering hysteria. Neither is attractive from the podium, nor useful.

1. Remember that no ideological conviction is worth a single broken body or a single broken heart.

2. Acknowledge that to no one is the complete truth vouchsafed about anything.

3. Acknowledge that you are no less prone to error than other human beings, male or female.

4. Acknowledge that though you may be dead right on this particular issue, others may think you are dead wrong and that they are dead right. And though *they* are dead wrong in their thinking, this does not necessarily ascribe deceit, malice, or moral turpitude to them.

5. Remember that your object is to persuade, gain converts, not recriminate.

---

[9]Read over Chapter 19, the section "Humility of Spirit," and see pages 197–199, *Sex, Power, and Pericles.*
[10]See Chapter 19 for more on this subject.

6. Remember that self-righteousness alienates, humility attracts.[11]

There's no need to delve any deeper than this into the subject.[12]

THE FEMALE SEX

As a gender, women need to acknowledge their strengths (oratorical passion) and weaknesses (emotional excess) and deal with them.

Males may find it more difficult to excel in a theatrical art like public speaking; women may find it easier to fail. But as women have shown in countless other fields, where they will, they prevail. Women have starred in combat at the school—throwing themselves with gusto into the fray, deliciously wicked, wonderfully funny, and *never* put off balance. But they are too few. Now that women are their own mistresses, they must finally master themselves.

---

[11]Much maligned St. Paul, to the Ephesians: "Get rid of all bitterness, all passion and anger, harsh words, slander, and malice of every kind. In place of these, be kind to one another, compassionate, and mutually forgiving . . ."

[12]For Christians. In *Centesimus Annus*, Pope John Paul II writes: "Nor does the Church close her eyes to the danger of fanaticism or fundamentalism among those who, in the name of an ideology which purports to be scientific or religious, claim the right to impose on others their own concept of what is true and good. Christian truth is not of this kind."

CHAPTER 22

PROFESSIONAL DETACHMENT

The public speaker must be *engagé*, yet *dégagé*; he must be passionately involved in what he is saying, yet professionally calculating; he must be mind and heart and soul committed, yet aloof.

He must be sincere, yet . . . no, not a hypocrite. He must be honest, yet . . . no, not duplicitous. He must assume two personalities: the one in action, delivering the address; the one in reserve, listening to himself, watching himself, striving with all his might at all times to edit and improve the performance . . . in which resides his honesty and sincerity, his passion and commitment, his professional absolute engagement in what he is doing.

I've described this ambiguous state as the mocking Mercutio in one's own garden. I've likened it to being at one and the same time Hamlet and the skilled professional actor playing Hamlet. No one can be so true and sincere as the actor who truly and sincerely, and if necessary, deviously, plots how best to reveal the psychology of the part he is called upon to play.

And so the speaker. You must pay attention to everything: voice, face, hands, body language. You must pitch your whole being into your performance, to the best of your ability, to the uttermost limit of your capacity, emotional and intellectual. You must believe as never have you believed, so that your audience may come to believe. Yet you must retain your spiritual independence, keeping that one step at a remove, the better instantly to gauge whether you are making the impact you wish to make, or whether you must modify your approach, tone down your intensity, amuse, entertain . . . when necessary, call up the reserves of passion and determination, storm the ramparts and take the city.

Step by step. Humble must you be, dedicated, the servant always of what you wish to say.

Leaf through this primer now and again, when you are preparing for a talk. Ponder what may not come easily to you. Rehearse what you sense you are deficient in. But do not mistake performance for reality. You are what you are before you step on stage; you return to what you are when you have stepped down from the stage. Don't permit the stage persona to invade, corrupt, and take possession of your true person. Only by maintaining an impervious wall of separation between the two will the performer on stage fully come into his own, driven by the will and the intelligence of the detached person. To thy own self be true . . . by surpassing your true self; not by acquiring the art of speaking in public . . . by mastering it.

APPENDICES

LETTERS FROM CEOs

Frederick J. Schwab, who heads up Porsche of North America, wrote me a letter so marvelous on the subject of business reports that I quote it in full:

> Time is the one commodity that is always in short supply. Therefore, "Rule One" should always be *to be concise* and *to the point*. Further, *the boss never likes to be surprised* [emphasis added]; advance notice of the subject, alternative solutions or suggestions, and reasons for the preferred result are always appreciated.
>
> When making the presentation, *don't read overheads or other visual aids* [emphasis added]. This is a common mistake that demonstrates a lack of preparation by the presenter and assumes the board has not read their advanced preparation booklet, or that they are unable to read.
>
> A good technical report regarding engineering, computer-controlled whatever, software applications, detailed economics, etc., must be easily understood by everyone in the audience regardless of their background. Don't try to impress or confuse as the desired answer will not be forthcoming . . . at least not in our organization.
>
> Finally, always realize you're selling both yourself and your ideas. These individuals want to have faith in you, and your confidence must show to be believable. Don't let the stature of your audience frighten you . . . just be well prepared.

So in summary, my five rules would be:

1. Remember you're selling both yourself and your ideas.

2. Be concise, and provide advance information supporting your position.

3. Don't read visual aids.

4. Use language understandable by the average-educated business person; don't try to impress or confuse.

5. When answering questions, if you don't know the answer just say so. Don't try to bluff your way through. Further, stick to your area of expertise with your opinions.

I hope these are not overly simplistic.

Far from which, they should be chiseled into stone over the portals of every school of business administration throughout the country.

Jim Ferguson comes down hard on jargon:

. . . by which I mean using initials, internal phrases or short-hand which might not be familiar to the listener. This is a partic-ular gripe of outside directors . . . the presentations I remember being most frustrating were ones where I was more or less of an outsider and was expected to know and understand situations when I simply didn't. There seemed to be an epidemic of this at one time at [a very old, distinguished, and major NYC bank], until one of the directors rebelled and asked that things be slowed down and more clearly spelled out.

His first, second, and fourth recommendations:

1. Be *the authority*, projecting confidence and control.

2. Gear the presentation to the characteristics of the audience, speaking neither up nor down . . .

4. Know something about the audience's "temperature" at the time of the presentation, and/or whatever "agendas" may be lurking.

"Jerry" Henry lists as positives:

1. Clarity about objectives.

2. Focus and simplicity.

3. Preparation.

4. Total honesty.

And as banes:

> . . . BS (obvious or subtle), rambling (shows lack of focus or preparation), and responding to questions too quickly (not very thoughtful).

Ed Russell advises:

1. Leave [something written] behind so I can revisit the conversation. Doesn't need to be fancy.

2. How important is this? Information or decision-making? Who will be impacted?

3. Tell me something I don't already know. Show some imagination.

4. Don't make it too complicated. Break it down into logical pieces.

5. Substance is more important than style.

Brian Lipke's is equally terse and mordant:

> Here are five points I think are most relevant when a subordinate is presenting a report to his immediate supervisor:

1. Be prepared! Know exactly what you are going to say before you start.

2. Give your report in crisp, concise points, versus a rambling monologue.

3. Do not get bogged down on details that may add color but serve no major point.

4. Be prepared to offer suggestions, alternatives, solutions, or actions to be taken.

5. Do not be negative. Do not blame others. Do not complain.

> I hope these points are helpful . . .

Indeed. My thanks again to all.

APPENDIX B

ERRORS IN PRONUNCIATION

The following tables of errors in pronunciation are taken from *Basic Public Speaking*, Third Edition, by Paul L. Soper (Oxford University Press, 1968) . . . with gratitude.

Misplacing the Accent

admir'able (ad'mirable)

applic'able (ap'plicable)

ce'ment (cement')

compar'able (com'parable)

combat'ant (com'batant)

despic'able (des'picable)

exemplar'y (exemp'lary)

exig'ency (ex'igency)

explic'able (ex'plicable)

finan'cier (financier')

formid'able (for'midable)

grim'ace (grimace')

hor'izon (hori'zon)

i'dea (ide'a)

impi'ous (im'pious)

impot'ent (im'potent)

incompar'able (incom'parable)

incongru'ous (incon'gruous)

infam'ous (in'famous)

in'terest'ed (in'terested)

irrepar'able (irrep'arable)

municip'al (munic'ipal)

prefer'able (pref'erable)

proj'ectile (projec'tile)

reg'ime (regime')

respite' (res'pite)

superflu'ous (super'fluous)

u'nited (unit'ed)

vehe'ment (ve'hement)

vag'ary (vagar'y)

vehi'cle (ve'hicle)

Addition of Sounds

attack-ted (attacked)
athaletics (athletics)
barbarious (barbarous)
colyum (column)
corpse (corps)
drawr (draw)
drownded (drowned)
elum (elm)
enterance (entrance)
ekscape (escape)
filum (film)
grievious (grievous)
height-th (height)

hinderance (hindrance)
idear (idea)
lightening (lightning)
mischievious (mischievous)
of-ten (of[t]en)
rememberance (remembrance)
sing-ger (singer)
stastistics (statistics)
sub-tle (su[b]tle)
sufferage (suffrage)
umberella (umbrella)
warsh (wash)

Omission of Sounds

accerate (accurate)
actully (actually)
assessory (accessory)
blong (belong)
canidate (candidate)
defnite (definite)
guarntee (guarantee)
jography (geography)
ineffecshal (ineffectual)
nuclus (nucleus)
particlar (particular)
pome (poem)

plice (police)
quite (quiet)
reconize (recognize)
resume (résumé)
sedimentry (sedimentary)
simlar (similar)
superntenent (superintendent)
sussinct (succinct)
temperture (temperature)
vilent (violent)
uzhal (usual)

Sound Substitutions

agin (again)
blaytant (blatant)
boquet (bouquet)
brochr (brochure)
calvary (cavalry)

capsl (capsule)
tshasm (chasm)
click (clique)
conscious (conscience)
crooks (crux)

Sound Substitutions

cullinary (culinary)

dictionury (dictionary)

diptheria (diphtheria)

dipthong (diphthong)

dis-hevel (dishevel)

fewtyle (futile)

gesture (g is soft)

genuwine (genuine)

gigantic (first g is soft)

hiccough (hiccup)

homidge (homage)

ullusion (illusion)

interduce (introduce)

irrevelant (irrelevant)

jist (just)

larnyx (larynx)

lenth (length)

loose (lose)

longgevity (longevity)

memor (memoir)

miradge (mirage)

preelude (prelude)

preform (perform)

prespiration (perspiration)

prestidge (prestige)

rench (rinse)

saloon (salon)

strenth (strength)

statue (stature)

substantuate (substantiate)

theayter (theater)

tedjius (tedious)

INDEX

Note: The *n.* after a page number refers to a note.

ABOUT THE AUTHOR

REID BUCKLEY has been a champion public speaker since his debating days at Yale University, where he starred on a team that scored national and international wins. During the turbulent 1960s and 1970s, he toured the United States, debating with liberal columnist Max Lerner in clashes frequently compared to the Lincoln-Douglas debates. He is the founder and head of The Buckley School of Public Speaking, which has graduated many leading figures in business and government. He is also author of *Speaking in Public: Buckley's Techniques for Winning Arguments and Getting Your Point Across* and *Sex, Power, and Pericles: Principles of Advanced Public Speaking.*